Sexual Love
and Western Morality

A Philosophical Anthology

Edited and with introductions by
   D. P. Verene

HARPER TORCHBOOKS

Harper & Row, Publishers
New York, Hagerstown, San Francisco, London

Published under the editorship of Charles M. Sherover.

CONTENTS

Introduction:
Sex in Western Thought
and Contemporary Society

What is sex? What relationships should prevail between the sexes? What is the relationship between sex and love? These questions and the subquestions that lie within them are fundamental to any understanding of human affairs and have been crucial in the development of Western morality.

Sex is a division which cuts across the human world and exists in various ways throughout the entire sphere of biological process. Although we use such terms as "person," "human being" and "man," they are abstractions from the way in which we actually exist. We exist as one sex or the other. Each of us encounters himself as existing within the body of a man or a woman. It is men and women and not "persons" who exist throughout history and create the world of human action. All societies and historical periods contain particular orientations toward the difference between the sexes and the nature of human sexuality. Each individual finds himself to be not only physically of one sex or the other but also to be part of a social structure which contains psychic and cultural frameworks which place him in a particular relationship to his own sexual nature and the sexes in a particular relationship to each other. Behind the customs and institutions relating to sex existing in any particular period in any particular society is the fundamental ethical question of how human beings ought to relate to their sexual natures and what relationships ought to prevail between the sexes in a society.

In contemporary society there is considerable discussion of sex and the nature of sexual morality. Much of this discussion, like much contemporary discussion of social and moral issues generally, is unconnected with historical views and is theoretically vague. It deals with issues of sex and morality in terms of surveys of attitudes, comparison of opinions, social statistics, journalistic commonplaces about human nature and the nature of society and broad arguments which do not derive from any systematic theory of man. Contemporary discussion often, although not always, proceeds apart from any contact with the views of sex that exist throughout the Western tradition. When sex is discussed in more than journalistic and immediate terms, the approach tends to be medical (e.g., the research of Masters and Johnson) or social scientific (e.g., Kinsey's studies of sexual behavior and the Institute for Sex Research) or psychoanalytic. Although such studies are of great value, little attention has been given to sex as a philosophical and ethical problem. This is largely due to the fact that philosophical and ethical thought during the past several decades has generally lost touch with the sphere of directly human problems. This is particularly true of Anglo-American philosophy which has been highly professionalized and largely oriented toward intramural discussions of technical problems involving logical and grammatical analysis. This is less true of continental philosophy and Catholic and Marxist thought.

This volume presents selections from the writings of major philosophers and thinkers in the ancient, medieval, modern and contemporary periods of Western thought as they relate to questions concerning the nature of sex, the sexes, and sexual love. These topics represent a set of interrelated problems which are part of the thought of each period. In the thought of these thinkers lie the origins of our contemporary views of sex and in it also lie a number of alternatives that have not been explored. It may seem surprising in itself that some of the thinkers in the volume have given attention to problems relating to sex at all as we are so accustomed to viewing classical philosophers as though they were only interested in meta-physical problems and abstract questions of ethical theory. This book can be approached as a broad picture of some of what has been thought about sex and sexual morality;[1] it may be approached in terms of specifically comparing what some influential thinkers have said about the meaning of the sex act, the status of women, the import of marriage, or the relationship of sex and love. It can also be simply regarded as calling attention in part to some often overlooked but often curious thoughts some important figures have had on sex.

1. This volume is not a history of sexual love. It presents only a number of prominent views on sex in a general historical order. Discussion of types of sexual customs and attitudes as they relate to the political and social life of their time can be found in such works as: Paul Brandt [Hans Licht, pseud.], *Sexual Life in Ancient Greece*, trans. J. H. Freese, and ed. Lawrence H. Dawson (London: Routledge & Kegan Paul, 1932); Otto Kiefer, *Sexual Life in Ancient Rome*, trans. Gilbert and Helen Highet (New York: Barnes & Noble, 1962); Morton M. Hunt, *The Natural History of Love* (New York: Alfred A. Knopf, 1959); Edward Westermarck, *A Short History of Marriage* (New York: Macmillan, 1926); and Denis de Rougemont, *Love in the Western World*, trans. Montgomery Belgion (New York: Pantheon, 1956). It should be noted that the present volume concentrates only on Western views of sex and does not include Eastern views. Eastern views on sex are sufficiently numerous and diverse so as to constitute an independent study of their own.

Sex is itself a vague notion. It refers in one sense to the genital and reproductive acts of persons and to the physiological differences of man and woman. This scientific and biological sense is perhaps the way it can be used most precisely, but the term sex ordinarily connotes more than this set of physical actions and differences between man and woman. Every society has an image of the masculine and the feminine and the roles that men and women are to play when they are acting in a manner distinctive to their sexual nature. It is through these images and the particular ways in which these roles are acted out that the physical act of sexual intercourse is made possible. The physical sexual act, itself describable in wholly physiological terms, is dependent upon some playing out of some socially and psychologically defined roles as preliminary to its initiation. The sexual act itself is never wholly physical but is through and through caught up in the mental and social experiences that the sexes have of themselves. This is also true of homosexual acts or of sexual acts that are not procreative in nature; that is, their physical dimension is only separable in thought from their psychic and social dimensions. Any sexual act, like any human act, is always at once something physical and mental.

Sex has a further meaning that goes beyond its biological and socio-psychological meanings. From Socrates' speech on the nature of *eros* in Plato's *Symposium* to Freud there is a concept in Western thought of sex as a force or power that is involved in the vital aspects of human existence. In this sense sex is often regarded as a kind of creative energy which exists within individuals and between them of which the physical act of procreation and the social and psychological images of the masculine and the feminine are only manifestations. Sex in this sense is a kind of thrust or drive acting within the human spirit and will and is closely connected to man's creative powers and the internal ordering of the human personality.

For Plato *eros* can lead the individual to an apprehension of beauty and the ultimate order of things. For Freud the sex instinct is involved in the ordering of the individual's personality and its power, and it can be frustrated and lead to pathological forms of mental life. This meaning of sex is one of the most difficult to define as each thinker in the Western tradition who deals with it approaches it differently, but there is a sense of sex which goes beyond the physical and social and is connected directly with the spiritual and mental dimension of human existence.

Questions concerning the relationship between the sexes in Western thought have centered on the nature of marriage and the role of women in society. Behind Western thought about marriage, exclusive of Greek and Roman thought, is the Judeo-Christian concept of monogamy which derives from the patriarchal structure of ancient Jewish society and the early Christian concept of marriage for life without divorce. At the center of this concept of marriage is the classic Christian denial of the body and the procreative model of the sex act. The body is separate from the soul and was seen by the early church fathers as the means to sin, as it is through the body that we experience the sensual pleasures that detract the soul from a pure relationship with God. Sex is seen on this view as necessary for the continuation of God's original creation of man through the act of procreation between man and woman, but it is also seen as a temptation to sin. Thus man's sexual activity should be limited to just that which is necessary to the continuance of the species. Other use of the sexual organs is a sin.

This concept of the sex act also places man in the primary position as the initiator and controller of the act and regards woman as a necessary but passive receptacle. Socially the woman is placed in a position that is analogous to her role in the sex act. In the Judeo-Christian society woman has been for the most part viewed as part of the total property relations of the man. Until the early decades of the twentieth century, women have been without civil rights. Although the position of women has varied from period to period and from one social and economic class to another within modern history, women as a class have had little control, except through men, over the ordering of society. This subordinate and subjected position of women has been the subject of women's rights and liberation movements since the mid-nineteenth century. The question of the position of women in society is one of the issues that make up the broad spectrum of challenges that contemporary society has made to the traditional concept of marriage with its accompanying proscriptions against sexual activity and enjoyment outside the procreatively-aimed sex act.

The question of the relationship between sex and love is involved in the fact that sex has a spiritual meaning that connects it with man's creative powers and which goes beyond its meaning as a physical act and as a set of social customs. The concept of sexual love overlies the social customs and institutions through which sexual activity actually occurs. Sexual love is usually regarded as a type of love among other types such as brotherly love, parental love, self-love, divine love or love of God. Love itself is generally thought of as a power that exists within man's ethical life through which he judges and shapes the customs of his social life. Love is generally regarded as a power of man to transcend the differences that exist between persons and in the world generally and to feel the unity of things. It is a power to bring together that which is apart and diverse, and it is thus a force that is close to the process of life itself. Sexual activity is ordinarily thought of as a concrete act of physical union which is an embodiment of this power. The sexual act (which need not be a procreative act or, in principle, a heterosexual act) can be seen as an ethical drama wherein two persons experience their ability to bring thir bodies and emotions together in a common union.

Sex and the drama of the sex act can be viewed both as a constant feature of human existence whereby the human species is itself continued and as a basic form of love. Sex, considered as a form of love, is seen as involved in the total set of ethical relationships that exist between persons. In an important sense there is no "sexual morality" in the sense of a special set of moral concepts and judgments that hold only for sexual acts and relationshps. If sex is a type of love, then the relationships that exist between persons in sexual activity are to be viewed ethically as only a particular version of those relationships that ought to exist generally between persons in all spheres of human activity. Sex, seen as a form of love, is connected to the basic power that continuously exists in various forms behind man's ethical life—the power of human loving. When the concept of love is joined with the concept of sex, sex becomes an act that can be regarded as at once deeply physical and sensual, mentally and emotionally structured and ethically significant.

These comments on the nature of sex, the sexes and sexual love are preliminary and are discussed further in the introductions to the various sections which follow and in the selections themselves. The reader may at his will follow out various of these issues from section to section. It is interesting, for example, to compare the judgments of Epictetus, Ovid, Augustine, Freud and de Sade on just how man is to relate to his sexual nature. Or, compare the concepts of marriage and of women voiced by Plato, Aristotle, Luther, Marx, Engels and de Beauvoir. Or, consider Plato's discussion of love in relation to the views of Hegel, Solovyov or Sartre.

The volume as a whole is divided into five sections, the first three of which contain statements from ancient, medieval and modern thought. They do not correspond one-to-one with these periods as some modern figures are included in the

Christian views of Section II, and Section III is limited to selections from writings of the mid-nineteenth and early twentieth centuries. Sections IV and V treat problems that are of particular interest to contemporary thought about the nature of love and the relationship of sex to social morality, but they include spokesmen from other than the twentieth century. All thought about sex in the Western tradition begins with the ancient Greeks in the sense that Western thought generally begins with them. But their sexual views and customs hold out to us attitudes and patterns of erotic behavior that are quite foreign to our contemporary concepts of sex, all of which are either derived from or are reactions against later Christian concepts of sex.

Section I presents several selections from Greek and Roman thought. The ancient Greeks were a sensual people who accepted human sexual activity in all of its forms and regarded them as natural to man and not as involving any intrinsic moral problems. The Greeks knew two kinds of sexual love—heterosexual and homosexual. The Greek love for boys is best understood in terms of the Greek ideal of beauty and customs of education. In ancient Greece there evolved a system of relationships between the older man and the boy, originating in Doric custom, in which the older man attached to himself a boy whom he undertook to cultivate and train in the arts of life. Men fraternized together from morning to evening in pursuit of beauty of body and soul, engaging in physical exercise on the playing fields and in conversation. Friendship was regarded as a precious possession and one of the most important features of human life. Sexual activity between men was seen as part of the total set of friendly relationships between men and was not considered in Greek society as incompatible with marriage or with heterosexual activity.

There were two major classes of women in ancient Greece—wives and *hetairae*. In addition there were prostitutes and domestic slave women. Greek wives spent their time bearing and rearing children and managing the affairs of their households. They had no part in public life. The *hetairae* were a special class of prostitutes or mistresses of high order. They were held in considerable regard by the Greeks for their education, wit and personalities, as well as for their sexual talents. Such women were often honored by having their statues erected in temples and other public buildings beside famous generals and statesmen. Female homosexuality was also known in ancient Greece, the primary figure of which is Sappho, whose love poems describe the delights of female homosexuality and the name of whose homeland, the island of Lesbos, is the origin of the term "lesbian."

The fact that the Greeks regarded sex as a natural human activity and not in itself involving far-reaching moral issues accounts for the fact that Plato and Aristotle seldom discuss sex as a particular topic in their works. Instead they are concerned with questions of the nature of love and friendship and the place the sexes should occupy in society. Since sex as such does not raise a moral issue for them, their discussions center on the spiritual characteristics of various human relationships of which only some involve sexual aspects. The ancient Greek society, like Western society generally, was male dominated— the only exception being the position enjoyed by the *hetairae*. For this reason Plato's proposal in the *Republic* that women should hold public office in the ideal state and be in all ways equal to men was more shocking to the Greek mind than anything said in his works about heterosexual or homosexual love.

Sexual life in ancient Rome tends to follow the course of the development of Roman civilization. In the early history of Rome when the Romans were an agrarian people, sex was more or less confined to a simple marriage system. As Rome developed, sophisticated forms of sensuality developed, and these finally degenerated into the violent spectacles of the Roman arena and the mass ethic of *panem et circenses*—food and sport. The Roman character was through and through practical and did not have the speculative and literary orientations of the Greek. Roman women, although they had no political rights, enjoyed more freedom than Greek women and exercised a certain influence on political affairs. The two basic approaches to sex in Roman thought come, on the one hand, from the Stoics such as Epictetus and Marcus Aurelius, who treat sex in terms of the general Stoic doctrine of self-denial and cultivation of the powers of the will over the pleasures of the body, and, on the other hand, from the poets such as Catullus and Ovid, who praise the erotic and endorse sensual pleasure and sexual love.

Section II portrays the Christian view of sex which enters Western thought in the first few centuries of the Christian era with the establishment of the Christian church. Early Christian views of sex and marriage are in large part a continuation of views found in ancient Jewish society which are connected to Egyptian customs and the code of Hammurabi. Ancient Jewish society placed the man in a completely dominant position over the woman in the marriage relationship and was generally a strongly patriarchal society. One of the socially radical factors in early Christian doctrine, and part of its clash with Jewish society, was its advocation of the abolishment of divorce. Under Mosaic law at the time of Jesus, divorce was permissible through a bill of divorcement, but the man could make it out himself, and divorce was practiced freely, creating a social problem of woman left without economic support. St. Paul advocates lifetime marriage and connects it with the view of woman's subservience to man. Paul generally regards marriage as a concession to the desires of the body. He states:

> It is well for a man not to touch a woman. But because of the
> temptation to immorality, each man should have his own wife
> and each woman her own husband. . . . A wife is bound to
> her husband as long as he lives. If the husband dies, she is free
> to be married to whom she wishes, only in the Lord. But in
> my judgment she is happier if she remains as she is.[2]

The views of sex, marriage and women found in St. Paul's
writings are taken up even more strongly by the early fathers
of the Christian church such as Tertullian and St. Ambrose,
both of whom regarded woman as a permanent possibility of
sin. St. Augustine, the first major thinker of the early centuries
of Christian theology, expressed many of the Christian sexual
doctrines in full form and connected the sex act with the problem of original sin. The doctrine of celibacy within the church
was not compulsory for the lower grades of clergy during the
first three centuries of the Christian era, and, in fact, the
struggle over celibacy for the clergy lasted a thousand years.
Complete celibacy was only very gradually made the rule. It
was not until Pope Leo IX (1048–1054) that chastity was
formally prescribed for priests such that to violate it was not
simply to engage in a breach of discipline but to commit
heresy, and it was not until 1074 under Gregory VII that all
priests were finally commanded to immediately put aside all
wives living with them. Sexual activity was widely engaged in
throughout the Middle Ages. Adulterous affairs were an art of
late Medieval courtly life and part of the total set of social
relationships between knights and ladies. Viewed against the
sexual activity of the Middle Ages, St. Thomas Aquinas's views
on marriage and fidelity of the thirteenth century seem somewhat less reactionary than they do today.

The Renaissance was an age of considerable interest in sex
and produced a number of works of literature with erotic
themes such as the sonnets of Aretino and the works of Rabe-

2. 1 Cor. 7:1–2; 39–40.

lais. Prior to such works but close to them in spirit is Boc-
caccio's *Decameron* of the mid-fourteenth century. In the early
1500s the Protestant Reformation began. Martin Luther along
with other founders of the Reformation such as Zwingli and
Calvin maintained that priests might marry, and within the
Reformation divorce became accepted and legalized. Luther's
reaction to the Church's rule of celibacy was partly founded on
the fact that it was being applied with a double standard,
being enforced for the lower levels of clergy while flaunted by
the higher officials in Rome. Interest in sex continued even
during the period of the Catholic Counter Reformation. In
1630 Molina's play, which created the figure of Don Juan, was
first performed and enjoyed considerable success.

The eighteenth century was a century with few inhibitions
about sexual activity. Sexual activity surrounded royal courts,
especially Versailles, and interest in sexual pleasure was wide-
spread throughout the aristocracy and within the society as a
whole. Two of the most famous memoirs of the period are
those of the Duc de Saint-Simon and Casanova. The *philos-
ophes* of the eighteenth century Enlightenment were divided
on the question of the relationships that should hold between
the sexes in society. Rousseau in his novel, *La Nouvelle Hél-
oïse,* sees the faults of conventional marriage as a social institution, but he comes out strongly against divorce and for marital
fidelity. In *Émile,* his treatise on education, Rousseau conceives a woman's education as relative to a man's and states
that a principle of the differences between the sexes is that
woman is by her nature to be for the delight of man. Diderot,
Helvétius, and Condorcet regard woman's secondary role in
society as the result of custom and differences of education
between men and women, and regard woman's societal position as a matter of injustice. David Hume and Immanuel
Kant, as is apparent from the selections from their writings at

the end of Section II, support the views of sexual morality and marriage of the Christian tradition.

Section III presents selections from nineteenth century and early twentieth century thought that attack the Christian view of sexual morality from various directions. It is evident that the Christian view of sex and marriage has never wholly been successful in directing man's actual sexual behavior, but in the mid-nineteenth and early twentieth centuries this view came under serious intellectual attack. Schopenhauer's theory of the sex instinct and its connection with the activity of the Will in nature puts forth a nontheistic explanation of sexual behavior. Nietzsche calls attention to the difficulties for an adequate theory of human action and history that are involved in the Christian ethic's denial of the body and the sublimation of the passions. Marx and Engels criticize the Christian concept of marriage and the role of women that has accompanied it by showing how it has served to support particular kinds of property relationships and the development of capitalism. Freud's theories on sex at the beginning of the twentieth century completely altered views on sex in Western thought, and sex became a subject for scientific investigation and something to be talked about openly in social conversation.

The concern of Marx and Engels with the place of women in society need not be regarded as unique to their thought but as part of a concern with women's rights that existed in the mid and late parts of the nineteenth century. The *Communist Manifesto* with its criticism of bourgeois marriage appeared in 1848. Marx's *Capital* appeared in 1867, the same year that John Stuart Mill made the first speech ever officially presented before the English Parliament in favor of women's rights. Two years later Mill published his essay on the *Subjection of Women.* In 1878 there was an international congress held on women's rights. Engels published his work on the *Origin of* the Family, Private Property and the State in 1884. Mill's work was actually preceded considerably by Mary Wollstonecraft's Vindication of the Rights of Woman in 1792. Writings and documents on women's rights of various sorts run throughout the nineteenth and twentieth centuries.

Section IV focuses on the theory of love which runs parallel to the attack on the Christian views of sexual morality of Section III. From the nineteenth century on there is an interest in developing a theory of love that is independent of church doctrine, although not necessarily independent of religious feeling or the spirit of Christianity, and in developing a theory of love that is more than a theory of manners such as is found in eighteenth century thought. Hegel's philosophy is at the base of this concern in that it develops a theory of human consciousness that shows the interdependence of all particular modes of consciousness within the total process of the development of human consciousness. Hegel's philosophy suggests the outlines of the problem of how one individual's existence is tied to the existence of others which since his thought has been central to theories of love and generally to theories of human relationships. Vladimir Sergeyevich Solovyov, late in the nineteenth century, developed a total philosophy of love based on a number of Hegelian-like principles which has exerted influence in the twentieth century on Nicolas Berdyaev's theory of man and his conception of ethics.

Kierkegaard, in the mid-nineteenth century, who argues against Hegelianism, is nonetheless concerned to develop a theory of love as part of his interpretation of Christian faith. Sartre develops an existentialist theory of human consciousness that is non-Christian and which contains detailed analysis of the being of the lover as a mode of human consciousness. Close to Sartre, and directly in the current tradition of phenomenological philosophy, are such figures as Merleau-Ponty and Emmanuel Levinas, who have given attention to the role of sex and of love in their analyses of the processes whereby consciousness structures the human world. From other generally existentialistic perspectives such thinkers as Ortega y Gasset have written works on the nature of love and its role in human affairs. Fromm, from a psychological and psychoanalytic perspective, applies a theory of love that is not incompatible with the tradition of philosophical idealism and existential analysis to the role that loving must play in creating the human relationships necessary for a desirable human world.

The selections that constitute Section V considered sex in its relationship to society and to social morality. The twentieth century is the inheritor of pioneer work done on psychological dimensions of sex in the late 1800s by such figures as Krafft-Ebing and Havelock Ellis. In contemporary society sex acts such as masturbation and oral-genital contact that were once seen as dangerous perversions have come through psychological and medical research to be seen as having a role in normal sex life. Their "unnaturalness" has come to be seen as largely based on cultural models of what is sexually normal and more specifically on the Christian model of the sex act as procreative. Since Freud there has been a general interest in research into human sexual activity and an interest in the freedom to discuss attitudes and social customs relating to sex. Sex investigation by social scientists has collected data on the actual sex habits, attitudes and practices of various strata of contemporary society. The development of anthropological thought has done much to make us aware of the diversity of sexual customs that exist in societies throughout the world.

Considerable attention has been given in contemporary thought to the amassing of information on sex and understanding its significance in human psychology, and most of the results of this research have been rapidly assimilated by the popular mind. Perhaps no other field of academic or scientific inquiry has had the results of its investigations so immediately enter ordinary thought. One of the fundamental questions that overrides the scientific investigation into sex is the ethical question of how society ought to be organized such that man can relate to his sexual nature and in so doing promote his own happiness. De Sade's proposal for a society in which all forms of sexual activity are permitted and encouraged, which appears as a selection in this section, is historically removed from contemporary thought, but it can be considered by the contemporary mind in a way that it could not by past eras, which were "morally" shocked by it or regarded it as pornographic fantasy. De Sade's concept of a society of absolute sexual freedom poses an ideal that is diametrically counter to the Christian ideal of restricting sexual activity to the procreative act performed within a monogamous marriage with the partners committed to each other for life. A generation ago Russell was regarded as a notorious advocate of free love. But Russell's proposals can be regarded as representing a position that takes neither of these extremes but stands more for the rational examination of sexual customs by society than for a particular set of sexual principles. De Beauvoir's analysis of the role of women in contemporary society argues that the civil rights gained for women in the early part of the twentieth century must be augmented by the creation in society of avenues of economic independence for women.

The final selection on the problem of the relation of sex to society is from the work of Rollo May and points to the fact that any understanding of the place of sex in contemporary society must take into account the entire orientation of contemporary life. The perspective implicit in May's analysis of the paradoxes of sex in contemporary life can be regarded as revisionary of the viewpoint present in Russell's thought. Russell's approach is exemplary of the commonly held view that we simply need to be more rational and critical in our approach to accepted sexual morality, and in the era in which Russell's view had its effect, the 1930s and 1940s, it was quite advanced. May's approach, however, suggests that it is not enough today to simply argue about the proper attitudes that should prevail toward sex. What we must come to understand is the way in which our contemporary attitudes toward sex and sexual freedom are tied to the total structuring of consciousness that makes advanced industrial civilization possible. One of the fundamental difficulties of contemporary life is that there exists, on the one hand, a total availability of scientific information on sex and, on the other hand, there is an inability of contemporary persons to experience the genuinely erotic dimension of human existence in the way, for example, the Greeks and other ancient peoples could.

Ultimately the reader must form his own judgments about how well philosophers and other thinkers who have written philosophically have thought about sex as an ethical and theoretical problem and how sex is to be understood in relation to contemporary society. Often philosophical thought that has dealt profoundly with metaphysical and ethical problems in a given age has but reflected the standard notions of its day when it has turned to questions of sex or the relations between the sexes. Although philosophers have in their personal lives often had admirable relationships with women, philosophers as a class have not thought highly of them, and there are, with only a few recent exceptions, no women philosophers. But regardless of what is to be made of what has been thought about sex in this context, we can hold to the point that if we are ever to understand the problems surrounding man's sexual nature and sexual morality, it is this kind of thought with which we must come to grips. Solutions to issues of contemporary interest that arise apart from historical orientation or simply from personal opinion are rarely of much lasting interest or of any general benefit to the altering of the human condition.

1

Greeks and Romans: Sex, Love and Eros

Love, sexuality and the relationships between the sexes are given considerable attention by classical thinkers. Regarded as problems inherent in the human world—aspects of life which all men face—they are proper subjects of philosophic inquiry. Classical philosophy, unlike much modern philosophy, is rarely technical in its subject matter, language or method of reasoning. Philosophical questions are thought of as questions open to all men as just those questions that arise in the course of all men's lives, the answers to which, if found, would affect all men equally. They are questions about the universal features of human experience, and the answers to them cannot, in principle, be hidden from any man who thinks straightforwardly in his own way, in his own language. Socrates, Plato, Aristotle, Epicurus, Lucretius, Epictetus, Marcus Aurelius and other ancient thinkers have no genuinely technical vocabulary or way of thinking. Their language is largely that of the marketplace of Athens and the citizenry of Rome, and their thought is open to all men who put their minds to it. The questions they discuss arise from the world of ordinary human experience, and their thought always leads us back to it.

The selections which follow are from Plato (429–347 B.C.), Aristotle (384–322 B.C.), Epictetus (A.D. 50–138) and Ovid (43 B.C.–A.D. 18). They discuss different types of love, friendship, the place of women in society and man's relationship to his sexual nature.

It seems natural that Plato and Aristotle, being in large part the founders of Western thought, should have discussed these questions as widely and deeply as they have. Love is a theme that runs throughout Plato's *Dialogues;* it constitutes part of Aristotle's ethical theory and plays a role in his concept of final causes. Epictetus and Ovid are representative of some of the intellectual attitudes present in the later part of the ancient period. Epictetus, being one of the prominent figures of Roman Stoicism, is representative of the general movement of classical thought from Athens to Rome, from the systems of Plato and Aristotle to the development of schools of thought centered around certain intellectual and moral premises. Epictetus sees sex as a problem for the moral will. According to Ovid, sex is a delight of the senses and love is to be made an erotic art. Plato, Aristotle, Epictetus and Ovid set before us a network of views which provide the basis for any subsequent or present day discussion of love, sex and the sexes. The views they express are as much of interest today as they were in their own time.

Plato's treatment of love occurs primarily in three dialogues —the *Lysis, Symposium* and *Phaedrus.* Of these the *Symposium* contains Plato's most complete and poetic discussion of love. The *Lysis* is one of Plato's early dialogues and is a discussion of friendship. The *Phaedrus* reflects many of the ideas about love that are expressed in the *Symposium* and connects them with a theory of the soul and with a discussion of the nature of rhetoric. The first two selections are the speeches of Aristophanes and Socrates in Plato's *Symposium*. The dialogue is devoted to the explanation of what love is and is organized around a series of speeches given by various persons with each person saying what he takes love to be. The speech of Aristophanes presents the myth of three sexes. It is a myth of the origin of the sexes which aims at picturing all the erotic relationships that are possible between the sexes—that between man and man, man and woman, and woman and woman. The speech of Socrates is presented by him as a discourse made to him by Diotima, a "prophetess," concerning the soul's ascent to an apprehension of absolute beauty under the impulse of love or *eros*.

Socrates maintains that love is to be identified with the lover and not the object of love. Love is the desire for immortality. This desire is manifest in the sexual unions of animals and of men in their drive for procreation. Ordinary men show this desire in their attempts to create offspring who will live after them. This desire also leads men to create social orders or states. This impulse can lead us on to the love of beauty which first appears as the love of beauty in other persons, then to beauty in the form of thoughts, laws and institutions. Finally, we can be led to the love of beauty itself. When we engage in this kind of love, we have made contact with that which is truly permanent and eternal in the world. In Socrates' speech love or *eros* is seen as a kind of self-motion of the soul in which it seeks to apprehend the rational order of things. This order is not visible to the eye, which sees only particular things and does not apprehend the total structure of which they are a part.

Socrates' speech in the *Symposium* is Plato's statement of

what has come to be called "Platonic love." "Platonic love" in
its literal and original meaning refers to the passion of the
individual for the apprehension of the rational order of things.
It does not, in Plato, mean a love between two persons that
does not involve sexual union, although this is what the term
has commonly come to mean. There is some basis for this
more popular meaning in Plato's discussion of friendship or
brotherly love in the *Lysis* and in the fact that in Socrates'
speech in the *Symposium* beauty is to be seen first in other
persons. But love is first and foremost for Plato a characteristic, and an essential characteristic, of the philosopher's nature.

Love or *eros* is a kind of self-motion of the soul in which it
seeks to apprehend the ultimate forms of things. The philosopher, as Socrates describes him at the beginning of his
speech, is literally a "lover of wisdom." Socrates' speech offers
a theory of what it means to be such a person. The philosopher
is presented as a figure who attempts to carry the impulse of
eros beyond its ordinary forms in order to gain an apprehension of that which is present in all of them. The activity of
philosophy is the attempt to love directly that element that is
being loved in all the lesser or more ordinary forms of loving.
In Socrates' speech we are shown that the activity of the
philosopher is to pass beyond the love of beautiful persons
and beauty in the form of various types of order to a love of
beauty itself. No particular beautiful thing is beauty itself. But
the reason for our attraction to it is that it presents to us
something of the nature of beauty itself. Beauty, for Plato, is
one of the Ideas or Forms that makes up the reality of the
world, its ultimate order. We only apprehend these Ideas or
Forms incompletely in the particular visible things around us.
Socrates' speech in the *Symposium* is one of Plato's first statements of his doctrine of Ideas or Forms. What emerges from it
for a theory of love is that the true lover is not the expert at

sexual love, nor the true friend, nor the lover of country and society, nor the lover of humanity. The true lover is one who would make over his own soul in accordance with *eros* such that he becomes a "lover of wisdom"—a seeker for the reality in all things.

The third selection from Plato which follows is from the *Republic* and is part of Plato's proposal of an ideal state, a state which is to be ruled by philosophers. After giving his account of the basic features of the ideal state, Plato takes up questions of what the relationship between the sexes ought to be, how children should be reared and the nature of marriage and the family. The selection which follows is from this part of his discussion. Earlier in the *Republic* Plato distinguishes between three classes of persons that are to exist in the ideal state—artisans, guardians and rulers. His proposal is not unique in having either the artisan or ruling class. All states require some persons who engage in the ordinary economic and practical activities of the state (artisans) and some persons who preform its legislative functions (rulers). The concept of the guardian class, however, is unique in Plato's theory. The guardians, generally speaking, are to be a class of educated persons whose duty it is to maintain the state both physically and spiritually. They are to be the preservers of culture and education and also its defenders or military. The rulers are selected out of the guardian class and are persons who undergo further education in order to attain the wisdom necessary to guide the state's course. Plato's conception of a guardian class has been one of the most controversial aspects of his theory of the state. It is in relation to the guardians that he makes his most radical social proposals.

Plato makes two fundamental proposals about the life of the guardians that were radical in his day and remain so in ours: (1) that women are to hold completely equal positions with men, i.e., they shall serve in the military equally, be eligible to become rulers, etc.; (2) all husbands, wives, children and property shall be held in common by the guardians and a system of eugenics shall be set up to assure the birth of only mentally and physically healthy children. This section of the *Republic* is, among other things, one of the first documents on the question of women's rights. The only difference between men and women in the ideal state is their role in the act of procreation. Plato derives his proposal that the guardians are to live communally and hold property only in common from the principle that: "friends have all things in common." The guardians are to have no private homes, marriages or parent relationships to the children they produce. They are to have no private families but are to be a family as a class such that all men stand to all women as husbands, all women to all men as wives, and all men and all women stand to all children as parents. Any analysis of women's rights and the desirability of the family as a basic social unit must begin with Plato's original and classic discussion of these questions.

One of Plato's strongest critics is Aristotle. The first of the selections from Aristotle is from his *Politics*. Here Aristotle argues that Plato's attempt to create a community of friends by having them hold husbands, wives and children in common will produce disunity, not unity in a state. By simply doing away with the various forms of friendship that are involved in the ordinary process of marriage, the family and the rearing of children, friendship itself will become so generalized that it will cease to exist. Although in a sense friends may have all things in common, friendship cannot simply exist as something general. It must exist in particular forms through which individuals relate to each other. The traditional forms of marriage and the family cannot simply be removed without something to replace them. Aristotle maintains that in such a state love will become "watery."

The second selection from Aristotle which follows is from

his *Ethics* and is his discussion of the types of friendship. Friendship, for Aristotle, is a primary element in human affairs as it was for all Greeks. In the *Politics* he calls friendship "the greatest good of states" and the preserver of their unity. In the *Ethics* he describes the types of friendship that exist on the basis of the object of love which each involves. He divides friendships into three classes—those of utility, of pleasure and of the type of love that exists between good men. The third type is the best relationship and is the most perfect form of human loving. Aristotle also endorses the notion of self-love. Love, Aristotle maintains, is not a term which refers only to relationships between individuals but can also describe the relationship an individual has to himself. By self-love Aristotle does not mean what is ordinarily thought of as egotism. He seems to have in mind more the ability to attribute human dignity to oneself. Before one can love others, one must regard oneself with a certain amount of esteem. It follows that Aristotle's third type of friendship of the love between good men involves the further condition that they are each lovers of self.

Epictetus sees true friendship to be possible only if men learn to employ their wills in accordance with virtue. Epictetus points to the fact that even the warmest and closest forms of human relationship such as between parent and child or blood relatives are subject to immediate dissolution if the smallest thing comes between the persons involved. This is because all such conventional relationships, even those of immediate family, depend upon some set of external conditions. If these conditions change, the relationship is threatened. True virtue depends upon men coming to grips with these external conditions and overcoming them by their wills. Desire for power and for property separate men from their wills and from each other. Unless these desires are conquered, they will always come between men. Virtue will never be possible. The desire for sexual pleasure must also be overcome as sexual pleasure involves man with his brutish nature. Sexual pleasure, for Epictetus, represents a loss of self-control.

In contrast to the Stoicism of Epictetus are Ovid's views in *The Art of Love*. Ovid regards love as an art that is practiced between man and woman for their mutual pleasure. Ovid's poem is a detailed description of how to practice the art of love, i. e., how to make oneself attractive to the opposite sex, how to meet and approach the opposite sex, how to conduct love affairs. The selection is taken from each of the three books of the poem. The first of the three books describes how a man is to find a mistress; the second describes how to keep her; and the third gives advice to women as to how they may do similarly. For Ovid, unlike Epictetus, sexual love is not brutish. It is part of man's humanity. Animals engage in sex acts but not in sexual love. Sexual love and its pleasure can only be experienced by humans as only humans raise their bodily functions to the level of an art. Ovid does not argue directly in this way as he is not writing in answer to Epictetus, but it is this argument that lies at the heart of his case. It should be noted that there is a certain equality of the sexes implied in Ovid's concept of the art of love. That is, it is conceived by him as an art in which both parties, man and woman, are to reciprocally achieve pleasure.

The thought of the Greek and Roman world raises fundamental questions about the nature of sex, the role the sexes are to play in society and the types of human love. The thought of Plato and Aristotle involves each of these areas and their thought about them differs considerably as do their philosophies as a whole. The comments and selections presented here do not involve all of the roles love plays in their thought. They concentrate on the role of love in their theories of man. The views of Epictetus and Ovid raise one of the most sweeping and fundamental questions relating to the philosophical theory of sex: Is man to regard his sexual nature as part of his animal nature which must be overcome if he is ever to be a moral being? Or, is man to regard his sexual nature as a positive part of his humanity, a bodily function that is to be raised to the level of a human art?

It should be noted that for Plato and Aristotle sex was not a "moral issue." Sex and sexual activity was regarded as something natural to man. Plato's *Dialogues* contain frequent references to both homosexual and heterosexual relationships without any moral tone attached to them. Both types of relationship are mentioned as natural and acceptable. There is in Greek thought and life little sense of there being "moral" or "immoral" forms in which sexual activity is supposed to take place. Sexual relationships, for Plato and Aristotle, are not in and of themselves moral problems. They are only problems insofar as they involve broader problems of human relationships or the functioning of society. It is only with the later Stoics, such as Epictetus, and the development of Christianity that sex itself becomes a moral problem.

1. PLATO: Origin of the Sexes

Plato (427–347 B.C.), a member of one of the leading families of
Athens, was expected to pursue a career in public life, but on meeting Socrates at an early age he decided to devote his life to philosophy. The ideas expressed in his **Dialogues** have shown themselves
to be the fountainhead of Western thought.

Aristophanes professed to open another vein of discourse; he
had a mind to praise Love in another way, unlike that either of
Pausanias or Eryximachus. Mankind, he said, judging by their
neglect of him, have never, as I think, at all understood the
power of Love. For if they had understood him they would

SOURCE: Plato, "Symposium," *The Dialogues of Plato,* 3d ed., trans. Benjamin Jowett (New York and London: Oxford University Press, 1892),
1:559–563.

surely have built noble temples and altars, and offered solemn sacrifices in his honor; but this is not done, and most certainly ought to be done; since of all the gods he is the best friend of men, the helper and the healer of the ills which are the great impediment to the happiness of the race. I will try to describe his power to you, and you shall teach the rest of the world what I am teaching you. In the first place, let me treat of the nature of man and what has happened to it; for the original human nature was not like the present, but different. The sexes were not two as they are now, but originally three in number; there was man, woman, and the union of the two, having a name corresponding to this double nature, which had once a real existence, but is now lost, and the word "Androgynous" is only preserved as a term of reproach. In the second place, the primeval man was round, his back and sides forming a circle; and he had four hands and four feet, one head with two faces, looking opposite ways, set on a round neck and precisely alike; also four ears, two privy members, and the remainder to correspond. He could walk upright as men now do, backwards or forwards as he pleased, and he could also roll over and over at a great pace, turning on his four hands and four feet, eight in all, like tumblers going over and over with their legs in the air; this was when he wanted to run fast. Now the sexes were three, and such as I have described them; because the sun, moon, and earth are three; and the man was originally the child of the sun, the woman of the earth, and the man-woman of the moon, which is made up of sun and earth, and they were all round and moved round and round like their parents. Terrible was their might and strength, and the thoughts of their hearts were great, and they made an attack upon the gods; of them is told the tale of Otys and Ephialtes who, as Homer says, dared to scale heaven, and would have laid hands upon the gods. Doubt reigned in the celestial councils. Should they kill them and annihilate the race with thunderbolts, as they had done the giants, then there would be an end of the sacrifices and worship which men offered to them; but, on the other hand, the gods could not suffer their insolence to be unrestrained. At last, after a good deal of reflection, Zeus discovered a way. He said: "Methinks I have a plan which will humble their pride and improve their manners; men shall continue to exist, but I will cut them in two and then they will be diminished in strength and increased in numbers; this will have the advantage of making them more profitable to us. They shall walk upright on two legs, and if they continue insolent and will not be quiet, I will split them again and they shall hop about on a single leg." He spoke and cut men in two, like a sorb-apple which is halved for pickling, or as you might divide an egg with a hair; and as he cut them one after another, he bade Apollo give the face and the half of the neck a turn in order that the man might contemplate the section of himself: he would thus learn a lesson of humility. Apollo was also bidden to heal their wounds and compose their forms. So he gave a turn to the face and pulled the skin from the sides all over that which in our language is called the belly, like the purses which draw in, and he made one mouth at the center, which he fastened in a knot (the same which is called the navel); he also molded the breast and took out most of the wrinkles, much as a shoemaker might smooth leather upon a last; he left a few, however, in the region of the belly and navel, as a memorial of the primeval state. After the division the two parts of man, each desiring his other half, came together, and throwing their arms about one another, entwined in mutual embraces, longing to grow into one, they were on the point of dying from hunger and self-neglect, because they did not like to do anything apart; and when one of the halves died and the other survived, the survivor sought another mate, man or woman as we call them—being the sections of entire men or women—and clung to that. They

were being destroyed, when Zeus in pity of them invented a
new plan: he turned the parts of generation round to the front,
for this had not been always their position, and they sowed the
seed no longer as hitherto like grasshoppers in the ground, but
in one another; and after the transposition the male generated
in the female in order that by the mutual embraces of man
and woman they might breed, and the race might continue; or
if man came to man they might be satisfied, and rest, and go
their ways to the business of life: so ancient is the desire of
one another which is implanted in us, reuniting our original
nature, making one of two, and healing the state of man. Each
of us when separated, having one side only, like a flat fish, is
but the indenture of a man, and he is always looking for his
other half. Men who are a section of that double nature which
was once called Androgynous are lovers of women; adulterers
are generally of this breed, and also adulterous women who
lust after men: the women who are a section of the woman do
not care for men, but have female attachments; the female
companions are of this sort. But they who are a section of the
male follow the male, and while they are young, being slices of
the original man, they hang about men and embrace them,
and they are themselves the best of boys and youths, because
they have the most manly nature. Some indeed assert that they
are shameless, but this is not true; for they do not act thus
from any want of shame, but because they are valiant and
manly, and have a manly countenance, and they embrace that
which is like them. And these when they grow up become our
statesmen, and these only, which is a great proof of the truth
of what I am saying. When they reach manhood, they are
lovers of youth, and are not naturally inclined to marry or
beget children—if at all, they do so only in obedience to the
law; but they are satisfied if they may be allowed to live with
one another unwedded; and such a nature is prone to love and
ready to return love, always embracing that which is akin to

him. And when one of them meets with his other half, the actual half of himself, whether he be a lover of youth or a lover of another sort, the pair are lost in an amazement of love and friendship and intimacy, and one will not be out of the other's sight, as I may say, even for a moment: these are the people who pass their whole lives together; yet they could not explain what they desire of one another. For the intense yearning which each of them has towards the other does not appear to be the desire of lover's intercourse, but of something else which the soul of either evidently desires and cannot tell, and of which she has only a dark and doubtful presentiment. Suppose Hephaestus, with his instruments, to come to the pair who are lying side by side and to say to them, "What do you two people want of one another?" they would be unable to explain. And suppose further, that when he saw their perplexity he said: "Do you desire to be wholly one; always day and night to be in one another's company? for if this is what you desire, I am ready to melt you into one and let you grow together, so that being two you shall become one, and while you live live a common life as if you were a single man, and after your death in the world below still be one departed soul instead of two—I ask whether this is what you lovingly desire, and whether you are satisfied to attain this?"—there is not a man of them who when he heard the proposal would deny or would not acknowledge that this meeting and melting into one another, this becoming one instead of two, was the very expression of his ancient need. And the reason is that human nature was originally one and we were a whole, and the desire and pursuit of the whole is called love. There was a time, I say, when we were one, but now because of the wickedness of mankind God has dispersed us, as the Arcadians were dispersed into villages by the Lacedaemonians. And if we are not obedient to the gods, there is a danger that we shall be split up again and go about in basso-relievo, like the profile figures having only half a nose which are sculptured on monuments, and that we shall be like tallies. Wherefore let us exhort all men to piety, that we may avoid evil, and obtain the good, of which Love is to us the lord and minister; and let no one oppose him—he is the enemy of the gods who opposes him. For if we are friends of the God and at peace with him, we shall find our own true loves, which rarely happens in this world at present. I am serious, and therefore I must beg Eryximachus not to make fun or to find any allusion in what I am saying to Pausanias and Agathon, who, as I suspect, are both of the manly nature, and belong to the class which I have been describing. But my words have a wider application— they include men and women everywhere; and I believe that if our loves were perfectly accomplished, and each one returning to his primeval nature had his original true love, then our race would be happy. And if this would be best of all, the best in the next degree and under present circumstances must be the nearest approach to such an union; and that will be the attainment of a congenial love. Wherefore, if we would praise him who has given to us the benefit, we must praise the god Love, who is our greatest benefactor, both leading us in this life back to our own nature, and giving us high hopes for the future, for he promises that if we are pious, he will restore us to our original state, and heal us and make us happy and blessed.

2. PLATO: Platonic Love

And now, taking my leave of you, I will rehearse a tale of love which I heard from Diotima of Mantineia, a woman wise in this and in many other kinds of knowledge, who in the days of old, when the Athenians offered sacrifice before the coming of the plague, delayed the disease ten years. She was my instructress in the art of love, and I shall repeat to you what she said to me, beginning with the admissions made by Agathon, which are nearly if not quite the same which I made to the wise woman when she questioned me: I think that this will be the easiest way, and I shall take both parts myself as well as I can. As you, Agathon, suggested, I must speak first of the

SOURCE: Plato, "Symposium," *The Dialogues of Plato*, 3d ed., trans. Benjamin Jowett (New York and London: Oxford University Press, 1892), 1:572–582.

being and nature of Love, and then of his works. First I said
to her in nearly the same words which he used to me, that
Love was a mighty god, and likewise fair; and she proved to
me as I proved to him that, by my own showing, Love was
neither fair nor good. "What do you mean, Diotima," I said, "is
love then evil and foul?" "Hush," she cried; "must that be foul
which is not fair?" "Certainly," I said. "And is that which is not
wise, ignorant? Do you not see that there is a mean between
wisdom and ignorance?" "And what may that be?" I said.
"Right opinion," she replied; "which, as you know, being incapable of giving a reason, is not knowledge (for how can
knowledge be devoid of reason? nor again, ignorance, for
neither can ignorance attain the truth), but is clearly something which is a mean between ignorance and wisdom." "Quite
true," I replied. "Do not then insist," she said, "that what is not
fair is of necessity foul, or what is not good evil; or infer that
because love is not fair and good he is therefore foul and evil;
for he is in a mean between them." "Well," I said, "Love is
surely admitted by all to be a great god." "By those who know
or by those who do not know?" "By all." "And how, Socrates,"
she said with a smile, "can Love be acknowledged to be a great
god by those who say that he is not a god at all?" "And who
are they?" I said. "You and I are two of them," she replied.
"How can that be?" I said. "It is quite intelligible," she replied;
"for you yourself would acknowledge that the gods are happy
and fair—of course you would—would you dare to say that
any god was not?" "Certainly not," I replied. "And you mean
by the happy, those who are the possessors of things good or
fair?" "Yes." "And you admitted that Love, because he was in
want, desires those good and fair things of which he is in
want?" "Yes, I did." "But how can he be a god who has no
portion in what is either good or fair?" "Impossible." "Then
you see that you also deny the divinity of Love."

"What then is Love?" I asked; "is he mortal?" "No." "What

then?" "as in the former instance, he is neither mortal nor
immortal, but in a mean between the two." "What is he,
Diotima?" "He is a great spirit ($\delta\alpha\acute{\iota}\mu\omega\nu$), and like all spirits he
is intermediate between the divine and the mortal." "And
what," I said, "is his power?" "He interprets," she replied,
"between gods and men, conveying and taking across to the
gods the prayers and sacrifices of men, and to men the commands and replies of the gods; he is the mediator who spans
the chasm which divides them, and therefore in him all is
bound together, and through him the arts of the prophet and
the priest, their sacrifices and mysteries and charms, and all
prophecy and incantation, find their way. For God mingles not
with man; but through Love all the intercourse and converse
of God with man, whether awake or asleep, is carried on. The
wisdom which understands this is spiritual; all other wisdom,
such as that of arts and handicrafts, is mean and vulgar. Now
these spirits or intermediate powers are many and diverse, and
one of them is Love." "And who," I said, "was his father, and
who his mother?" "The tale," she said, "will take time; nevertheless I will tell you. On the birthday of Aphrodite there was
a feast of the gods, at which the god Poros or Plenty, who is
the son of Metis or Discretion, was one of the guests. When
the feast was over, Penia or Poverty, as the manner is on such
occasions, came about the doors to beg. Now Plenty, who was
the worse for nectar (there was no wine in those days), went
into the garden of Zeus and fell into a heavy sleep; and
Poverty considering her own straitenened circumstances,
plotted to have a child by him, and accordingly she lay down
at his side and conceived Love, who partly because he is
naturally a lover of the beautiful, and because Aphrodite is
herself beautiful, and also because he was born on her birthday, is her follower and attendant. And as his parentage is, so
also are his fortunes. In the first place he is always poor, and
anything but tender and fair, as the many imagine him; and he

is rough and squalid, and has no shoes, nor a house to dwell in; on the bare earth exposed he lies under the open heaven, in the streets, or at the doors of houses, taking his rest; and like his mother he is always in distress. Like his father too, whom he also partly resembles, he is always plotting against the fair and good; he is bold, enterprising, strong, a mighty hunter, always weaving some intrigue or other, keen in the pursuit of wisdom, fertile in resources; a philosopher at all times, terrible as an enchanter, sorcerer, sophist. He is by nature neither mortal nor immortal, but alive and flourishing at one moment when he is in plenty, and dead at another moment, and again alive by reason of his father's nature. But that which is always flowing in is always flowing out, and so he is never in want and never in wealth; and, further, he is in a mean between ignorance and knowledge. The truth of the matter is this: No god is a philosopher or seeker after wisdom, for he is wise already; nor does any man who is wise seek after wisdom. Neither do the ignorant seek after wisdom. For herein is the evil of ignorance, that he who is neither good nor wise is nevertheless satisfied with himself: he has no desire for that of which he feels no want." "But who then, Diotima," I said, "are the lovers of wisdom, if they are neither the wise nor the foolish?" "A child may answer that question," she replied; "they are those who are in a mean between the two; Love is one of them. For wisdom is a most beautiful thing, and Love is of the beautiful; and therefore Love is also a philosopher or lover of wisdom, and being a lover of wisdom is in a mean between the wise and the ignorant. And of this too his birth is the cause; for his father is wealthy and wise, and his mother poor and foolish. Such, my dear Socrates, is the nature of the spirit Love. The error in your conception of him was very natural, and as I imagine from what you say, has arisen out of a confusion of love and the beloved, which made you think that love was all beautiful. For the beloved is the truly beautiful, and delicate, and perfect, and blessed; but the principle of love is of another nature, and is such as I have described."

I said: "O thou stranger woman, thou sayest well; but, assuming Love to be such as you say, what is the use of him to men?" "That, Socrates," she replied, "I will attempt to unfold: of his nature and birth I have already spoken; and you acknowledge that love is of the beautiful. But some one will say: Of the beautiful in what, Socrates and Diotima?—or rather let me put the question more clearly, and ask: When a man loves the beautiful, what does he desire?" I answered her "That the beautiful may be his." "Still," she said, "the answer suggests a further question: What is given by the possession of beauty?" "To what you have asked," I replied, "I have no answer ready." "Then," she said, "let me put the word 'good' in the place of the beautiful, and repeat the question once more: If he who loves loves the good, what is it then that he loves?" "The possession of the good," I said. "And what does he gain who possesses the good?" "Happiness," I replied; "there is less difficulty in answering that question." "Yes," she said, "the happy are made happy by the acquisition of good things. Nor is there any need to ask why a man desires happiness; the answer is already final." "You are right," I said. "And is this wish and this desire common to all? and do all men always desire their own good, or only some men?—what say you?" "All men," I replied; "the desire is common to all." "Why, then," she rejoined, "are not all men, Socrates, said to love, but only some of them? whereas you say that all men are always loving the same things." "I myself wonder," I said, "why this is." "There is nothing to wonder at," she replied; "the reason is that one part of love is separated off and receives the name of the whole, but the other parts have other names." "Give an illustration," I said. She answered me as follows: "There is poetry, which, as you know, is complex and manifold. All creation or passage of non-being into being is poetry or making, and the processes of all art are creative; and the masters of arts are all poets or makers." "Very true." "Still," she said, "you know that they are not called poets, but have other names; only that portion of the art which is separated off from the rest, and is concerned with music and metre, is termed poetry, and they who possess poetry in this sense of the word are called poets." "Very true," I said. "And the same holds of love. For you may say generally that all desire of good and happiness is only the great and subtle power of love; but they who are drawn towards him by any other path, whether the path of money-making or gymnastics or philosophy, are not called lovers—the name of the whole is appropriated to those whose affection takes one form only—they alone are said to love, or to be lovers." "I dare say," I replied, "that you are right." "Yes," she added, "and you hear people say that lovers are seeking for their other half; but I say that they are seeking neither for the half of themselves, nor for the whole, unless the half or the whole be also a good. And they will cut off their own hands and feet and cast them away, if they are evil; for they love not what is their own, unless perchance there be some one who calls what belongs to him the good, and what belongs to another the evil. For there is nothing which men love but the good. Is there anything?" "Certainly, I should say, that there is nothing." "Then," she said, "the simple truth is, that men love the good." "Yes," I said. "To which must be added that they love the possession of the good?" "Yes, that must be added." "And not only the possession, but the everlasting possession of the good?" "That must be added too." "Then love," she said, "may be described generally as the love of the everlasting possession of the good?" "That is most true."

"Then if this be the nature of love, can you tell me further," she said, "what is the manner of the pursuit? what are they doing who show all this eagerness and heat which is called love? and what is the object which they have in view? Answer me." "Nay, Diotima," I replied, "if I had known, I should not have wondered at your wisdom, neither should I have come to learn from you about this very matter." "Well," she said, "I will teach you:—The object which they have in view is birth in beauty, whether of body or soul." "I do not understand you," I said; "the oracle requires an explanation." "I will make my meaning clearer," she replied. "I mean to say, that all men are bringing to the birth in their bodies and in their souls. There is a certain age at which human nature is desirous of procreation —procreation which must be in beauty and not in deformity; and this procreation is the union of man and woman, and is a divine thing; for conception and generation are an immortal principle in the mortal creature, and in the inharmonious they can never be. But the deformed is always inharmonious with the divine, and the beautiful harmonious. Beauty, then, is the destiny or goddess of parturition who presides at birth, and therefore, when approaching beauty, the conceiving power is propitious, and diffusive, and benign, and begets and bears fruit: at the sight of ugliness she frowns and contracts and has a sense of pain, and turns away, and shrivels up, and not without a pang refrains from conception. And this is the reason why, when the hour of conception arrives, and the teeming nature is full, there is such a flutter and ecstacy about beauty whose approach is the alleviation of the pain of travail. For love, Socrates, is not, as you imagine, the love of the beautiful only." "What then?" "The love of generation and of birth in beauty." "Yes," I said. "Yes, indeed," she replied. "But why of generation?" "Because to the mortal creature, genera-tion is a sort of eternity and immortality," she replied; "and if, as has been already admitted, love is of the everlasting posses-sion of the good, all men will necessarily desire immortality together with good: Wherefore love is of immortality."

All this she taught me at various times when she spoke of love. And I remember her once saying to me, "What is the cause, Socrates, of love, and the attendant desire? See you not how all animals, birds, as well as beasts, in their desire of procreation, are in agony when they take the infection of love, which begins with the desire of union; whereto is added the care of offspring, on whose behalf the weakest are ready to battle against the strongest even to the uttermost, and to die for them, and will let themselves be tormented with hunger or suffer anything in order to maintain their young. Man may be supposed to act thus from reason; but why should animals have these passionate feelings? Can you tell me why?" Again I replied that I did not know. She said to me: "And do you expect ever to become a master in the art of love, if you do not know this?" "But I have told you already, Diotima, that my ignorance is the reason why I come to you; for I am conscious that I want a teacher; tell me then the cause of this and of the other mysteries of love." "Marvel not," she said, "if you believe that love is of the immortal, as we have several times acknowledged; for here again, and on the same principle too, the mortal nature is seeking as far as is possible to be everlasting and immortal: and this is only to be attained by generation, because generation always leaves behind a new existence in the place of the old. Nay even in the life of the same individual there is succession and not absolute unity: a man is called the same, and yet in the short interval which elapses between youth and age, and in which every animal is said to have life and identity, he is undergoing a perpetual process of loss and reparation—hair, flesh, bones, blood, and the whole body are always changing. Which is true not only of the body, but also of the soul, whose habits, tempers, opinions, desires, pleasures, pains, fears, never remain the same in any one of us, but are always coming and going; and equally true of knowledge, and what is still more surprising to us mortals, not only do the sciences in general spring up and decay, so that in respect of them we are never the same; but each of them individually experiences a like change. For what is implied in the word "recollection," but the departure of knowledge, which is ever being forgotten, and is renewed and preserved by recollection, and appears to be the same although in reality new, according to that law of succession by which all mortal things are preserved, not absolutely the same, but by substitution, the old worn-out mortality leaving another new and similar existence behind—unlike the divine, which is always the same and not another? And in this way, Socrates, the mortal body, or mortal anything, partakes of immortality; but the immortal in another way. Marvel not then at the love which all men have of their offspring; for that universal love and interest is for the sake of immortality."

I was astonished at her words, and said: "Is this really true, O thou wise Diotima?" And she answered with all the authority of an accomplished sophist: "Of that, Socrates, you may be assured;—think only of the ambition of men, and you will wonder at the senselessness of their ways, unless you consider how they are stirred by the love of an immortality of fame. They are ready to run risks of all kinds and greater far than they would have run for their children, and to spend money and undergo any sort of toil, and even to die, for the sake of leaving behind them a name which shall be eternal. Do you imagine that Alcestis would have died to save Admetus, or Achilles to avenge Patroclus, or your own Codrus in order to preserve the kingdom for his sons, if they had not imagined that the memory of their virtues, which still survives among us, would be immortal? Nay," she said, "I am persuaded that all men do all things, and the better they are the more they do them, in hope of the glorious fame of immortal virtue; for they desire the immortal.

"Those who are pregnant in the body only, betake themselves to women and beget children—this is the character of their love; their offspring, as they hope, will preserve their memory and give them the blessedness and immortality which they desire in the future. But souls which are pregnant—for there certainly are men who are more creative in their souls than in their bodies—conceive that which is proper for the soul to conceive or contain. And what are these conceptions?—wisdom and virtue in general. And such creators are poets and all artists who are deserving of the name inventor. But the greatest and fairest sort of wisdom by far is that which is concerned with the ordering of states and families, and which is called temperance and justice. And he who in youth has the seed of these implanted in him and is himself inspired, when he comes to maturity desires to beget and generate. He wanders about seeking beauty that he may beget offspring—for in deformity 'he will beget nothing—and naturally embraces the beautiful rather than the deformed body; above all when he finds a fair and noble and well-nurtured soul, he embraces the two in one person, and to such an one he is full of speech about virtue and the nature and pursuits of a good man; and he tries to educate him; and at the touch of the beautiful which is ever present to his memory, even when absent, he brings forth that which he had conceived long before, and in company with him tends that which he brings forth; and they are married by a far nearer tie and have a closer friendship than those who beget mortal children, for the children who are their common offspring are fairer and more immortal. Who, when he thinks of Homer and Hesiod and other great poets, would not rather have their children than ordinary human ones? Who would not emulate them in the creation of children such as theirs, which have preserved their memory and given them everlasting glory? Or who would not have such children as Lycurgus left behind him to be the saviors, not only of Lacedaemon, but of Hellas, as one may say? There is Solon, too, who is the revered father of Athenian laws; and many others there are in many other places, both among Hellenes and barbarians, who have given to the world many noble works, and have been the parents of virtue of every kind; and many temples have been raised in their honor for the sake of children such as theirs; which were never raised in honor of any one, for the sake of his mortal children.

"These are the lesser mysteries of love, into which even you, Socrates, may enter; to the greater and more hidden ones which are the crown of these, and to which, if you pursue them in a right spirit, they will lead, I know not whether you will be able to attain. But I will do my utmost to inform you, and do you follow if you can. For he who would proceed aright in this matter should begin in youth to visit beautiful forms; and first, if he be guided by his instructor aright, to love one such form only—out of that he should create fair thoughts; and soon he will of himself perceive that the beauty of one form is akin to the beauty of another; and then if beauty of form in general is his pursuit, how foolish would he be not to recognize that the beauty in every form is one and the same! And when he perceives this he will abate his violent love of the one, which he will despise and deem a small thing, and will become a lover of all beautiful forms; in the next stage he will consider that the beauty of the mind is more honorable than the beauty of the outward form. So that if a virtuous soul have but a little comeliness, he will be content to love and tend him, and will search out and bring to the birth thoughts which may improve the young, until he is compelled to contemplate and see the beauty of institutions and laws, and to understand that the beauty of them all is of one family, and that personal beauty is a trifle; and after laws and institutions he will go on to the sciences, that he may see their beauty, being not like a servant in love with the beauty of one youth or man or institution, himself a slave mean and narrow-minded, but drawing towards and contemplating the vast sea of beauty, he will create many fair and noble thoughts and notions in boundless love of wisdom; until on that shore he grows and waxes strong, and at last the vision is revealed to him of a single science, which is the science of beauty everywhere. To this I will proceed; please to give me your very best attention:

"He who has been instructed thus far in the things of love, and who has learned to see the beautiful in due order and succession, when he comes toward the end will suddenly perceive a nature of wondrous beauty (and this, Socrates, is the final cause of all our former toils)—a nature which in the first place is everlasting, not growing and decaying, or waxing and waning; secondly, not fair in one point of view and foul in another, or at one time or in one relation or at one place fair, at another time or in another relation or at another place foul, as if fair to some and foul to others, or in the likeness of a face or hands or any other part of the bodily frame, or in any form of speech or knowledge, or existing in any other being, as for example, in an animal, or in heaven, or in earth, or in any other place; but beauty absolute, separate, simple, and everlasting, which without diminution and without increase, or any change, is imparted to the ever-growing and perishing beauties of all other things. He who from these ascending under the influence of true love, begins to perceive that beauty, is not far from the end. And the true order of going, or being led by another, to the things of love, is to begin from the beauties of earth and mount upwards for the sake of that other beauty, using these as steps only, and from one going on to two, and from two to all fair forms, and from fair forms to fair practices, and from fair practices to fair notions, until from fair notions he arrives at the notion of absolute beauty, and at last knows what the essence of beauty is. This, my dear Socrates," said the stranger of Mantineia, "is that life above all others which man should live, in the contemplation of beauty

absolute; a beauty which if you once beheld, you would see
not to be after the measure of gold, and garments, and fair
boys and youths, whose presence now entrances you; and you
and many alone would be content to live seeing them only and
conversing with them without meat or drink, if that were
possible—you only want to look at them and to be with them.
But what if man had eyes to see the true beauty—the divine
beauty, I mean, pure and clear and unalloyed, not clogged
with the pollutions of mortality and all the colors and van-
ities of human life—thither looking, and holding converse with
the true beauty simple and divine? Remember how in that
communion only, beholding beauty with the eye of the mind,
he will be enabled to bring forth, not images of beauty, but
realities (for he has hold not of an image but of a reality), and
bringing forth and nourishing true virtue to become the friend
of God and be immortal, if mortal man may. Would that be an
ignoble life?"

Such, Phaedrus—and I speak not only to you, but to all of
you—were the words of Diotima; and I am persuaded of their
truth. And being persuaded of them, I try to persuade others,
that in the attainment of this end human nature will not easily
find a helper better than love. And therefore, also, I say that
every man ought to honor him as I myself honor him, and
walk in his ways, and exhort others to do the same, and praise
the power and spirit of love according to the measure of my
ability now and ever.

The words which I have spoken, you, Phaedrus, may call an
encomium of love, or anything else which you please.

3. PLATO: Women's Rights

First, then, whether the question is to be put in jest or in earnest, let us come to an understanding about the nature of woman: Is she capable of sharing either wholly or partially in the actions of men, or not at all? And is the art of war one of those arts in which she can or can not share? That will be the best way of commencing the inquiry, and will probably lead to the fairest conclusion.

That will be much the best way.

Shall we take the other side first and begin by arguing against ourselves; in this manner the adversary's position will not be undefended.

SOURCE: Plato, "Republic," *The Dialogues of Plato,* 3d ed., trans. Benjamin Jowett (New York and London: Oxford University Press, 1892), 3:144–159.

Why not? he said.

Then let us put a speech into the mouths of our opponents. They will say: "Socrates and Glaucon, no adversary need convict you, for you yourselves, at the first foundation of the State, admitted the principle that everybody was to do the one work suited to his own nature." And certainly, if I am not mistaken, such an admission was made by us. "And do not the natures of men and women differ very much indeed?" And we shall reply: Of course they do. Then we shall be asked, "Whether the tasks assigned to men and to women should not be different, and such as are agreeable to their different natures?" Certainly they should. "But if so, have you not fallen into a serious inconsistency in saying that men and women, whose natures are so entirely different, ought to perform the same actions?"—What defence will you make for us, my good Sir, against any one who offers these objections?

That is not an easy question to answer when asked suddenly; and I shall and I do beg of you to draw out the case on our side.

These are the objections, Glaucon, and there are many others of a like kind, which I foresaw long ago; they made me afraid and reluctant to take in hand any law about the possession and nurture of women and children.

By Zeus, he said, the problem to be solved is anything but easy.

Why yes, I said, but the fact is that when a man is out of his depth, whether he has fallen into a little swimming bath or into mid ocean, he has to swim all the same.

Very true.

And must not we swim and try to reach the shore: we will hope that Arion's dolphin or some other miraculous help may save us?

I suppose so, he said.

Well then, let us see if any way of escape can be found. We

acknowledged—did we not? that different natures ought to have different pursuits, and that men's and women's natures are different. And now what are we saying?—that different natures ought to have the same pursuits,—this is the inconsistency which is charged upon us.

Precisely.

Verily, Glaucon, I said, glorious is the power of the art of contradiction!

Why do you say so?

Because I think that many a man falls into the practice against his will. When he thinks that he is reasoning, he is really disputing, just because he cannot define and divide, and so know that of which he is speaking; and he will pursue a merely verbal opposition in the spirit of contention and not of fair discussion.

Yes, he replied, such is very often the case; but what has that to do with us and our argument?

A great deal; for there is certainly a danger of our getting unintentionally into a verbal opposition.

In what way?

Why we valiantly and pugnaciously insist upon the verbal truth, that different natures ought to have different pursuits, but we never considered at all what was the meaning of sameness or difference of nature, or why we distinguished them when we assigned different pursuits to different natures and the same to the same natures.

Why, no, he said, that was never considered by us.

I said: Suppose that by way of illustration we were to ask the question whether there is not an opposition in nature between bald men and hairy men; and if this is admitted by us, then, if bald men are cobblers, we should forbid the hairy men to be cobblers, and conversely?

That would be a jest, he said.

Yes, I said, a jest; and why? because we never meant when

we constructed the State, that the opposition of natures should extend to every difference, but only to those differences which affected the pursuit in which the individual is engaged; we should have argued, for example, that a physician and one who is in mind a physician may be said to have the same nature.

True.

Whereas the physician and the carpenter have different natures?

Certainly.

And if, I said, the male and female sex appear to differ in their fitness for any art or pursuit, we should say that such pursuit or art ought to be assigned to one or the other of them; but if the difference consists only in women bearing and men begetting children, this does not amount to a proof that a woman differs from a man in respect of the sort of education she should receive; and we shall therefore continue to maintain that our guardians and their wives ought to have the same pursuits.

Very true, he said.

Next, we shall ask our opponent how, in reference to any of the pursuits of arts of civic life, the nature of a woman differs from that of a man?

That will be quite fair.

And perhaps he, like yourself, will reply that to give a sufficient answer on the instant is not easy; but after a little reflection there is no difficulty.

Yes, perhaps.

Suppose then that we invite him to accompany us in the argument, and then we may hope to show him that there is nothing peculiar in the constitution of women which would affect them in the administration of the State.

By all means.

Let us say to him: Come now, and we will ask you a question:—when you spoke of a nature gifted or not gifted in any respect, did you mean to say that one man will acquire a thing easily, another with difficulty; a little learning will lead the one to discover a great deal; whereas the other, after much study and application, no sooner learns than he forgets; or again, did you mean, that the one has a body which is a good servant to his mind, while the body of the other is a hindrance to him?— would not these be the sort of differences which distinguish the man gifted by nature from the one who is ungifted?

No one will deny that.

And can you mention any pursuit of mankind in which the male sex has not all these gifts and qualities in a higher degree than the female? Need I waste time in speaking of the art of weaving, and the management of pancakes and preserves, in which womankind does really appear to be great, and in which for her to be beaten by a man is of all things the most absurd?

You are quite right, he replied, in maintaining the general inferiority of the female sex: although many women are in many things superior to many men, yet on the whole what you say is true.

And if so, my friend, I said, there is no special faculty of administration in a state which a woman has because she is a woman, or which a man has by virtue of his sex, but the gifts of nature are alike diffused in both; all the pursuits of men are the pursuits of women also, but in all of them a woman is inferior to a man.

Very true.

Then are we to impose all our enactments on men and none of them on women?

That will never do.

One woman has a gift of healing, another not; one is a musician, and another has no music in her nature?

Very true.

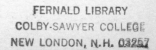

And one woman has a turn for gymnastic and military exercises, and another is unwarlike and hates gymnastics?

Certainly.

And one woman is a philosopher, and another is an enemy of philosophy; one has spirit, and another is without spirit?

That is also true.

Then one woman will have the temper of a guardian, and another not. Was not the selection of the male guardians determined by differences of this sort?

Yes.

Men and women alike possess the qualities which make a guardian; they differ only in their comparative strength or weakness.

Obviously.

And those women who have such qualities are to be selected as the companions and colleagues of men who have similar qualities and whom they resemble in capacity and in character?

Very true.

And ought not the same natures to have the same pursuits?

They ought.

Then, as we were saying before, there is nothing unnatural in assigning music and gymnastic to the wives of the guardians—to that point we come round again.

Certainly not.

The law which we then enacted was agreeable to nature, and therefore not an impossibility or mere aspiration; and the contrary practice, which prevails at present, is in reality a violation of nature.

That appears to be true.

We had to consider, first, whether our proposals were possible, and secondly whether they were the most beneficial?

Yes.

And the possibility has been acknowledged?

Yes.

The very great benefit has next to be established?

Quite so.

You will admit that the same education which makes a man a good guardian will make a woman a good guardian; for their original nature is the same?

Yes.

I should like to ask you a question.

What is it?

Would you say that all men are equal in excellence, or is one man better than another?

The latter.

And in the commonwealth which we were founding do you conceive the guardians who have been brought up on our model system to be more perfect men, or the cobblers whose education has been cobbling?

What a ridiculous question!

You have answered me, I replied: Well, and may we not further say that our guardians are the best of our citizens?

By far the best.

And will not their wives be the best women?

Yes, by far the best.

And can there be anything better for the interests of the State than that the men and women of a State should be as good as possible?

There can be nothing better.

And this is what the arts of music and gymnastic, when present in such manner as we have described, will accomplish?

Certainly.

Then we have made an enactment not only possible but in the highest degree beneficial to the State?

True.

Then let the wives of our guardians strip, for their virtue will be their robe, and let them share in the toils of war and the defence of their country; only in the distribution of labors the lighter are to be assigned to the women, who are the weaker natures, but in other respects their duties are to be the same. And as for the man who laughs at naked women exercising their bodies from the best of motives, in his laughter he is plucking, "A fruit of unripe wisdom," and he himself is ignorant of what he is laughing at, or what he is about;—for that is, and ever will be, the best of sayings, *That the useful is the noble and the hurtful is the base*.

Very true.

Here, then, is one difficulty in our law about women, which we may say that we have now escaped; the wave has not swallowed us up alive for enacting that the guardians of either sex should have all their pursuits in common; to the utility and also to the possibility of this arrangement the consistency of the argument with itself bears witness.

Yes, that was a mighty wave which you have escaped.

Yes, I said, but a greater is coming; you will not think much of this when you see the next.

Go on; let me see.

The law, I said, which is the sequel of this and of all that has preceded, is to the following effect—"that the wives of our guardians are to be common, and their children are to be common, and no parent is to know his own child, nor any child his parent."

Yes, he said, that is a much greater wave than the other; and the possibility as well as the utility of such a law are far more questionable.

I do not think, I said, that there can be any dispute about the very great utility of having wives and children in common; the possibility is quite another matter, and will be very much disputed.

I think that a good many doubts may be raised about both.

You imply that the two questions must be combined, I replied. Now I meant that you should admit the utility; and in this way, as I thought, I should escape from one of them, and then there would remain only the possibility.

But that little attempt is detected, and therefore you will please to give a defence of both.

Well, I said, I submit to my fate. Yet grant me a little favor: let me feast my mind with the dream as day dreamers are in the habit of feasting themselves when they are walking alone; for before they have discovered any means of effecting their wishes—that is a matter which never troubles them—they would rather not tire themselves by thinking about possibilities; but assuming that what they desire is already granted to them, they proceed with their plan, and delight in detailing what they mean to do when their wish has come true—that is a way which they have of not doing much good to a capacity which was never good for much. Now I myself am beginning to lose heart, and I should like, with your permission, to pass over the question of possibility at present. Assuming therefore the possibility of the proposal, I shall now proceed to inquire how the rulers will carry out these arrangements, and I shall demonstrate that our plan, if executed, will be of the greatest benefit to the State and to the guardians. First of all, then, if you have no objection, I will endeavor with your help to consider the advantages of the measure; and hereafter the question of possibility.

I have no objection; proceed.

First, I think that if our rulers and their auxiliaries are to be worthy of the name which they bear, there must be willingness to obey in the one and the power of command in the other; the guardians must themselves obey the laws, and they must also imitate the spirit of them in any details which are entrusted to their care.

That is right, he said.

You, I said, who are their legislator, having selected the

men, will now select the women and give them to them;—they must be as far as possible of like natures with them; and they must live in common houses and meet at common meals. None of them will have anything specially his or her own; they will be together, and will be brought up together, and will associate at gymnastic exercises. And so they will be drawn by a necessity of their natures to have intercourse with each other —necessity is not too strong a word, I think?

Yes, he said;—necessity, not geometrical, but another sort of necessity which lovers know, and which is far more convincing and constraining to the mass of mankind.

True, I said; and this, Glaucon, like all the rest, must proceed after an orderly fashion; in a city of the blessed, licentiousness is an unholy thing which the rulers will forbid.

Yes, he said, and it ought not to be permitted.

Then clearly the next thing will be to make matrimony sacred in the highest degree, and what is most beneficial will be deemed sacred?

Exactly.

And how can marriages be made most beneficial?—that is a question which I put to you, because I see in your house dogs for hunting, and of the nobler sort of birds not a few. Now, I beseech you, do tell me, have you ever attended to their pairing and breeding?

In what particulars?

Why, in the first place, although they are all of a good sort, are not some better than others?

True.

And do you breed from them all indifferently, or do you take care to breed from the best only?

From the best.

And do you take the oldest or the youngest, or only those of ripe age?

I choose only those of ripe age.

And if care was not taken in the breeding, your dogs and birds would greatly deteriorate?

Certainly.

And the same of horses and of animals in general?

Undoubtedly.

Good heavens! my dear friend, I said, what consummate skill will our rulers need if the same principle holds of the human species!

Certainly, the same principle holds; but why does this involve any particular skill?

Because, I said, our rulers will often have to practice upon the body corporate with medicines. Now you know that when patients do not require medicines, but have only to be put under a regimen, the inferior sort of practitioner is deemed to be good enough; but when medicine has to be given, then the doctor should be more of a man.

That is quite true, he said; but to what are you alluding?

I mean, I replied, that our rulers will find a considerable dose of falsehood and deceit necessary for the good of their subjects: we were saying that the use of all these things regarded as medicines might be of advantage.

And we were very right.

And this lawful use of them seems likely to be often needed in the regulations of marriages and births.

How so?

Why, I said, the principle has been already laid down that the best of either sex should be united with the best as often, and the inferior with the inferior, as seldom as possible; and that they should rear the offspring of the one sort of union, but not of the other, if the flock is to be maintained in first-rate condition. Now these goings on must be a secret which the rulers only know, or there will be a further danger of our herd, as the guardians may be termed, breaking out into rebellion.

Very true.

Had we not better appoint certain festivals at which we will bring together the brides and bridegrooms, and sacrifices will be offered and suitably hymeneal songs composed by our poets: the number of weddings is a matter which must be left to the discretion of the rulers, whose aim will be to preserve the average of population? There are many other things which they will have to consider, such as the effects of wars and diseases and any similar agencies, in order as far as this is possible to prevent the State from becoming either too large or too small.

Certainly, he replied.

We shall have to invent some ingenious kind of lots which the less worthy may draw on each occasion of our bringing them together, and then they will accuse their own ill-luck and not the rulers.

To be sure, he said.

And I think that our braver and better youth, besides their other honors and rewards, might have greater facilities of intercourse with women given them; their bravery will be a reason, and such fathers ought to have as many sons as possible.

True.

And the proper officers, whether male or female or both, for offices are to be held by women as well as by men—

Yes—

The proper officers will take the offspring of the good parents to the pen or fold, and there they will deposit them with certain nurses who dwell in a separate quarter; but the offspring of the inferior, or of the better when they chance to be deformed, will be put away in some mysterious, unknown place, as they should be.

Yes, he said, that must be done if the breed of the guardians is to be kept pure.

They will provide for their nurture, and will bring the

mothers to the fold when they are full of milk, taking the greatest possible care that no mother recognizes her own child; and other wet-nurses may be engaged if more are required. Care will also be taken that the process of suckling shall not be protracted too long; and the mothers will have no getting up at night or other trouble, but will hand over all this sort of thing to the nurses and attendants.

You suppose the wives of our guardians to have a fine easy time of it when they are having children.

Why, said I, and so they ought. Let us, however, proceed with our scheme. We were saying that the parents should be in the prime of life?

Very true.

And what is the prime of life? May it not be defined as a period of about twenty years in a woman's life, and thirty in a man's?

Which years do you mean to include?

A woman, I said, at twenty years of age may begin to bear children to the State, and continue to bear them until forty; a man may begin at five-and-twenty, when he has passed the point at which the pulse of life beats quickest, and continue to beget children until he be fifty-five.

Certainly, he said, both in men and women those years are the prime of physical as well as of intellectual vigor.

Any one above or below the prescribed ages who takes part in the public hymeneals shall be said to have done an unholy and unrighteous thing; the child of which he is the father, if it steals into life, will have been conceived under auspices very unlike the sacrifices and prayers, which at each hymeneal priestesses and priests and the whole city will offer, that the new generation may be better and more useful than their good and useful parents, whereas his child will be the offspring of darkness and strange lust.

Very true, he replied.

And the same law will apply to any one of those within the prescribed age who forms a connection with any women in the prime of life without the sanction of the rulers; for we shall say that he is raising up a bastard to the State, uncertified and unconsecrated.

Very true, he replied.

This applies, however, only to those who are within the specified age: after that we allow them to range at will, except that a man may not marry his daughter or his daughter's daughter, or his mother or his mother's mother; and women, on the other hand, are prohibited from marrying their sons or fathers, or son's son or father's father, and so on in either direction. And we grant all this, accompanying the permission with strict orders to prevent any embryo which may come into being from seeing the light; and if any force a way to the birth, the parents must understand that the offspring of such an union cannot be maintained, and arrange accordingly.

That also, he said, is a reasonable proposition. But how will they know who are fathers and daughters, and so on?

They will never know. The way will be this:—dating from the day of the hymeneal, the bridegroom who was then married will call all the male children who are born in the seventh and the tenth month afterwards his sons, and the female children his daughters, and they will call him father, and he will call their children his grandchildren, and they will call the elder generation grandfathers and grandmothers. All who were begotten at the time when their fathers and mothers came together will be called their brothers and sisters, and these, as I was saying, will be forbidden to intermarry. This, however, is not to be understood as an absolute prohibition of the marriage of brothers and sisters; if the lot favors them, and they receive the sanction of the Pythian oracle, the law will allow them.

Quite right, he replied.

Such is the scheme, Glaucon, according to which the guardians of our State are to have their wives and families in common. And now you would have the argument show that this community is consistent with the rest of our polity, and also that nothing can be better—would you not?

Yes, certainly.

Shall we try to find a common basis by asking of ourselves what ought to be the chief aim of the legislator in making laws and in the organization of a State,—what is the greatest good, and what is the greatest evil, and then consider whether our previous description has the stamp of the good or of the evil?

By all means.

Can there be any greater evil than discord and distraction and plurality where unity ought to reign? or any greater good than the bond of unity?

There cannot.

And there is unity where there is community of pleasures and pains—where all the citizens are glad or grieved on the same occasions of joy and sorrow?

No doubt.

Yes; and where there is no common but only private feeling a State is disorganized—when you have one half of the world triumphing and the other plunged in grief at the same events happening to the city or the citizens?

Certainly.

Such differences commonly originate in a disagreement about the use of the terms "mine" and "not mine," "his" and "not his."

Exactly so.

And is not that the best-ordered State in which the greatest number of persons apply the terms "mine" and "not mine" in the same way to the same thing?

Quite true.

Or that again which most nearly approaches to the condition

of the individual—as in the body, when but a finger of one of us is hurt, the whole frame, drawn towards the soul as a center and forming one kingdom under the ruling power therein, feels the hurt and sympathizes all together with the part affected, and we say that the man has a pain in his finger; and the same expression is used about any other part of the body, which has a sensation of pain at suffering or of pleasure at the alleviation of suffering.

Very true, he replied; and I agree with you that in the best-ordered State there is the nearest approach to this common feeling which you describe.

Then when any one of the citizens experiences any good or evil, the whole State will make his case their own, and will either rejoice or sorrow with him?

Yes, he said, that is what will happen in a well-ordered State.

It will now be time, I said, for us to return to our State and see whether this or some other form is most in accordance with these fundamental principles.

Very good.

Our State like every other has rulers and subjects?

True.

All of whom will call one another citizens?

Of course.

But is there not another name which people give to their rulers in other States?

Generally they call them masters, but in democratic States they simply call them rulers.

And in our State what other name besides that of citizens do the people give the rulers?

They are called saviors and helpers, he replied.

And what do the rulers call the people?

Their maintainers and foster-fathers.

And what do they call them in other States?

Slaves.

And what do the rulers call one another in other States?

Fellow-rulers.

And what in ours?

Fellow-guardians.

Did you ever know an example in any other State of a ruler who would speak of one of his colleagues as his friend and of another as not being his friend?

Yes, very often.

And the friend he regards and describes as one in whom he has an interest, and the other as a stranger in whom he has no interest?

Exactly.

But would any of your guardians think or speak of any other guardian as a stranger?

Certainly he would not; for every one whom they meet will be regarded by them either as a brother or sister, or father or mother, or son or daughter, or as the child or parent of those who are thus connected with him.

Capital, I said; but let me ask you once more: Shall they be a family in name only; or shall they in all their actions be true to the name? For example, in the use of the word "father," would the care of a father be implied and the filial reverence and duty and obedience to him which the law commands; and is the violator of these duties to be regarded as an impious and unrighteous person who is not likely to receive much good either at the hands of God or of man? Are these to be or not to be the strains which the children will hear repeated in their ears by all the citizens about those who are intimated to them to be their parents and the rest of their kinsfolk?

These, he said, and none other; for what can be more ridiculous than for them to utter the names of family ties with the lips only and not to act in the spirit of them?

Then in our city the language of harmony and concord will

be more often heard than in any other. As I was describing before, when any one is well or ill, the universal word will be "with me it is well" or "it is ill."

Most true.

And agreeably to this mode of thinking and speaking, were we not saying that they will have their pleasures and pains in common?

Yes, and so they will.

And they will have a common interest in the same thing which they will alike call "my own," and having this common interest they will have a common feeling of pleasure and pain?

Yes, far more so than in other States.

And the reason of this, over and above the general constitution of the State, will be that the guardians will have a community of women and children?

That will be the chief reason.

And this unity of feeling we admitted to be the greatest good, as was implied in our own comparison of a well-ordered State to the relation of the body and the members, when affected by pleasure or pain?

That we acknowledged, and very rightly.

Then the community of wives and children among our citizens is clearly the source of the greatest good to the State?

Certainly.

And this agrees with the other principle which we were affirming—that the guardians were not to have houses or lands or any other property; their pay was to be their food, which they were to receive from the other citizens, and they were to have no private expenses; for we intended them to preserve their true character of guardians.

Right, he replied.

Both the community of property and the community of families, as I am saying, tend to make them more truly guardians; they will not tear the city in pieces by differing about "mine" and "not mine"; each man dragging any acquisition which he has made into a separate house of his own, where he has a separate wife and children and private pleasures and pains; but all will be affected as far as may be by the same pleasures and pains because they are all of one opinion about what is near and dear to them, and therefore they all tend towards a common end.

Certainly, he replied.

4. ARISTOTLE: Politics and the Sexes

Aristotle (384–322 B.C.) was a pupil in the Platonic Academy until Plato's death. He became the tutor of Alexander the Great and founded his own school in Athens, the Lyceum, in which research was conducted into almost all areas of the natural world and history.

I

Our purpose is to consider what form of political community is best of all for those who are most able to realize their ideal of life. We must therefore examine not only this but

SOURCE: Aristotle, "Politica," vol. X, trans. Benjamin Jowett, *The Works of Aristotle,* ed. W. D. Ross (Oxford: Clarendon Press, 1921). This selection is book II, chapters I–IV.

other constitutions, both such as actually exist in well-governed states, and any theoretical forms which are held in esteem; that what is good and useful may be brought to light. And let no one suppose that in seeking for something beyond them we are anxious to make a sophistical display at any cost; we only undertake this inquiry because all the constitutions with which we are acquainted are faulty.

We will begin with the natural beginning of the subject. Three alternatives are conceivable: The members of a state must either have (1) all things or (2) nothing in common, or (3) some things in common and some not. That they should have nothing in common is clearly impossible, for the constitution is a community, and must at any rate have a common place—one city will be in one place, and the citizens are those who share in that one city. But should a well-ordered state have all things, as far as may be, in common, or some only and not others? For the citizens might conceivably have wives and children and property in common, as Socrates proposes in the *Republic* of Plato. Which is better, our present condition, or the proposed new order of society?

II

There are many difficulties in the community of women. And the principle on which Socrates rests the necessity of such an institution evidently is not established by his arguments. Further, as a means to the end which he ascribes to the state, the scheme, taken literally, is impracticable, and how we are to interpret it is nowhere precisely stated. I am speaking of the premise from which the argument of Socrates proceeds, "that the greater the unity of the state the better." Is it not obvious that a state may at length attain such a degree of unity as to be no longer a state?—since the nature of a state is to be a plurality, and in tending to greater unity, from being a state, it becomes a family, and from being a family, an individual; for the family may be said to be more one than the state, and the individual than the family. So that we ought not to attain this greatest unity even if we could, for it would be the destruction of the state. Again, a state is not made up only of so many men, but of different kinds of men; for similars do not constitute a state. It is not like a military alliance. The usefulness of the latter depends upon its quantity even where there is no difference in quality (for mutual protection is the end aimed at), just as a greater weight of anything is more useful than a less (in like manner, a state differs from a nation, when the nation has not its population organized in villages, but lives an Arcadian sort of life); but the elements out of which a unity is to be formed differ in kind. Wherefore the principle of compensation, as I have already remarked in the *Ethics,* is the salvation of states. Even among freemen and equals this is a principle which must be maintained, for they cannot all rule together, but must change at the end of a year or some other period of time or in some order of succession. The result is that upon this plan they all govern; just as if shoemakers and carpenters were to exchange their occupations, and the same persons did not always continue shoemakers and carpenters. And since it is better that this should be so in politics as well, it is clear that while there should be continuance of the same persons in power where this is possible, yet where this is not possible by reason of the natural equality of the citizens, and at the same time it is just that all should share in the government (whether to govern be a good thing or a bad), an approximation to this is that equals should in turn retire from office and should, apart from official position, be treated alike. Thus the one party rule and the others are ruled in turn, as if they were no longer the same persons. In like manner when they hold office, there is a variety in the offices held. Hence it is evident that a city is not by nature one in that sense which some persons affirm; and that what is said to be the greatest good of cities is in reality their destruction; but surely the good of things must be that which preserves them. Again, in another point of view, this extreme unification of the state is clearly not good; for a family is more self-sufficing than an individual, and a city than a family, and a city only comes into being when the community is large enough to be self-sufficing. If then self-sufficiency is to be desired, the lesser degree of unity is more desirable than the greater.

III

But, even supposing that it were best for the community to have the greatest degree of unity, this unity is by no means proved to follow from the fact "of all men saying 'mine' and 'not mine' at the same instant of time," which, according to Socrates, is the sign of perfect unity in a state. For the word "all" is ambiguous. If the meaning be that every individual says "mine" and "not mine" at the same time, then perhaps the result at which Socrates aims may be in some degree accomplished; each man will call the same person his own son and the same person his own wife, and so of his property and of all that falls to his lot. This, however, is not the way in which people would speak who had their wives and children in common; they would say "all" but not "each." In like manner their property would be described as belonging to them, not severally but collectively. There is an obvious fallacy in the term "all": like some other words, "both," "odd," "even," it is ambiguous, and even in abstract argument becomes a source of logical puzzles. That all persons call the same thing mine in the sense in which each does so may be a fine thing, but it is impracticable; or if the words are taken in the other sense, such a unity in no way conduces to harmony. And there is another objection to the proposal. For that which is common to the greatest number has the least care bestowed upon it. Every one thinks chiefly of his own, hardly at all of the common interest; and only when he is himself concerned as an individual. For besides other considerations, everybody is more inclined to neglect the duty which he expects another to fulfill; as in families many attendants are often less useful than a few. Each citizen will have a thousand sons who will not be his sons individually, but anybody will be equally the son of anybody, and will therefore be neglected by all alike. Further, upon this principle, every one will use the word "mine" of one who is prospering or the reverse, however small a fraction he may himself be of the whole number; the same boy will be "my son," "so and so's son," the son of each of the thousand, or whatever be the number of the citizens; and even about this he will not be positive; for it is impossible to know who chanced to have a child, or whether, if one came into existence, it has survived. But which is better—for each to say "mine" in this way, making a man the same relation to two thousand or ten thousand citizens, or to use the word "mine" in the ordinary and more restricted sense? For usually the same person is called by one man his own son whom another calls his own brother or cousin or kinsman—blood relation or connection by marriage either of himself or of some relation of his, and yet another his clansman or tribesman; and how much better is it to be the real cousin of somebody than to be a son after Plato's fashion! Nor is there any way of preventing brothers and children and fathers and mothers from sometimes recognizing one another; for children are born like their parents, and they will necessarily be finding indications of their relationship to one another. Geographers declare such to be the fact; they say that in part of Upper Libya, where the women are common, nevertheless the children who are born are assigned to their respective fathers on the ground of their likeness. And some women, like the females of other animals—

for example, mares and cows—have a strong tendency to produce offspring resembling their parents, as was the case with the Pharsalian mare called Honest.

IV

Other evils, against which it is not easy for the authors of such a community to guard, will be assaults and homicides, voluntary as well as involuntary, quarrels and slanders, all which are most unholy acts when committed against fathers and mothers and near relations, but not equally unholy when there is no relationship. Moreover, they are much more likely to occur if the relationship is unknown, and, when they have occurred, the customary expiations of them cannot be made. Again, how strange it is that Socrates, after having made the children common, should hinder lovers from carnal intercourse only, but should permit love and familiarities between father and son or between brother and brother, than which nothing can be more unseemly, since even without them love of this sort is improper. How strange, too, to forbid intercourse for no other reason than the violence of the pleasure, as though the relationship of father and son or of brothers with one another made no difference.

This community of wives and children seems better suited to the husbandmen than to the guardians, for if they have wives and children in common, they will be bound to one another by weaker ties, as a subject class should be, and they will remain obedient and not rebel. In a word, the result of such a law would be just the opposite of that which good laws ought to have, and the intention of Socrates in making these regulations about women and children would defeat itself. For friendship we believe to be the greatest good of states and the preservative of them against revolutions; neither is there anything which Socrates so greatly lauds as the unity of the state which he and all the world declare to be created by friendship. But the unity which he commends would be like that of the lovers in the *Symposium,* who, as Aristophanes says, desire to grow together in the excess of their affection, and from being two to become one, in which case one or both would certainly perish. Whereas in a state having women and children common, love will be watery; and the father will certainly not say "my son," or the son "my father." As a little sweet wine mingled with a great deal of water is imperceptible in the mixture, so, in this sort of community, the idea of relationship which is based upon these names will be lost; there is no reason why the so-called father should care about the son, or the son about the father, or brothers about one another. Of the two qualities which chiefly inspire regard and affection—that a thing is your own and that it is your only one—neither can exist in such a state as this.

Again, the transfer of children as soon as they are born from the rank of husbandmen or of artisans to that of guardians, and from the rank of guardians into a lower rank, will be very difficult to arrange; the givers or transferrers cannot but know whom they are giving and transferring, and to whom. And the previously mentioned evils, such as assaults, unlawful loves, homicides, will happen more often amongst those who are transferred to the lower classes, or who have a place assigned to them among the guardians; for they will no longer call the members of the class they have left brothers, and children, and fathers, and mothers, and will not, therefore, be afraid of committing any crimes by reason of consanguinity. Touching the community of wives and children, let this be our conclusion.

5. ARISTOTLE: Types of Love

I

After what we have said, a discussion of friendship would naturally follow, since it is a virtue or implies virtue, and is besides most necessary with a view to living. For without friends no one would choose to live, though he had all other goods; even rich men and those in possession of office and of dominating power are thought to need friends most of all; for what is the use of such prosperity without the opportunity of beneficence, which is exercised chiefly and in its most laudable form towards friends? Or how can prosperity be guarded and

SOURCE: Aristotle, "Ethica Nicomachea," vol. IX, *The Works of Aristotle,* ed. and trans. W. D. Ross (Oxford: Clarendon Press, 1915). This selection is book VIII, chapters I–IV and book IX, chapter VIII.

preserved without friends? The greater it is, the more exposed is it to risk. And in poverty and in other misfortunes men think friends are the only refuge. It helps the young, too, to keep from error; it aids older people by ministering to their needs and supplementing the activities that are failing from weakness; those in the prime of life it stimulates to noble actions—"two going together"—for with friends men are more able both to think and to act. Again, parent seems by nature to feel it for offspring and offspring for parent, not only among men but among birds and among most animals; it is felt mutually by members of the same race, and especially by men, whence we praise lovers of their fellowmen. We may see even in our travels how near and dear every man is to every other. Friendship seems too to hold states together, and lawgivers to care more for it than for justice; for unanimity seems to be something like friendship, and this they aim at most of all, and expel faction as their worst enemy; and when men are friends they have no need of justice, while when they are just, they need friendship as well, and the truest form of justice is thought to be a friendly quality.

But it is not only necessary but also noble; for we praise those who love their friends, and it is thought to be a fine thing to have many friends; and again we think it is the same people that are good men and are friends.

Not a few things about friendship are matters of debate. Some define it as a kind of likeness and say like people are friends, whence come the sayings "like to like," "birds of a feather flock together," and so on; others on the contrary say "two of a trade never agree." On this very question they inquire for deeper and more physical causes, Euripides saying that "parched earth loves the rain, and stately heaven when filled with rain loves to fall to earth," and Heraclitus that "it is what opposes that helps" and "from different tones comes the fairest tune" and "all things are produced through strife";

while Empedocles, as well as others, expresses the opposite view that like aims at like. The physical problems we may leave alone (for they do not belong to the present inquiry); let us examine those which are human and involve character and feeling, e.g., whether friendship can arise between any two people or people cannot be friends if they are wicked, and whether there is one species of friendship or more than one. Those who think there is only one because it admits of degrees have relied on an inadequate indication; for even things different in species admit of degree. We have discussed this matter previously.

II

The kinds of friendship may perhaps be cleared up if we first come to know the object of love. For not everything seems to be loved but only the lovable, and this is good, pleasant, or useful; but it would seem to be that by which some good or pleasure is produced that is useful, so that it is the good and the pleasant that are lovable as ends. Do men love, then, *the* good, or what is good for *them?* These sometimes clash. So too with regard to the pleasant. Now it is thought that each loves what is good for himself, and that the good is without qualification lovable, and what is good for each man is lovable for him; but each man loves not what is good for him but what seems good. This however will make no difference; we shall just have to say that this is "that which seems lovable." Now there are three grounds on which people love; of the love of lifeless objects we do not use the word "friendship"; for it is not mutual love, nor is there a wishing of good to the other (for it would surely be ridiculous to wish wine well; if one wishes anything for it, it is that it may keep, so that one may have it oneself); but to a friend we say we ought to wish what is good for his sake. But to those who thus wish good we ascribe only goodwill, if the wish is not reciprocated; goodwill when it *is* reciprocal being friendship. Or must we add "when it is recognized"? For many people have goodwill to those whom they have not seen but judge to be good or useful; and one of these might return this feeling. These people seem to bear goodwill to each other; but how could one call them friends when they do not know their mutual feelings? To be friends, then, they must be mutually recognized as bearing goodwill and wishing well to each other for one of the aforesaid reasons.

III

Now these reasons differ from each other in kind; so, therefore, do the corresponding forms of love and friendship. There are therefore three kinds of friendship, equal in number to the things that are lovable; for with respect to each there is a mutual and recognized love, and those who love each other wish well to each other in that respect in which they love one another. Now those who love each other for their utility do not love each other for themselves but in virtue of some good which they get from each other. So too with those who love for the sake of pleasure; it is not for their character that men love ready-witted people, but because they find them pleasant. Therefore those who love for the sake of utility love for the sake of what is good for *themselves*, and those who love for the sake of pleasure do so for the sake of what is pleasant to *themselves*, and not in so far as the other is the person loved but in so far as he is useful or pleasant. And thus these friendships are only incidental; for it is not as being the man he is that the loved person is loved, but as providing some good or pleasure. Such friendships, then, are easily dissolved, if the parties do not remain like themselves; for if the one party is no longer pleasant or useful the other ceases to love him.

Now the useful is not permanent but is always changing. Thus when the motive of the friendship is done away, the friendship is dissolved, inasmuch as it existed only for the ends in question. This kind of friendship seems to exist chiefly between old people (for at that age people pursue not the pleasant but the useful) and, of those who are in their prime or young, between those who pursue utility. And such people do not live much with each other either; for sometimes they do not even find each other pleasant; therefore they do not need such companionship unless they are useful to each other; for they are pleasant to each other only in so far as they rouse in each other hopes of something good to come. Among such friendships people also class the friendship of host and guest. On the other hand the friendship of young people seems to aim at pleasure; for they live under the guidance of emotion, and pursue above all what is pleasant to themselves and what is immediately before them; but with increasing age their pleasures become different. This is why they quickly become friends and quickly cease to be so; their friendship changes with the object that is found pleasant, and such pleasure alters quickly. Young people are amorous too; for the greater part of the friendship of love depends on emotion and aims at pleasure; this is why they fall in love and quickly fall out of love, changing often within a single day. But these people do wish to spend their days and lives together; for it is thus that they attain the purpose of their friendship.

Perfect friendship is the friendship of men who are good, and alike in virtue; for these wish well alike to each other *qua* good, and they are good in themselves. Now those who wish well to their friends for their sake are most truly friends; for they do this by reason of their own nature and not incidentally; therefore their friendship lasts as long as they are good—and goodness is an enduring thing. And each is good without qualification and to his friend, for the good are both good without qualification and useful to each other. So too they are pleasant; for the good are pleasant both without qualification and to each other, since to each his own activities and others like them are pleasurable, and the actions of the good *are* the same or like. And such a friendship is as might be expected permanent, since there meet in it all the qualities that friends should have. For all friendship is for the sake of good or of pleasure—good or pleasure either in the abstract or such as will be enjoyed by him who has the friendly feeling—and is based on a certain resemblance; and to a friendship of good men all the qualities we have named belong in virtue of the nature of the friends themselves; for in the case of this kind of friendship the other qualities also are alike in both friends, and that which is good without qualification is also without qualification pleasant, and these are the most lovable qualities. Love and friendship therefore are found most and in their best form between such men.

But it is natural that such friendships should be infrequent; for such men are rare. Further, such friendship requires time and familiarity; as the proverb says, men cannot know each other till they have "eaten salt together"; nor can they admit each other to friendship or be friends till each has been found lovable and been trusted by each. Those who quickly show the marks of friendship to each other wish to be friends, but are not friends unless they both are lovable and know the fact; for a wish for friendship may arise quickly, but friendship does not.

IV

This kind of friendship, then, is perfect both in respect of duration and in all other respects, and in it each gets from each in all respects the same as, or something like what, he gives; which is what ought to happen between friends. Friendship for the sake of pleasure bears a resemblance to this kind; for good people too *are* pleasant to each other. So too does friendship for the sake of utility; for the good are also useful to each other. Among men of these inferior sorts too, friendships are most permanent when the friends get the same thing from each other (e.g., pleasure), and not only that but also from the same source, as happens between ready-witted people, not as happens between lover and beloved. For these do not take pleasure in the same things, but the one in seeing the beloved and the other in receiving attentions from his lover; and when the bloom of youth is passing the friendship sometimes passes too (for the one finds no pleasure in the sight of the other, and the other gets no attentions from the first); but many lovers on the other hand are constant, if familiarity has led them to love each other's characters, these being alike. But those who exchange not pleasure but utility in their amour are both less truly friends and less constant. Those who are friends for the sake of utility part when the advantage is at an end; for they were lovers not of each other but of profit.

For the sake of pleasure or utility, then, even bad men may be friends of each other, or good men of bad, or one who is neither good nor bad may be a friend to any sort of person, but for their own sake clearly only good men can be friends; for bad men do not delight in each other unless some advantage come of the relation.

The friendship of the good too and this alone is proof against slander; for it is not easy to trust any one's talk about a man who has long been tested by oneself; and it is among good men that trust and the feeling that "he would never wrong me" and all the other things that are demanded in true friendship are found. In the other kinds of friendship, however, there is nothing to prevent these evils arising.

For men apply the name of friends even to those whose

motive is utility, in which sense states are said to be friendly (for the alliances of states seem to aim at advantage), and to those who love each other for the sake of pleasure, in which sense children are called friends. Therefore we too ought perhaps to call such people friends, and say that there are several kinds of friendship—firstly and in the proper sense that of good men *qua* good, and by analogy the other kinds; for it is in virtue of something good and something akin to what is found in true friendship that they are friends, since even the pleasant is good for the lovers of pleasure. But these two kinds of friendship are not often united, nor do the same people become friends for the sake of utility and of pleasure; for things that are only incidentally connected are not often coupled together.

Friendship being divided into these kinds, bad men will be friends for the sake of pleasure or of utility, being in this respect like each other, but good men will be friends for their own sake, i.e. in virtue of their goodness. These, then, are friends without qualification; the others are friends incidentally and through a resemblance to these. . . .

The question is also debated, whether a man should love himself most, or some one else. People criticize those who love themselves most, and call them self-lovers, using this as an epithet of disgrace, and a bad man seems to do everything for his own sake, and the more so the more wicked he is—and so men reproach him, for instance, with doing nothing of his own accord—while the good man acts for honor's sake, and the more so the better he is, and acts for his friend's sake, and sacrifices his own interest.

But the facts clash with these arguments, and this is not surprising. For men say that one ought to love best one's best friend, and a man's best friend is one who wishes well to the object of his wish for his sake, even if no one is to know of it;

and these attributes are found most of all in a man's attitude towards himself, and so are all the other attributes by which a friend is defined; for, as we have said, it is from this relation that all the characteristics of friendship have extended to our neighbors. All the proverbs, too, agree with this, e.g., "a single soul," and "what friends have is common property," and "friendship is equality," and "charity begins at home"; for all these marks will be found most in a man's relation to himself; he is his own best friend and therefore ought to love himself best. It is therefore a reasonable question, which of the two views we should follow; for both are plausible.

Perhaps we ought to mark off such arguments from each other and determine how far and in what respects each view is right. Now if we grasp the sense in which each school uses the phrase "lover of self," the truth may become evident. Those who use the term as one of reproach ascribe self-love to people who assign to themselves the greater share of wealth, honors, and bodily pleasures; for these are what most people desire, and busy themselves about as though they were the best of all things, which is the reason, too, why they become objects of competition. So those who are grasping with regard to these things gratify their appetites and in general their feelings and the irrational element of the soul; and most men are of this nature (which is the reason why the epithet has come to be used as it is—it takes its meaning from the prevailing type of self-love, which is a bad one); it is just, therefore, that men who are lovers of self in this way are reproached for being so. That it is those who give themselves the preference in regard to objects of this sort that most people usually call lovers of self is plain; for if a man were always anxious that he himself, above all things, should act justly, temperately, or in accordance with any other of the virtues, and in general were always to try to secure for himself the honorable course, no one will call such a man a lover of self or blame him.

But such a man would seem more than the other a lover of self; at all events he assigns to himself the things that are noblest and best, and gratifies the most authoritative element in himself and in all things obeys this; and just as a city or any other systematic whole is most properly identified with the most authoritative element in it, so is a man; and therefore the man who loves this and gratifies it is most of all a lover of self. Besides, a man is said to have or not to have self-control according as his reason has or has not the control, on the assumption that this is the man himself; and the things men have done on a rational principle are thought most properly their own acts and voluntary acts. That this is the man himself, then, or is so more than anything else, is plain, and also that the good man loves most this part of him. Whence it follows that he is most truly a lover of self, of another type than that which is a matter of reproach, and as different from that as living according to a rational principle is from living as passion dictates, and desiring what is noble from desiring what seems advantageous. Those, then, who busy themselves in an exceptional degree with noble actions all men approve and praise; and if *all* were to strive towards what is noble and strain every nerve to do the noblest deeds, everything would be as it should be for the common weal, and every one would secure for himself the goods that are greatest, since virtue is the greatest of goods.

Therefore the good man should be a lover of self (for he will both himself profit by doing noble acts, and will benefit his fellows), but the wicked man should not; for he will hurt both himself and his neighbors, following as he does evil passions. For the wicked man, what he does clashes with what he ought to do, but what the good man ought to do he does; for reason in each of its possessors chooses what is best for itself, and the good man obeys his reason. It is true of the good man too that he does many acts for the sake of his friends and his country, and if necessary dies for them; for he will throw away both wealth and honors and in general the goods that are objects of competition, gaining for himself nobility; since he would prefer a short period of intense pleasure to a long one of mild enjoyment, a twelvemonth of noble life to many years of humdrum existence, and one great and noble action to many trivial ones. Now those who die for others doubtless attain this result; it is therefore a great prize that they choose for themselves. They will throw away wealth too on condition that their friends will gain more; for while a man's friend gains wealth he himself achieves nobility; he is therefore assigning the greater good to himself. The same too is true of honor and office; all these things he will sacrifice to his friend; for this is noble and laudable for himself. Rightly then is he thought to be good, since he chooses nobility before all else. But he may even give up actions to his friend; it may be nobler to become the cause of his friend's acting than to act himself. In all the actions, therefore, that men are praised for, the good man is seen to assign to himself the greater share in what is noble. In this sense, then, as has been said, a man should be a lover of self; but in the sense in which most men are so, he ought not.

6. EPICTETUS: Sex and Self-Denial

Epictetus (A.D. 50–138) was a slave who belonged to a member of
the Emperor Nero's bodyguard. He was freed and lived in Rome
until the expulsion of philosophers by the Emperor Domitian. He
left Rome and founded a school which he headed until his death.
He is one of the most prominent of the Roman Stoics and exerted
an influence on another prominent Stoic—the Emperor Marcus
Aurelius.

On Friendship

A man naturally loves those things in which he is interested.
Now do men take an interest in things evil? Certainly not. Do

SOURCE: Epictetus, *The Discourses and Manual*, 2 vols., trans. P. E.
Matheson (Oxford: Clarendon Press, 1916). The selection is taken from
book II, chapters XVIII and XXII. Reprinted by permission of the
Clarendon Press, Oxford.

they take interest in what does not concern them? No, they do not. It follows then that they are interested in good things alone, and if interested in them, therefore love them too. Whoever then has knowledge of good things, would know how to love them; but how could one who cannot distinguish good things from evil and things indifferent from both have power to love? Therefore the wise man alone has power to love.

"Nay, how is this?" says one. "I am not wise, yet I love my child."

By the gods, I am surprised, to begin with, at your admission that you are not wise. What do you lack? Do you not enjoy sensation, do you not distinguish impressions, do you not supply your body with the food that is suited to it, and with shelter and a dwelling? How is it then that you admit that you are foolish? I suppose because you are often disturbed and bewildered by your impressions, and overcome by their persuasive powers, so that the very things that at one moment you consider good you presently consider bad and afterwards indifferent; and, in a word, you are subject to pain, fear, envy, confusion, change: that is why you confess yourself to be foolish. And do you not change in your affections? Do you believe at one time that wealth and pleasure and mere outward things are good, and at another time that they are evil, and do you not regard the same persons now as good, now as bad, and sometimes feel friendly towards them, sometimes unfriendly, and now praise, now blame them?

"Yes. I am subject to these feelings."

Well then; do you think a man can be a friend to anything about which he is deceived?

"Not at all."

Nor can he whose choice of a friend is subject to change bear good will to him?

"No, he cannot."

Can he who first reviles a man and then admires him?

"No, he cannot."

Again, did you never see curs fawning on one another and playing with one another, so that you say nothing could be friendlier? But to see what friendship is, throw a piece of meat among them and you will learn. So with you and your dear boy: throw a bit of land between you, and you will learn how your boy wishes to give you a speedy burial, and you pray for the boy to die. Then you cry out again, "What a child I have reared! He is impatient to bury me." Throw a pretty maid between you and suppose you both love her, you the old man, and he the young man. Or suppose you throw a bit of glory between you. And if you have to risk your life, you will use the words of Admetus' father: "You love the light; shall not your father love it?" [Euripides, *Alcestis*, 691] Do you think that he did not love his own child when it was small, and was not distressed when it had the fever, and did not often say, "Would it were I who had the fever instead!"? yet when the event came close upon him, see what words they utter! Were not Eteocles and Polynices born of the same mother and the same father? Were they not reared together, did they not live together, drink together, sleep together, often kiss one another, so that if one had seen them he would, no doubt, have laughed at the paradoxes of philosophers on friendship. Yet when the bit of meat, in the shape of a king's throne, fell between them, see what they say:

> E. *Where wilt stand upon the tower?*
> P. *Wherefore dost thou ask me this?*
> E. *I will face thee then and slay thee.*
> P. *I desire thy blood no less:*
>
> [Euripides, *The Phoenissae*, 621]

Yes, such are the prayers they utter!

For be not deceived, every creature, to speak generally, is

attached to nothing so much as to its own interest. Whatever then seems to hinder his way to this, be it a brother or a father or a child, the object of his passion or his own lover, he hates him, guards against him, curses him. For his nature is to love nothing so much as his own interest; this is his father and brother and kinsfolk and country and god. At any rate, when the gods seem to hinder us in regard to this we revile even the gods and overthrow their statues and set fire to their temples, as Alexander ordered the shrines of Asclepius to be burnt when the object of his passion died. Therefore if interest, religion and honor, country, parents and friends are set in the same scale, then all are safe; but if interest is in one scale, and in the other friends and country and kindred and justice itself, all these are weighed down by interest and disappear. For the creature must needs incline to that side where "I" and "mine" are; if they are in the flesh, the ruling power must be there; if in the will, it must be there; if in external things, it must be there.

If then I identify myself with my will, then and only then shall I be a friend and son and father in the true sense. For this will be my interest—to guard my character for good faith, honor, forbearance, self-control, and service of others, to maintain my relations with others. But if I separate myself from what is noble, then Epicurus' statement is confirmed, which declares that "there is no such thing as the noble or at best it is but the creature of opinion."

It was this ignorance that made the Athenians and Lacedaemonians quarrel with one another, and the Thebans with both, and the Great King with Hellas, and the Macedonians with Hellas and the King, and now the Romans with the Getae; and yet earlier this was the reason of the wars with Ilion. Paris was the guest of Menelaus, and any one who had seen the courtesies they used to one another would not have believed one who denied that they were friends. But a morsel was thrown between them, in the shape of a pretty woman, and for that there was war! So now, when you see friends or brothers who seem to be of one mind, do not therefore pronounce upon their friendship, though they swear to it and say it is impossible for them to part with one another. The Governing Principle of the bad man is not to be trusted; it is uncertain, irresolute, conquered now by one impression, now by another. The question you must ask is, not what others ask, whether they were born of the same parents and brought up together and under the charge of the same slave; but this question only, where they put their interest—outside them or in the will. If they put it outside, do not call them friends, any more than you can call them faithful, or stable, or confident, or free; nay, do not call them even men, if you are wise. For it is no human judgment which makes them bite one another and revile one another and occupy deserts or market-places like wild beasts and behave like robbers in the law-courts; and which makes them guilty of profligacy and adultery and seduction and the other offences men commit against one another. There is one judgment and one only which is responsible for all this—that they set themselves and all their interests elsewhere than in their will. But if you hear that these men in very truth believe the good to lie only in the region of the will and in dealing rightly with impressions, you need trouble yourself no more as to whether a man is son or father, whether they are brothers, or have been familiar companions for years; I say, if you grasp this one fact and no more, you may pronounce with confidence that they are friends, as you may that they are faithful and just. For where else is friendship but where faith and honor are, where men give and take what is good, and nothing else?

"But he has paid me attention all this time: did he not love me?"

How do you know, slave, whether he has paid you this attention, as a man cleans his boots, or tends his beast? How do you know whether, when you have lost your use as a paltry vessel, he will not throw you away like a broken plate?

"But she is my wife and we have lived together this long time."

How long did Eriphyle live with Amphiaraus, ay, and was mother of many children?—But a necklace came between them.

"What do you mean by a necklace?"

Man's judgment about good and evil. This was the brutish element, this was what broke up the friendship, which suffered not the wife to be true to her wedlock, nor the mother to be a mother indeed. So let every one of you, who is anxious himself to be friend to another, or to win another for his friend, uproot these judgments, hate them, drive them out of his mind. If he does that, then first he will never revile himself or be in conflict with himself, he will be free from change of mind, and self-torture; secondly he will be friendly to his neighbor, always and absolutely, if he be like himself, and if he be unlike, he will bear with him, be gentle and tender with him, considerate to him as one who is ignorant and in error about the highest matters; not hard upon any man, for he knows of a certainty Plato's saying, "No soul is robbed of the truth save involuntarily."

But if you fail to do this, you may do everything else that friends do—drink together and live under the same roof and sail in the same ship and be born of the same parents; well, the same may be true of snakes, but neither they nor you will be capable of friendship so long as you retain these brutish and revolting judgments.

How We Must Struggle against Impressions

Every habit and every faculty is confirmed and strengthened by the corresponding acts, the faculty of walking by

walking, that of running by running. If you wish to have a
faculty for reading, read; if for writing, write. When you have
not read for thirty days on end, but have done something else,
you will know what happens. So if you lie in bed for ten days,
and then get up and try to take a fairly long walk, you will see
how your legs lose their power. So generally if you wish to
acquire a habit for anything, do the thing; if you do not wish
to acquire the habit, abstain from doing it, and acquire the
habit of doing something else instead. The same holds good in
things of the mind: when you are angry, know that you have
not merely done ill, but that you have strengthened the habit,
and, as it were, put fuel on the fire. When you yield to carnal
passion you must take account not only of this one defeat, but
of the fact that you have fed your incontinence and strengthened it. For habits and faculties are bound to be affected by
the corresponding actions; they are either implanted if they
did not exist before, or strengthened and intensified if they
were there already. This is exactly how philosophers say that
morbid habits spring up in the mind. For when once you
conceive a desire for money, if reason is applied to make you
realize the evil, the desire is checked and the Governing Principle recovers its first power; but if you give it no medicine to
heal it, it will not return to where it was, but when stimulated
again by the appropriate impression it kindles to desire quicker
than before. And if this happens time after time it ends by
growing hardened, and the weakness confirms the avarice in a
man. For he who has a fever and gets quit of it is not in the
same condition as before he had it, unless he has undergone a
complete cure. The same sort of thing happens with affections
of the mind. They leave traces behind them like weals from a
blow, and if a man does not succeed in removing them, when
he is flogged again on the same place his weals turn into sores.
If, then, you wish not to be choleric, do not feed the angry
habit, do not add fuel to the fire. To begin with, keep quiet,

and count the days when you were not angry. I used to be angry every day, then every other day, then every three days, then every four. But if you miss thirty days, then sacrifice to God: for the habit is first weakened and then wholly destroyed.

I kept free from distress today, and again next day, and for two or three months after; and when occasions arose to provoke it, I took pains to check it.

Know that you are doing well.

Today when I saw a handsome woman I did not say to myself, "Would that she were mine!" and "Blessed is her husband!" For he who says that will say, "Blessed is the adulterer!" Nor do I picture the next scene: the woman present and disrobing and reclining by my side. I pat myself on the head and say, "Bravo, Epictetus, you have refuted a pretty fallacy, a much prettier one than the so-called 'Master.'" And if, though the woman herself, poor thing, is willing and beckons and sends to me, and even touches me and comes close to me, I still hold aloof and conquer: the refutation of this fallacy is something greater than the argument of "The Liar," or the "Resting" argument. This is a thing to be really proud of, rather than of propounding the "Master" agrument.

How, then, is this to be done? Make up your mind at last to please your true self, make up your mind to appear noble to God; set your desires on becoming pure in the presence of your pure self and God. "Then when an impression of that sort assails you," says Plato [*Laws*, 854b], "go and offer expiatory sacrifices, go as a suppliant and sacrifice to the gods who avert evil": it is enough even if "you withdraw to the society of the good and noble" and set yourself to compare them with yourself, whether your pattern be among the living or the dead. Go to Socrates and see him reclining with Alcibiades and making light of his beauty. Consider what a victory, what an Olympic triumph, he won over himself—and knew it—what place he thus achieved among the followers of Heracles! a victory that deserves the salutation, "Hail, admirable victor, who hast conquered something more than these wornout boxers and pancratiasts and the gladiators who are like them"! If you set these thoughts against your impression, you will conquer it, and not be carried away by it. But first of all do not be hurried away by the suddenness of the shock, but say, "Wait for me a little, impression. Let me see what you are, and what is at stake: let me test you." And, further, do not allow it to go on picturing the next scene. If you do, it straightway carries you off whither it will. Cast out this filthy impression and bring in some other impression, a lovely and noble one, in its place. I say, if you acquire the habit of training yourself thus, you will see what shoulders you get, what sinews, what vigor; but now you have only paltry words and nothing more.

The man who truly trains is he who disciplines himself to face such impressions. Stay, unhappy man! be not carried away. Great is the struggle, divine the task; the stake is a kingdom, freedom, peace, an unruffled spirit. Remember God, call Him to aid and support you, as voyagers call in storm to the Dioscuri. Can any storm be greater than that which springs from violent impressions that drive out reason? For what is storm itself but an impression? Take away the fear of death, and you may bring as much thunder and lightning as you will, and you will discover what deep peace and tranquillity is in your mind. But if you once allow yourself to be defeated and say that you will conquer hereafter, and then do the same again, be sure that you will be weak and miserable; you will never notice hereafter that you are going wrong, but will even begin to provide excuses for your conduct: and then you will confirm the truth of Hesiod's words, "A dilatory man is ever wrestling with calamities." [*Works and Days,* 413]

7. OVID: Erotic Love

Ovid (43 B.C.–A.D. 18) was born of wealthy parents and lived most
of his adult life in Rome. Toward the end of his life he fell into dis-
favor with the Emperor Augustus and was exiled. Until his exile he
lived an exceptionally comfortable life, admired by men and idolized
by women. His love poems have a place in the development of
Western literature and rank alongside such Oriental works of erotic
literature as the **Kama Sutra.**

I

If anyone among this people knows not the art of loving, let
him read my poem, and having read be skilled in love. By skill

SOURCE: Ovid, *The Art of Love and Other Poems,* trans. J. H. Motzley
(Cambridge, Mass.: Harvard University Press, 1939), 1:13–17; 2:111–
117; 3:123–124, 173–175. Reprinted by permission of the publisher
and The Loeb Classical Library.

swift ships are sailed and rowed, by skill nimble chariots are driven: by skill must Love be guided. Well fitted for chariots and pliant reins was Automedon, and Tiphys was the helmsman of the Haemonian ship: me hath Venus set over tender Love as master in the art; I shall be called the Tiphys and Automedon of Love. Wild indeed is he, and apt often to fight against me; but he is a boy, tender his age and easily controlled. The son of Philyra made the boy Achilles accomplished on the lyre, and by his peaceful art subdued those savage passions. He who terrified his friends so often and so often his foes, cowered, we are told, before an aged man. Those hands that Hector was to feel, he held out to the lash obediently, when his master bade. Chiron taught Aeacides, I am Love's teacher: a fierce lad each, and each born of a goddess. Yet even the bull's neck is burdened by the plough, and the high-mettled steed champs the bridle with his teeth; and to me Love shall yield, though he wound my breast with his bow, and whirl aloft his brandished torch. The more violently Love has pierced and branded me, the better shall I avenge the wound that he has made: I will not falsely claim that my art is thy gift, O Phoebus, nor am I taught by the voice of a bird of the air, neither did Clio and Clio's sisters appear to me while I kept flocks in thy vale, O Ascra: experience inspires this work: give ear to an experienced bard; true will be my song: favor my enterprise, O mother of Love. Keep far away, ye slender fillets, emblems of modesty, and the long skirt that hides the feet in its folds. Of safe love-making do I sing, and permitted secrecy, and in my verse shall be no wrong-doing.

First, strive to find an object for your love, you who now for the first time come to fight in warfare new. The next task is, to win the girl that takes your fancy; the third, to make love long endure. This is my limit, this the field whose bound my chariot shall mark, this the goal my flying wheel shall graze.

While yet you are at liberty and can go at large with loosened rein, choose to whom you will say, "You alone please me." She will not come floating down to you through the tenuous air, she must be sought, the girl whom your glance approves. Well knows the hunter where to spread his nets for the stag, well knows he in what glen the boar with gnashing teeth abides; familiar are the copses to fowlers, and he who holds the hook is aware in what waters many fish are swimming; you too, who seek the object of a lasting passion, learn first what places the maidens haunt. I will not bid you in your search set sails before the wind, nor, that you may find, need a long road be travelled. Though Perseus brought Andromeda from the dusky Indians, though the Phrygian lover carried off a Grecian girl, yet Rome will give you so many maidens and so fair that, "Here," you will say, "is all the beauty of the world." As numerous as the crops upon Gargara, as the grape-bunches of Methymna, as the fishes that lurk within the sea, or the birds among the leaves, as many as are the stars of heaven, so many maidens doth thine own Rome contain: the mother of Aeneas still dwells in the city of her son. Are you attracted by early and still ripening years? a real maid will come before your eyes. Would you have a full-grown beauty? a thousand such will please you, and, try as you will, you know not which to choose. Or do you perchance prefer a later and staider age? still more numerous, believe me, will be their array. . . .

II

Particularly forbear to reproach a woman with her faults, faults which many have found it useful to feign otherwise. Her complexion was not made a reproach against Andromeda by him on whose either foot was a swift moving pinion. All thought Andromache too big: Hector alone deemed her of moderate size. Grow used to what you bear ill: you will bear it well; age eases many a smart, but love feels everything at first. While the graft is newly growing in the green bark, let any breeze but shake the weakling shoot, 'twill fall; soon, strengthened by time, this same tree will withstand the winds, and stoutly bear its adopted fruits. Time itself removes all faults from the body, and what was a blemish ceases to be a hindrance. Nostrils in youth cannot bear the hides of bulls; when years of habit have tamed them the odor is not noticed. With names you can soften shortcomings; let her be called swarthy, whose blood is blacker than Illyrian pitch; if cross-eyed, she is like Venus: yellow-haired, like Minerva; call her slender whose thinness impairs her health; if short, call her trim; if stout, of full body; let its nearness to a virtue conceal a fault.

Ask not how old she be, nor under what consul she was born; these are the duties of the stern Censor: particulary so, if she is past her prime, if the flower of her age is over, and already she is plucking out the whitening hairs. Profitable, ye lovers, is that or even a later age; that field will bear, that field must be sown. Endure the toil, while your strength and years permit; soon bent old age will come with silent foot. Cleave the sea with oars, or the earth with the plough, or exert your warlike hands in savage battle, or bring to women's service your bodily strength and vigor and diligence: this too is warfare, this too calls for your powers. Add this, that they have greater acquaintance with their business, and they have experience, which alone gives skill, upon their side: they make good the waste of years by elegance, and by their pains contrive not to seem old. According to your taste they will embrace you in a thousand ways; no picture could devise more modes than they. They need no spur to enjoy their pleasure: let both man and woman feel what delights them equally. I hate embraces which leave not each outworn; that is why a boy's love appeals to me but little. I hate her who gives because she must, and who, herself unmoved, is thinking of her wool. Pleasure given as a duty has no charms for me; for me let no woman be dutiful. I like to hear the words that confess rapture, that beg me hold back and stay awhile. May I see my mistress in frenzy, with eyes that confess defeat; may she be languid, and long refuse to be embraced. These joys, which come quickly after seven lusters, nature has not granted to early youth. Let those who hasten drink new liquor; for me let a jar put down under ancient consuls pour forth its ancestral wine. Neither can the plane tree, save it be mature, resist the sun, and new-sprung meads injure naked feet. What? would you be able to prefer Hermione to Helen, and was Gorge fairer than her mother? whoever you are that wish to approach charms that are mature, if you will play your part, you will win a fitting reward.

Lo! the conscious couch has received two lovers: tarry, O Muse, at the closed door of their chamber. Of their own accord, without your aid, they will utter eloquent speech, nor will the left hand lie idle on the bed. Their fingers will find what to do in those parts where Love plies his weapons unperceived. Most valiant Hector of old did thus with Andromache, nor in war alone did he avail. Thus did the great Achilles with the Lyrnesian captive, when weary from the foe he burdened the soft couch. By those hands didst thou suffer thyself to be touched, Briseis, that were ever imbued in Phrygian blood; was it this very thing, wanton one, that delighted thee, that a conqueror's hands should caress thy limbs? Believe me, love's bliss must not be hastened, but gradually lured on by slow delay. When you have found the place where a woman loves to be touched, let not shame prevent you from touching it. You will see her eyes shooting tremulous gleams, as the sun often glitters in clear water. Then she will complain, then she will lovingly murmur, and sweetly sigh, and utter words that fit the sport. But neither do you, spreading too full sail, leave your mistress behind, nor let her outstrip your speed; haste side by side to the goal: then is pleasure full, when man and woman lie vanquished both together. This is the tenor you must keep, when dallying is free, and no fear urges on the secret work. When delay is dangerous, it is best to press on with all oars, and to spur the galloping horse.

My task is finished: give me the palm, ye grateful lovers, and bring wreaths of myrtle for my scented locks. As great as was Podalirius among the Greeks in the art of healing, or Aeacides in might of hand, or Nestor in understanding, as great as was Calchas at the sacrifice, or Telamon's son in arms, or Automedon in the chariot, so great a lover am I. Celebrate me, the prophet, O ye men; sing my praises, let my name be sung in all the world. I have given you armor; Vulcan gave armor to Achilles; do ye conquer, as he conquered, by virtue of the gift. But whosoever shall by my steel lay low the Amazon, let him inscribe upon his spoils "NASO WAS MY MASTER."

Lo! the young women are begging me to give them counsel: you will be my poetry's next care.

III

. . . While she inspires me, seek precepts here, O women, whom propriety and the laws and your own rights permit. Now already be mindful of the old age which is to come; thus no hour will slip wasted from you. While you can, and still are in your spring-time, have your sport; for the years pass like flowing water; the wave that has gone by cannot be called back, the hour that has gone by cannot return. You must employ your time: time glides on with speedy foot, nor is that which follows so good as that which went before. These plants, now withering, I saw as violet-beds; from this thorn was a pleasing garland given me. That day will come when you, who now shut out your lovers, will lie, a cold and lonely

old woman, through the night; nor will your door be broken in
a nightly brawl, nor will you find your threshold strewn with
roses in the morning. How quickly, ah, me! is the body fur-
rowed by wrinkles, and the color fled that once was in that
lovely face! And the white hairs that you swear have been
there since maidenhood will suddenly be scattered over all
your head. Serpents put off their age with their frail skins, nor
are stags made old by casting their horns: our charms flee
without our aid; pluck the flower, which save it be plucked
will basely wither. Besides, childbirth shortens the period of
youth: a field grows old by continual harvesting. Latmian
Endymion brings no blush to thee, O Moon, nor is Cephalus a
prize that shames the roseate goddess; though Adonis, whom
she mourns, be granted to Venus, whence has she her Aeneas
and Harmonia? Study, ye mortal folk, the examples of the
goddesses, nor deny your joys to hungry lovers. Though they
at last deceive you, what do you lose? those joys abide;
though they take a thousand pleasures, naught is lost therefrom. Iron is worn away, and flints are diminished by use; that
part endures, and has no fear of loss. What forbids to take
light from a light that is set before you, or who would guard
vast waters upon the cavernous deep? And yet does any
woman say to a man, "It is not expedient"?[1] tell me, what are
you doing, save wasting the water that you will draw? Nor do
my words make you vile, but forbid you to fear unreal loss;
there is no loss in your giving. But though the blasts of a
stronger wind will soon impel me, while I am still in harbor,
let a light breeze bear me on. . . .

What remains I blush to tell; but kindly Dione says, "What
brings a blush is before all else my business." Let each woman
know herself; from your own bodies fix your methods; one

---

1. For a woman to give herself to a man is no more wasteful than taking a light from a torch, or using water when it is needed. In fact, not to
do so is itself a waste. [Author's note.]

fashion does not suit all alike. Let her who is fair of face re-
cline upon her back; let those whose backs please them be seen
from behind. Milanion bore Atalanta's legs upon his shoulders;
if they are comely, let them be taken thus. A small woman
should ride astride; because she was tall, his Theban bride
never sat Hector like a horse. A woman whose long flanks
deserve to be seen should press the coverlets with her knees,
her neck bent backward somewhat. If her thighs be youthful
and her breasts without blemish, her lover should stand, and
she herself lie slantwise on the couch. Nor think it unbecoming
to loose your hair, like the Phylleian mother, and bend back
your neck amid flowing tresses. And you whose belly Lucina
has marked with wrinkles, like the swift Parthian, use a back-
ward-turned steed. There are a thousand modes of love; a
simple one, and least fatiguing, is when the woman lies upon
her right side, half-reclined. But neither Phoebus' tripods nor
horned Ammon will tell you more truth than does my Muse: if
an art I have learnt by long experience be trustworthy, give
credence: my poems will warrant for its truth. Let the woman
feel love's act, unstrung to the very depths of her frame, and
let that act delight both alike. Nor let winning sounds and
pleasant murmurs be idle, nor in the midst of the play let
naughty words be hushed. You to whom nature has denied the
sensation of love, counterfeit the sweet bliss with lying sounds.
Unhappy the woman for whom that place, whereof man and
woman ought to have joy alike, is dull and unfeeling. Only,
when you pretend, see that you are not caught: win assurance
by your movements and even by your eyes. Let your words
and panting breath make clear your pleasure; ah, for shame!
that part of your body has its secret signs. She that after love's
joys will ask a lover for reward will not wish her prayers to
have much weight. And let not light into your room by all the
windows; it is better that much of your body should be
hidden.

Our sport is ended: it is time to step down from the swans whose necks have drawn my car. As once the youths, so now let the women, my votaries, write upon their spoils, NASO WAS OUR MASTER.

II

The Tradition of Christian Thought: Marriage, Monogamy and Fidelity

The Christian tradition is the source of our present-day conventional attitudes toward sex and the relations between the sexes. The thought of Plato and Aristotle has had a wide influence on the shaping of ideas about man and society in Western intellectual life, but it has not had the same effect on the basic life attitudes and customs around which Western society is organized. These attitudes and customs have largely grown out of religious ideas which entered Western thought and life with the beginning of Christianity and dominated it throughout the Middle Ages. This is particularly true of our attitudes toward sex. Our conventional moral feelings about the sexual act stem from the Christian tradition, but not from the ancient Greeks. The views the Greeks held on sexual love, the place of sex in human experience and the role of women in the ideal society are grasped by us today as a series of intellectual perspectives. We do not easily make contact with the life attitudes that lie behind them. The conventional attitudes toward sex that we feel acting on us in contemporary life are quite different than those in terms of which Plato and Aristotle wrote.

For the Greeks, and to some extent for the Romans, sex was not a moral issue. Sex was regarded as a natural condition of human life and as such was something to be reflected on and understood, rather than something on which to pass moral judgment. In and of itself sex raised no special or far-reaching moral problems. Outside of some of the views of the Roman Stoics, which are close to Christian views, it is with the introduction of Christianity into the Western tradition that sex and man's sexual behavior becomes a primary moral problem. Our own conventional attitudes toward sex have their origin in the views of such thinkers as Augustine (A.D. 354–430), Thomas Aquinas (A.D. 1225–1274) and Martin Luther (A.D. 1483–1546). Their views on sex seem surprisingly familiar to the attitudes that we have absorbed since childhood simply by growing up in Western culture. They argue for sexual intercourse only after marriage, for monogamous marriage for life, against promiscuity and fornication, for the idea that a woman's proper place is in the home so as to rear children. If one holds conservative and conventional sexual views, one finds here a host of good arguments. If one holds a liberal or experimentalist approach to sexual matters, one finds here a view of things that he feels must be gotten beyond. In either case we find just those ideas that form the basis of conventional Western morality. The basis of our attitudes toward sex is not in the Puritan ethic as many popular writers picture it. The Puritans have special relevance to American attitudes, but the real origins of our attitudes toward sexual morality go back deeper in human thought to the Middle Ages.

The attitude of Plato and Aristotle toward man's sexual nature—that it is something to be reflected on and understood in relation to other types of man's activities—appears today as something almost futuristic. Plato's position on women, if it is seen as ahead of its time, must be seen as at least twenty-four centuries ahead of its time. For sexual activity not to be singled out as an area of human activity that raises particular moral problems is very difficult for the post-Christian mind to comprehend. The very mention in conversation that someone is a "moral" or an "immoral" man or that his "morals are questionable" has the effect for most people of being a summary comment on the person's sexual activities. The rest of his character—whether he is kindly or brutish, honest or devious, etc.—is ignored and his total moral orientation is gauged by his sexual conduct. Morality itself is largely equated in ordinary circles of society with keeping one's behavior in accordance with certain sexual customs of the Christian tradition.

We may ask, how does this come about? How are Greco-Roman views of sexuality transformed into Christian views? Generally speaking, Augustine and Aquinas were concerned to join the ideas of Christian scripture with the ideas of Greek thought. Augustine's thought has as its background Platonic philosophy, and the thought of Aquinas is a Christian interpretation of Aristotle. The key notion that is present in Christian thought, but is absent in Greek thought and is crucial for an understanding of the shift to the Christian view of sex, is—*sin*. The concept that sex is to be understood through its relation to the idea of sin is basic to the approach of Augustine and Aquinas and later to the Reformation-Protestant approach of Luther.

It is through the concept of sin that sex becomes a moral issue. The concept of sin—both of original sin and of particular sins that man can commit—is the basis from which Christian philosophers introduce the distinction between moral and immoral forms of sexual behavior. Every society—whether ancient, traditional, primitive or "advanced industrial"—makes distinctions by custom and law between types of sexual activity that are to be condoned and types that are to be condemned. What is unique to the Christian tradition is not the creation of distinctions between acceptable and unacceptable forms of sexual activity; it is the creation of these distinctions in terms of a theory of man's relationship to God and the future of his soul. The notion of the soul in Christian thought about sex serves to direct the idea of sin.

To view man as having a soul is to locate man's nature in a spiritual substance that is in the real order of things separate and distinct from his body. My soul, on this view, is something wholly spiritual and nonmaterial, as is God. As an individual person I must relate to my body and my bodily activities in such a way as to always attempt to orient my soul toward God. My body is my imperfection, and it is to be regarded by me as fundamentally an instrument with which I must work as I progress toward my salvation. To have a body is every human's trial. Thus personal morality in classical Christian thought becomes largely body-denying morality based upon a set of restrictions on man's bodily activities. Classical Christian morality directs me to relate to activities that heavily involve the passions of my body only in certain ways (only through marriage, etc.) and not in others. This is done in order that I can relate properly to my soul and relate my soul properly to God.

Augustine is the first major thinker to join Christian doctrine with philosophical thought and is also the first major figure of the Middle Ages. The selection is from the *City of God*. In this work generally Augustine is concerned to show not only the superiority and rationality of the Christian religion over pagan religions and practices but also how Christian doctrine can be a guide for the affairs of men. Augustine is specifically concerned with how sexual lust comes about and how its existence in man is resolvable with Christian doctrine. What troubles Augustine in these passages is that the sexual act, performed within marriage and for the purposes of procreation, depends upon lust or "the stirrings of obscene heat" in order to activate the sex organs. Christian morality involves man controlling his bodily appetites through his will. Our will is the agency through which we direct our bodily movements. Unless suffering from a nervous disorder or paralysis, we can will to move an arm or a leg, to walk or run, but we cannot move our sexual organs into action at will. They seem to be completely moved by bodily stimulations. The Christian can resist through his will the temptations to have illicit sexual relations toward which his bodily appetites may incline him. But he must submit to and even follow these lusts if he is to engage in sexual action in its licit form—the having of children in marriage. It also troubles Augustine that in the sex act man loses momentary mental control of himself. The true Christian, he states, "would prefer to beget children without this kind of lust" (part II).

The difficulty of Augustine's problem may not be readily seen from a modern point of view. But given his approach to Christianity, it is a genuine problem: if man is to perfect himself by exercising his will and mind and thus make himself more like God, who is pure will and pure mind, how can he do so if there are aspects of his existence that seem permanently placed outside the power of his will and mental faculties? The explanation of Augustine's connection of sexual lust with original sin lies in the difficulty of solving this paradox. The irreducible element of lust in the sex act and hence in the continuance of man as a species is seen by Augustine as part of original sin. As such lust is part of man's finitude—an aspect of human existence that can never be overcome but must be continually fought against. It is part of the state in which man must live since he has been expelled from his original Paradise. This is why Augustine is concerned to argue (part X) that if human beings had remained in Paradise they would have been able to control their genital organs in procreation through acts of will. His arguments for this from the existence of persons who can wiggle their ears, swallow and regurgitate objects, imitate bird calls and animal sounds and produce flatulent musical notes at will are extraordinary.

Thomas Aquinas, writing much later out of a much different historical and cultural period, approaches the problem of man's sexual nature in a different tone. The selection is from the *Summa Contra Gentiles*. The thought of Thomas Aquinas is largely the intellectual basis for the doctrines of the Catholic faith; thus one finds in it the theological argument that lies behind the sexual attitudes and practices of a large part of the world's population. The *Summa Contra Gentiles* is an attempt by Aquinas to present a statement of the total truth about things. In its four books he discusses the nature of God himself, the nature and order of God's creation, God's relation to man and God's providence over him, and the meaning of virtually all of the major tenets of Christianity. Aquinas's discussion of sex occurs as part of his general discussion of the relationship between God and man. He presents his case clearly, offering an argument for each point, with each point forming part of the argument of his total case. It is not a case, however, that is being simply argued on its own merits. Ultimately its acceptance or rejection depends upon the acceptance or rejection of the truth of Christian scripture of which it is an interpretation.

The points he makes are familiar. They have been the subject of well-known arguments within Catholicism in our own day. Since many of the points he makes are views on sex held widely in Western culture, they are present in various forms in most contemporary discussions of sex. In the passages which follow Aquinas argues: (1) that sexual intercourse should only be engaged in for the purpose of having children and not simply for pleasure; (2) that it should only be engaged in by persons who are married; (3) contraception by artificial means is sinful and wrong (he compares this to a sin next to homicide); (4) performance of the sexual act with anyone other than one's wife is sinful and illicit; (5) marriage is to be for life between one man and one woman; and (6) intermarriage between close relatives is improper and is to be forbidden. Aquinas's arguments for these points vary with each of them, but behind all of them is the general argument that man has a particular nature that is part of the order of things, and he is to act in accordance with it. This notion that each being has its own end and purpose which it is to attain is repeated on all levels of his argument. A good example of this and an argument that has caused much contemporary controversy is his argument against contraception. He argues (part I, paragraphs 4 and 5) that as the whole of a person should attain its end so should each of its parts. Thus, Aquinas argues, the proper end of semen once emitted is the procreation of the species, and all measures taken to interrupt this process are sinful.

Martin Luther, a founder of Protestant Christianity, initiated theological ideas that differ widely from Catholicism, yet many of his basic ideas on sex do not differ. He is against fornication, premarital sexual relations, adultery and for marriage, fidelity, chasteness on the part of the unmarried, insofar as marriage is to be undertaken for the primary purpose of having children. These ideas are written into the Christian tradition and they are endorsed and supported by Luther. Perhaps the two major differences between a Catholic and a classic Protestant position on sex is that Protestant sects generally have come to allow contraception (although not necessarily abortion) and divorce (although the traditional marriage ceremony acts as if marriage is for life). The Catholic position has stood firm against any form of artificial birth control and against any second marriage of persons once separated.

The passages from Luther that make up the selection occur in various places in his works. They are of interest not so much because they present a Protestant point of view as because of their tone and because of some of the subjects on which Luther comments. One of the most interesting of these is his treatment of the role of women. Luther argues that women by nature are made for the care of infants and the home. As he says: "For God did not create this sex to rule. . . . Woman was created for the benefit (*usum*) of man, that is, for the prudent and sensible training of children. Everyone does best when he does that for which he was created." Luther quotes scripture to support his position. It is clear for Luther that in the natural order of things women have a place just next to, but never equal to men.

A particular male point of view runs throughout the discussions of sex of Augustine, Aquinas and Luther. Women are always there passively in the background. They are never active in the problem. This comes out in many ways. Note that Augustine in discussing how on occasion the mind is alive with sexual lust but the body does not comply (part II) appears to have in mind the sometimes-encountered experience of the failure of the male genitals to produce erection. Aquinas speaks of it being a sin for *a man* to arrange for the emission of semen apart from the purpose of having children (part I, paragraph 9). He would appear to have in mind *coitus interruptus,* an act of the male. He also argues that marriage should be indivisible because a woman naturally needs a man to govern her as "the male is both more perfect in reasoning and stronger in his powers" (part II, paragraph 3). Luther seems to regard one of the major features of marriage and reasons to recommend it that it serves as a remedy for fornication. In discussing the question of legalized prostitution he says: "By the grace of God a good remedy for fornication is marriage or the prospect of marriage." The direction of Luther's approach is from the problem of the male's temptation to sin. His advice for the male who feels the temptation of the flesh too strongly is to take a wife. The woman's being is defined through the man's. It is just these views of the relationship between the sexes that have in our own day become the subject of debate over women's rights and position in society (see Section V).

Hume and Kant, who are included in this section, are eighteenth century figures and are separated from Augustine, Aquinas and Luther by considerable historical and philosophical distance, yet both argue strongly for the morality of the traditional Christian views on sex. Hume considers arguments for and against polygamy and its alternative, a series of monogamous relationships periodically divorced. He concludes that the difficulties involved in either are greater than "our present European practice with regard to marriage." Kant argues for sexual relations only in marriage. He views all forms of nonheterosexuality—masturbation, homosexuality and intercourse with animals—as unnatural acts, degrading to the human species. He regards these acts as below animal nature which "make man unworthy of his humanity. He no longer deserves to be a person."

It is interesting that Hume and Kant, who in their central philosophical doctrines so completely revised the course of human thought, should so readily reflect what is simply conventional thought and custom in these matters. There is, however, an important shift from Augustine, Aquinas and Luther that is implicit in their approach. Hume and Kant argue their case for the Christian sexual ethic directly. They do not settle their case by appeals to scripture or reason that is in the end based on it. Kant's arguments about morality in sexual relationships, like his ethical theory generally, are rationalistic and in many ways insightful. His argument that the proper sexual relationship must be one in which the two persons approach each other as subjects and neither is made an object is a view that is at the heart of much contemporary thought about sex, although many contemporary thinkers would not agree with Kant that this is possible only in marriage. Hume's approach, typical of his philosophy generally, reviews what he has available as the facts and draws conclusions on the basis of what seem to be the consequences of various practices for current social custom. Because Kant and Hume base their case on appeals to reason and evidence rather than authority and faith, their approach has implicit in it, in principle, the possibility of a thoroughly critical examination of sexual ethics, although much of what they say is quite ordinary thinking by otherwise extraordinary minds.

8. AUGUSTINE: Sexual Lust and Original Sin

Saint Augustine (A.D. 354–430) was born and educated in North Africa and was for the first part of his life a teacher of rhetoric in Italy. He was converted to Christianity in 386 and subsequently returned to North Africa, founded a monastic community and became Bishop of Hippo. His life spanned a substantial period of the decline of the Roman Empire in which the old Roman pagan traditions were giving way to Christianity.

I

On the justice of the retribution that was meted out to the first human beings for their disobedience.

Man, as we know, scorned the bidding of God who had created him, who had made him in his own image, who had

Source: St. Augustine, *City of God,* trans. Philip Levine (Cambridge, Mass.: Harvard University Press, 1966), 4:345–401. Copyright 1966 by the President and Fellows of Harvard College. Reprinted by permission of the publisher and The Loeb Classical Library.

placed him above the other animals, who had established him
in paradise, who had provided him with an abundance of all
things and of security, and who had not laden him with commands that were numerous or onerous or difficult but had
propped him up for wholesome obedience with one very brief
and easy command, whereby he sought to impress upon this
creature, for whom free service was expedient, that he was the
Lord. Therefore, as a consequence, just condemnation followed, and this condemnation was such that man, who would
have been spiritual even in flesh if he had observed the order,
became carnal in mind as well. Moreover, this man who had
pleased himself in his pride was then granted to himself by
God's justice; yet this was not done in such a way that he was
completely in his own power, but that he disagreed with himself and so led, under the rule of the one with whom he agreed
when he sinned, a life of cruel and wretched slavery in place
of the freedom for which he had conceived a desire. He was
willingly dead in spirit and unwillingly destined to die in
body; a deserter of the eternal life, he was doomed also to
eternal death, unless he were freed by grace. Whoever thinks
that condemnation of this sort is either excessive or unjust
surely does not know how to gauge the magnitude of wickedness in sinning when the opportunity for not sinning was so
ample.

Just as Abraham's obedience is not undeservedly celebrated
as great because he was ordered to do a very difficult thing,
namely, to slay his son, so in paradise disobedience was all the
greater because the command that was given would have
involved no difficulty. And just as the obedience of the Second
Man is the more laudable because "he became obedient unto
death," so the disobedience of the first man is the more
abominable because he became disobedient unto death. For
where the proposed punishment for disobedience is great and

the command of the Creator is easy to obey, who can adequately expound how grave an evil it is not to obey when an easy matter has been ordered by so mighty a power and is attended by the terror of such awful punishment?

To put it briefly then, in the punishment of that sin the requital for disobedience was no other than disobedience. For man's wretchedness consists only in his own disobedience to himself, wherefore, since he would not do what he then could, he now has a will to do what he cannot. In paradise, to be sure, man could not do everything whatsoever even before he sinned, yet, whatever he could not do, he did not have a will to do, and in that way he could do everything that he would. Now, however, as we recognize in his offspring and as holy Scripture attests, "Man has become like vanity." For who can count up all the things that man has a will to do but cannot as long as he is disobedient to himself, that is, as long as his very mind and even his flesh, which is lower, are disobedient to his will? For even against his will his mind is very often agitated and his flesh feels pain, grows old, dies and suffers whatever else we suffer; but we should not suffer all this against our will if our being in every way and in every part gave obedience to our will.

Someone may perhaps protest that the flesh is unable to serve us because of what it suffers. But what difference does it make how this happens? It only matters that through the justice of God, who is our master and to whom we his subjects refused service, our flesh, which had been subject to us, is troublesome by its insubordination, though we by our insubordination to God have succeeded only in being troublesome to ourselves and not to him. For he does not need our service as we need that of the body; so that what we get is punishment for us, but what we did was none for him. Further, the so-called pains of the flesh are pains of the soul that exist in and proceed from the flesh. For what pain or desire does the flesh experience by itself apart from a soul?

When we say that the flesh feels desire or pain, we mean that it is either man himself, as I have argued, or some part of the soul affected by what the flesh experiences, whether it be harsh and painful or gentle and pleasant. Pain of the flesh is only a vexation of the soul arising from the flesh and a sort of disagreement with what is done to the flesh, just as the pain of the mind that we call grief is a disagreement with the things that have happened to us against our will. But grief is generally preceded by fear, which is also something in the soul and not in the flesh. Pain of the flesh, on the other hand, is not preceded by anything like fear on the part of the flesh that is felt in the flesh before the pain. Pleasure, however, is preceded by a certain craving that is felt in the flesh as its own desire, such as hunger, thirst and the desire that is mostly called lust when it affects the sex organs, though this is a general term applicable to any kind of desire.

Even anger itself, so the ancients defined it, is nothing but a lust for revenge, although at times a man vents his anger even upon inanimate objects, where no effect of vengeance can be felt, and in his rage smashes his style or breaks his reed pen when it writes badly. But even this lust, though rather irrational, is a sort of lust for revenge and something like a shadowy reflection, as it were, of the principle or retribution whereby they who do evil must suffer evil. There is then a lust for revenge, which is called anger; there is a lust for possessing money, which is termed greed; there is a lust for winning at any price, which is termed obstinacy; and there is a lust for bragging, which is termed vainglory. There are many different kinds of lust, of which some have special designations also while others have none. No one, for example, would find it easy to say what the lust to be overlord is called, though, as even civil wars attest, it exercises a very powerful influence in the minds of tyrants.

II

On the evil of lust, a term which, though it is applicable to many vices, is especially ascribed to the stirrings of obscene heat.

Therefore, although there are lusts for many things, yet when the term lust is employed without the mention of any object, nothing comes to mind usually but the lust that excites the shameful parts of the body. Moreover, this lust asserts its power not only over the entire body, nor only externally, but also from within. It convulses all of a man when the emotion in his mind combines and mingles with the carnal drive to produce a pleasure unsurpassed among those of the body. The effect of this is that at the very moment of its climax there is an almost total eclipse of acumen and, as it were, sentinel alertness. But surely any friend of wisdom and holy joys, who lives in wedlock but knows, as the Apostle admonished, "how to possess his bodily vessel in holiness and honor, not in the disease of lust like the gentiles who do not know God," would prefer, if he could, to beget children without this kind of lust. For he would want his mind to be served, even in this function of engendering offspring, by the parts created for this kind of work, just as it is served by the other members, each assigned to its own kind of work. They would be set in motion when the will urged, not stirred to action when hot lust surged.

But not even those who are enamoured of this pleasure are aroused whether to marital intercourse or to the uncleanness of outrageous vice just when it is their will. At times the urge intrudes uninvited; at other times it deserts the panting lover, and although desire is ablaze in the mind, the body is frigid. In this strange fashion lust refuses service not only to the will to procreate but also to the lust for wantonness; and though for the most part it solidly opposes the mind's restraint, there are times when it is divided even against itself and, having aroused the mind, inconsistently fails to arouse the body.

III

On the nakedness of the first human beings, which seemed to them base and shameful after they sinned.

It is reasonable then that we should feel very much ashamed of such lust, and reasonable too that those members which it moves or does not move by its own right, so to speak, and not in full subjection to our will, should be called pudenda or shameful parts as they were not before man sinned; for we read in Scripture: "They were naked, and not embarrassed." And the reason for this is not that they were unaware of their nakedness, but that their nakedness was not yet base because lust did not yet arouse those members apart from their will, and the flesh did not yet bear witness, so to speak, through its own disobedience against the disobedience of man.

For the first human beings had not been created blind, as the ignorant multitude think, since Adam saw the animals upon which he bestowed names, and of Eve we read: "The woman saw that the tree was good for food and that it was a delight for the eyes to behold." Accordingly, their eyes were not closed, but they were not open, that is, attentive so as to recognize what a boon the cloak of grace afforded them, in that their bodily members did not know how to oppose their will. When this grace was lost and punishment in kind for their disobedience was inflicted, there came to be in the action of the body a certain shameless novelty, and thereafter nudity was indecent. It drew their attention and made them embarrassed.

This is why Scripture says of them, after they had violated God's command in open transgression: "And the eyes of both were opened, and they discovered that they were naked, and they sewed fig leaves together and made themselves aprons." "The eyes of both," we are told, "were opened," yet not that they might see, since they could see already, but that they might distinguish between the good that they had lost and the evil into which they had fallen. This also explains why the tree itself, which was to enable them to make such a distinction if they laid hands on it to eat its fruit in spite of the prohibition, was named for that fact and called the tree of the knowledge of good and evil. For experience of discomfort in sickness gives a clearer insight into the joys of health as well.

Accordingly, "they realized that they were naked," stripped naked, that is, of the grace that kept nakedness of body from embarrassing them before the law of sin came into opposition with their minds. Thus they learned what they would more fortunately not have known if through belief in God and obedience to his word they had refrained from an act that would compel them to find out by experience what harm unbelief and disobedience could do. Therefore, embarrassed by their flesh's disobedience, a punishment that bore witness to their own disobedience, "they sewed fig leaves together and made themselves aprons (*campestria*)," that is, loin-cloths, a term employed by certain translators. (Moreover, though *campestria* is a Latin word, it derives its origin from the practice of young men who used to cover up their pudenda while they exercised in the nude on the so-called *campus* or field. Hence, those who are so girt are commonly designated as *campestrati*.) Thus modesty, prompted by a sense of shame, covered what was disobediently aroused by lust against a will condemned for disobedience.

Ever since that time, this habit of concealing the pudenda has been deeply ingrained in all peoples, descended, as they are, from the original stock. In fact, certain barbarians do not expose those parts of the body even in the bath but wash with their coverings on. In the dark retreats of India too certain men who practice philosophy in the nude (and hence are called gymnosophists) nevertheless use coverings for their genitals, though they have none for the other parts of the body.

IV

On the sense of shame in sexual intercourse, whether promiscuous or marital.

Let us consider the act itself that is accomplished by such lust, not only in every kind of licentious intercourse, for which hiding-places are prerequisite to avoid judgment before human tribunals, but also in the practice of harlotry, a base vice that has been legalized by the earthly city. Although in the latter case the practice is not under the ban of any law of this city, nevertheless even the lust that is allowed and free of penalty shuns the public gaze. Because of an innate sense of shame even brothels have made provision for privacy, and unchastity found it easier to do without the fetters of legal prohibition than shamelessness did to eliminate the secret nooks of that foul business.

But this harlotry is called a base matter even by those who are base themselves, and although they are enamoured of it, they dare not make public display of it. What of marital intercourse, which has for its purpose, according to the terms of the marriage contract, the procreation of children? Lawful and respectable though it is, does it not seek a chamber secluded from witnesses? Before the bridegroom begins even to caress his bride, does he not first send outside all servants and even his own groomsmen as well as any who had been permitted to enter for kinship's sake, whatever the tie? And since, as a certain "supreme master of Roman eloquence" also maintains, all right actions wish to be placed in the light of day, that is, are eager to become known, this right action also desires to become known, though it still blushes to be seen. For who does not know what goes on between husband and wife for the procreation of children? Indeed, it is for the achievement of this purpose that wives are married with such ceremony. And yet, when the act for the birth of children is being consummated, not even the children that may already have been born from the union are allowed to witness it. For this right action does indeed seek mental light for recognition of it, but it shrinks from visual light. What is the reason for this if not that something by nature fitting and proper is carried out in such a way as to be accompanied also by something of shame as punishment?

V

That anger and lust, parts that are stirred in man with such harmful effect that they must be checked and curbed by wisdom, did not exist in that sound state of his being before he sinned.

Here we have the reason why those philosophers too who came closer to the truth admitted that anger and lust are faulty divisions of the soul. They reasoned that these emotions proceed in a confused and disorderly way to engage even in acts that wisdom forbids and that consequently they stand in need of a controlling and rational mind. This third part of the soul, according to them, resides in a sort of citadel to rule the other two parts in order that, as it commands and they serve, justice in man may be preserved among all the parts of the soul.

Now as for these two divisions of the soul, those philosophers confess that they are vicious even in a wise and temperate man. It is for this reason that the mind by repression and restraint curbs and recalls them from things that they are wrongly moved to do, but allows them to follow any course that the law of wisdom has sanctioned. Anger, for example, is permitted for the display of a just compulsion, and lust for the duty of propagating offspring. But these divisions, I maintain, were not vicious in paradise before man sinned, for they were not set going against a right will in pursuit of anything that made it necessary to check them with the guiding reins, as it were, of reason.

For in so far as these emotions are now set going in this way and controlled with more or less ease or difficulty, yet still controlled, by restraint and opposition on the part of those who lead temperate, just and holy lives, this is by no means a healthy state due to nature; it is a morbid condition due to guilt. Moreover, if modesty does not conceal the actions prompted by anger and the other emotions in every word and deed as it does those of lust in which the sexual organs are used, the reason is simply that in other cases the members of the body are not put into operation by the emotions themselves but by the will, after it has consented to them, for it has complete control in the employment of such members. No one who utters a word in anger or even strikes a person could do so if his tongue or hand were not set in motion at the command, so to speak, of his will; and these members can also be set in motion by the same will even when there is no anger. But in the case of the sexual organs, lust has somehow brought them so completely under its rule that they are incapable of activity if this one emotion is lacking and has not sprung up spontaneously or in answer to a stimulus. Here is the cause of shame, here is what blushingly avoids the eye of onlookers; and a man would sooner put up with a crowd of spectators when he is wrongly venting his anger upon another than with the gaze of a single individual even when he is rightly having intercourse with his wife.

VI

On the utterly absurd indecency of the Cynics.

Those canine philosophers, or Cynics,[1] were not aware of this fact when they expounded a view offensive to human modesty, a view that can only be termed canine, that is, base and shameless. They held that since the act is lawful when it is done with a wife, no one should feel ashamed to do it openly and engage in marital intercourse on any street or square. Nevertheless, our natural sense of shame has been victorious over this heretical notion. There is, to be sure, a tradition that Diogenes once ostentatiously performed such an act because he thought that his school would win more publicity in this way, that is, if its shamelessness was more sensationally impressed upon the memory of mankind. The later Cynics, however, have abandoned any such practice, and modesty has prevailed over error, that is, the instinct among men to feel ashamed before other men has prevailed over the doctrine that men should make it their aim to be like dogs.

Hence I prefer to think that Diogenes and others who reputedly did such a thing rather acted out the motions of lying together before the eyes of men who really did not know what was done under the cloak. I do not believe that there could have been any achievement of such pleasure under the glare of human gaze. For those philosophers did not blush to seem willing to lie together in a place where lust itself would have blushed to rear its head. Even now we see that there are still Cynic philosophers among us. They are the ones who not only wrap themselves in a cloak but also carry a club.[2] Yet

1. The term is derived from the Greek κύων meaning "dog."
2. Their club is thought to recall a traditional attribute of Hercules, who was their favorite model.

none of them dares to behave so, for it would bring down upon any who had dared a shower, if not of stones, at any rate of spittle from the outraged public.

Human nature then doubtless feels shame at this lust, and rightly so. For its disobedience, which subjected the sexual organs to its impulses exclusively and wrested them from control by the will, is a sufficient demonstration of the punishment that was meted out to man for that first disobedience. And it was fitting that this punishment should show itself particularly in that part of the body which engenders the very creature that was changed for the worse through that first great sin. No one can be delivered from the meshes of that sin unless the offence that was committed to the common disaster of all and punished by the justice of God when all men existed in but one, is expiated in each man singly by the grace of God.

VII

That the blessing of increase in human fertility given before sin was not forfeited through transgression but alloyed with the disease of lust.

Far be it then from us to believe that the couple that were placed in paradise would have fulfilled through this lust, which shamed them into covering those organs, the words pronounced by God in his blessing: "Increase and multiply and fill the earth." For it was only after man sinned that this lust arose; it was after man sinned that his natural being, retaining the sense of shame but losing that dominance to which the body was subject in every part, felt and noticed, then blushed at and concealed that lust. The nuptial blessing, however, whereby the pair, joined in marriage, were to increase and multiply and fill the earth, remained in force even when they sinned, yet it was given before they sinned, for its purpose was to make it clear that the procreation of children is a part of the glory of marriage and not of the punishment of sin.

There are, nevertheless, in our own day men who must surely lack knowledge of that former happiness in paradise, for they believe that children could only have been engendered by the means with which they are personally acquainted, that is, by lust, which, as we see, causes embarrassment even to the honorable state of marriage. Some of these men not merely reject outright but unbelievingly deride the holy Scriptures, in which we read that after sin nakedness caused shame and the organs of shame were covered. Others among them, on the other hand, accept and honor the Scriptures but hold that the words "Increase and multiply" are not to be taken as referring to carnal fertility because some similar statement is also found with reference to the soul: "Thou wilt multiply me with strength in my soul." Relying on this passage, they interpret allegorically the words that follow in *Genesis:* "Both fill the earth and be masters of it." By earth they understand the flesh which the soul fills with its presence and over which it has greatest mastery when it is multiplied in inner strength, or virtue. But carnal offspring, they maintain, could no more have been born then than now without lust, which arose after man sinned, was observed with embarrassment and concealed, and they would not have been born in paradise but only outside it, as in fact happened. For it was after the first couple had been sent away from there that they united to beget children and did beget them.

VIII

On the matrimonial bond as originally established and blessed by God.

I myself, however, have no doubt at all that to increase, multiply and fill the earth in accordance with the blessing of

God is a gift of marriage and that God established this institution from the beginning before man's fall by the creation of male and female; the difference in sex is in any case clear enough in the flesh. It was also with this work of God that the blessing itself was connected, for immediately after the scriptural words: "Male and female he created them," there was added: "And God blessed them, and God said to them: 'Increase and multiply and fill the earth and be masters of it,'" and so on.

Granted that all this can without impropriety be taken in a spiritual sense, yet we cannot understand "male" and "female" as figurative terms referring to any analogy in a single human being on the ground that in him, as we know, there is one element that rules and another that is ruled. As the bodies of different sex make abundantly clear, it is the height of absurdity to deny that male and female were created as they were to increase, multiply and fill the earth by begetting offspring. For when the Lord was asked whether it was permitted to divorce one's wife on any grounds whatever, since Moses allowed the Israelites to give a bill of divorcement on account of their hardness of heart, his reply did not concern the spirit which commands and the flesh which obeys, or the rational mind which rules and the irrational desire which is ruled, or the contemplative virtue which is superior and the active virtue which is subordinate, or the understanding of the mind and the sensation of the body, but it plainly referred to the marriage tie which binds both sexes to one another. In this answer he said: "Have you not read that he who made them from the beginning made them male and female, and said, 'For this reason a man shall leave his father and mother and be joined to his wife, and the two shall become one flesh'? So they are no longer two but one flesh. What therefore God has joined together, let not man put asunder."

There is no doubt then that from the very beginning male

and female were fashioned in quite the same way as we see and know two human beings of different sex to be now and that they are called "one" either because of their union or because of the origin of the female, who was created from the side of the male. For the Apostle too invoked this first example, which God instituted as a precedent, to admonish each and every one that husbands should love their wives.

IX

Whether procreation would have been allowed even in paradise if no one had sinned, or whether the principle of chastity would have fought there against the ardor of lust.

When anyone says that there would have been no copulation or generation if the first human beings had not sinned, does he not imply that man's sin was required to complete the number of saints? For if by not sinning they would have continued to be solitary because, so some think, they could not have produced offspring if they had not sinned, then surely sin was required before there could not be just two but many righteous persons. But if that is too absurd to believe, we must rather believe that even if no one had sinned, a sufficiently large number of saints would have come into existence to populate that supremely happy city—as large a number, that is, as are now being gathered through the grace of God from the multitude of sinners, and as will be, so long as "the children of this world" beget and are begotten.

This leads to the conclusion that if no sin had been committed, that marriage, being worthy of the happiness of paradise, would have produced offspring to be loved, yet no lust to cause shame. But there is now no example with which to illustrate how this could have been effected. Nevertheless, that is no reason why it should seem incredible that the will, which is now obeyed by so many members, might also have been

obeyed in the absence of this lust by that one part as well.
Consider how, when we choose, we set our hands and feet in
motion to do the things that are theirs to do, how we manage
this without any conflict and with all the facility that we see
both in our own case and in that of others, especially among
workers in all kinds of physical tasks, where a natural capacity
that is too weak and slow is fitted for its employment by the
application of greater dexterity and effort. May we not similarly believe that those organs of procreation could, like the
others, have served mankind by obedience to the decision of
the will for the generation of children even if there had been
no lust inflicted as punishment for the sin of disobedience?

When in his discussion of the different forms of rule in his
work entitled *On the Commonwealth* Cicero drew an analogy
for his purpose from human nature, did he not say that the
members of the body are ruled like children because of their
readiness to obey, whereas the depraved parts of the soul are
constrained like slaves by a harsher rule? No doubt, in the
order of nature, the soul ranks above the body, yet the soul
itself finds it easier to rule the body than to rule itself. Nevertheless, this lust that we are now discussing is something all
the more shameful because under its effect the soul neither
succeeds in ruling itself so as to have no lust at all nor controls
the body completely in such a way that the organs of shame
are set in motion by the will rather than by lust. Indeed, if
such were the case, they would not be organs of shame.

As things now stand, the soul is ashamed of the body's
opposition to it, for the body is subject to it because of its
lower nature. When the soul opposes itself in the case of other
emotions, it feels less ashamed because when it is vanquished
by itself, the soul is its own vanquisher. Although this victory
of soul over soul is disorderly and morbid because it is a
victory of constituents that should be subject to reason, yet it
is a victory of its own constituents and therefore, as was said, a

self-conquest. For when the soul vanquishes itself in an orderly fashion and thus subordinates its irrational emotions to the rule of a rational purpose, such a victory is laudable and virtuous, provided that its purpose in turn is subordinate to God. Still, the soul feels less ashamed when it is not obeyed by its own depraved constituents than when its will and bidding are not heeded by the body, which is different from it and inferior to it and has a substance that has no life without it.

But when a curb is imposed by the will's authority on the body's other members, without which those organs that are excited by lust in defiance of the will cannot fulfill their craving, chastity is safeguarded, not because the pleasure of sinning has disappeared, but because it is not allowed to appear. If culpable disobedience had not been punished with disobedience in retribution, then doubtless the marriage in paradise would not have experienced this resistance, this opposition, this conflict of will and lust or, at any rate, the deficiency of lust as against the sufficiency of will; rather, the will would have been obeyed not only by other members of the body but by all alike.

Under those circumstances, the organ created for this work would have sown its seed upon the field of generation as the hand does now upon the earth. And though I am now hampered by modesty when I wish to treat this subject in greater detail, and am compelled to apologize to chaste ears and to ask their pardon, there would then have been no reason for this to happen. Discussion, free and unencumbered by any fear of obscenity, would range over every aspect that might occur to the thought of anyone who reflected on bodily parts of this sort. There would not even be words that could be called obscene, but all our talk on this subject would be as decent as what we say in speaking about the other members of the body. Accordingly, if anyone approaches in a wanton spirit what I have written here, let him shun any guilt on his own part, not the natural facts. Let him censure the deeds of his own depravity, not the words of my necessity. Herein I shall very readily be pardoned by the chaste and devout reader or listener as long as I refute the scepticism which relies for argument not on the faith in things unexperienced, but on the perception of things experienced. For these words of mine will give no offence to the reader who is not appalled by the Apostle's censure of the appalling immoralities of the women who "exchanged natural relations for unnatural," especially since I am not, like the Apostle, now bringing up and censuring damnable lewdness. Still, in explaining, as best I can, the working of human generation I try, like him, to avoid the use of lewd terms.

X

That if human beings had remained innocent and had earned the right to stay in paradise by their obedience, they would have used their genital organs for the procreation of offspring in the same way as they used the rest, that is, at the discretion of the will.

The seed of offspring then would have been sown by the man and received by the woman at such time and in such amount as was needed, their genital organs being directed by the will and not excited by lust. For we move at our bidding not only those members which have joints and solid bones, like hands, feet and fingers, but we can at will shake and move, stretch and extend, twist and bend or contract and stiffen even the parts that are slackly composed of soft muscular tissue, like those which the will moves, as far as it can, in the mouth and face. Indeed, even the lungs, which, except for the marrows, are the most delicate of all the internal organs and for that reason are sheltered in the cavity of the chest, are made to function in this way for the purpose of drawing in and expelling the breath and uttering or modulating a sound;

for just as bellows serve the will of blacksmiths or organists, so lungs serve the will of anyone who blows out or draws in his breath or speaks or shouts or sings.

I shall not dwell on the natural endowment of certain animals in connection with the covering that clothes their entire body; suffice it to say that if in any part of it they feel anything that should be driven off, they are able to make it move just at the point where they feel the object and to dislodge with a quiver of their hide not only flies settled upon them but also spears sticking in them. Granted that man does not have this faculty, yet surely it does not follow that the creator was unable to grant it to such animate beings as he chose. Hence man himself too may once have commanded even from his lower members an obedience that by his own disobedience he has lost. For it was not difficult for God to design him in such a way that even what now is moved in his flesh only by lust was then moved only by his will.

Certain human beings too, as we know, have natural endowments that are quite different from those of others and remarkable for their very rarity. They can at will do with their bodies some things that others find utterly impossible to imitate and scarcely credible to hear. For some people can actually move their ears, either one at a time or both together. Other people, without moving their head, can bring all the scalp that is covered with hair to the forefront and then draw it back again at will. Others can swallow an astonishing number of different objects and then, with a very slight contraction of their diaphragm, bring forth, as though from a bag, whatever item they please in perfect condition. Certain people mimic and render so expertly the utterances of birds and beasts, as well as of any other human beings, that it is impossible to tell the difference unless they are seen. Some people produce at will without any stench such rhythmical sounds from their fundament that they appear to be making music even from that quarter. From my own experience I know of a man who used to perspire at will. Certain people are known to weep at will and to shed a flood of tears.

But here is something far more incredible, a spectacle that a large number of our own brethren very recently witnessed. There was a certain presbyter, Restitutus by name, in the parish of the church of Calama. Whenever he pleased (and he used to be asked to do it by those who desired to have a firsthand knowledge of the amazing phenomenon), he would withdraw from his senses to an accompaniment of cries as of some person in distress and lie still exactly like a dead man. In this state he not only was completely insensitive to pinching and pricking but at times was even burned by the application of fire and yet felt no pain except afterwards from the wound. Proof that his body remained motionless, not through deliberate effort, but through absence of feeling was provided by the fact that, like someone deceased, he showed no sign of breathing. Nevertheless, he later reported that he could hear people talking, as though from a distance, if they spoke distinctly enough.

The body then, as we have seen, even now remarkably serves certain people beyond the ordinary limits of nature in many kinds of movement and feeling although they are living our present wretched life in perishable flesh. That being so, what is there to keep us from believing that human members may have served the human will without lust for the procreation of offspring before the sin of disobedience and the consequent punishment of deterioration? Man therefore was handed over to himself because he forsook God in his self-satisfaction, and since he did not obey God, he could not obey even himself. From this springs the more obvious wretchedness whereby man does not live as he chooses. For if he lived as he chose, he would deem himself happy; but yet he would not be happy even so if he lived an indecent life.

XI

On the true happiness, which our present life does not possess.

Yet, if we are to regard the matter more closely, only a happy man lives as he chooses, and only a righteous man is happy. But even the righteous man himself will not live as he chooses until he arrives where he both is wholly free from death, deception and injury and is assured that he will always so remain. For this is what our nature seeks, and it will not be fully and perfectly happy unless it attains what it seeks. But who among us now can live as he chooses when the very matter of living is not in his power? For he chooses to live but is compelled to die. How then does he live as he chooses if he does not live as long as he chooses? But if he should choose to die, how can he live as he chooses when he does not choose to live? And if a person should choose to die, not because he does not choose to live, but in order to have a better life after death, then he does not yet live as he chooses, but will so live when by dying he has attained to what he chooses.

But, presto, let him live as he chooses, since he has dragooned and ordered himself not to choose what he cannot have, but to choose what he can have, just as we read in Terence:

> *Since what you will you cannot do,*
> *Then will to do what you can do.*

Is such a person happy because he is wretched patiently? No, indeed, for the happy life belongs to no one who does not love it. Moreover, if a man does love it and have it, he must love it above all other things since whatever else is loved must be loved for the sake of this happy life. Further, if it is loved as much as it deserves to be loved—and unless a person loves the happy life itself as it deserves, he is not happy—the man who so loves it cannot help but wish it to be eternal. Life therefore will be happy when it is eternal.

XII

That we must believe that the happy pair who lived in paradise could have fulfilled the function of generation without shameful desire.

Accordingly, man lived in paradise just as he chose for as long a time as his choice coincided with God's command. He lived in the enjoyment of God, whose goodness ensured his goodness. He lived without any want and had it in his power always to live such a life. He had food at hand against hunger, drink against thirst and the tree of life against the decay of old age. There was no deterioration in the body or arising from it to cause any discomfort to any of his senses. There was no fear of disease from within or of injury from without. He had perfect health in his flesh and complete tranquillity in his soul.

Just as in paradise it was neither too hot nor too cold, so in its occupant there was no interference from desire or fear to thwart his good will. There was no depressing gloom at all, no unreal gaiety. True joy emanated continuously from God, for whom there glowed "love from a pure heart and a good conscience and sincere faith." Between husband and wife there was a loyal partnership springing from honest love; there was a harmonious alertness of mind and body and an effortless observance of God's command. No one suffered from weariness in his leisure, no one was overcome with sleep against his will.

In such facility of living and such felicity of mankind, far be it from us to suspect that it was impossible for the seed of offspring to be sown without the infection of lust; rather, the sexual organs could have been set in motion by the same authority of the will as the other bodily members. The husband, exempt from all seductive goading of passion, could have come to rest on his wife's bosom with peace of mind undisturbed and pristine state of body intact. Granted that we cannot prove this by actual experiment, yet that is no reason why we should refuse to believe that when those parts of the body were not impelled by turbulent ardor but brought into play by a voluntary exercise of capacity as the need arose, the male seed could then be introduced into the wife's uterus without damage to her maidenhead, even as now the menstrual flow can issue from an maiden's uterus without any such damage. For the seed could be injected through the same passage as that by which the menses can be ejected. Just as for parturition the womb of the female would not have been unclosed by any groan of travail but by some impulse when the time was ripe, so for impregnation and conception the two sexes would have been brought together not by lustful appetite but by exercise of the will.

The matters of which I am speaking now provoke shame. I am, to be sure, trying to conceive, as best I can, what they might have been like before they became a cause for shame; yet, for the reason stated, my discussion must rather be curbed by modesty that calls me back than further advanced by my eloquence, inadequate as it is. Not even those who were in a position to experience what I am describing did experience it, since their sin came first and thus they incurred exile from paradise before they could unite with one another dispassionately and deliberately in the work of propagating their kind. Hence it is impossible that when this subject is mentioned, it should now bring before our imagination anything but our own experience of turbulent lust rather than any speculative notion of a calm act of will.

Consequently, a sense of shame impedes my speech, though my mind is not at a loss for matter. Nevertheless, God almighty, who is the supreme and supremely good creator of all things, who supports and rewards all good will but abandons and condemns all bad will and orders both alike, surely did not lack a plan by which he could complete the set number of citizens foreordained in his wisdom for his city even from among the condemned human race. Since the entire mass of mankind has been condemned from its diseased root, as it were, he does not now select them by their deserts but by his grace, and he manifests his bounty to those who have been delivered not only in his treatment of them but also in his dealing with those who have not been delivered. For each one can see that he has been rescued from evils by a kindness that is not owed to him but freely given when he becomes exempt from participation in the fate of those in whose just punishment he had shared. There was no reason then why God should not have created men of whom he had foreknowledge that they would sin. For that enabled him to exhibit in them and through them both the due reward of their guilt and the gift of his grace, and as long as he was creator and disposer, the perverse disorder of transgressors could not pervert the right order of creation.

9. AQUINAS: The Divinity of Marriage

Saint Thomas Aquinas (1225–1274) was born in the castle of Roccasecca near Naples and was educated at the University of Naples. He entered the Dominican order against the wishes of his family which led to his kidnapping by his brothers, who held him prisoner for about a year. He subsequently went to the University of Paris and after several years of study and lecturing became a member of the faculty of theology. In 1272 he returned to Naples and later died on a journey to Lyons. All of his works were written within a twenty-year period while he was teaching; they comprise a total system of thought.

I

The reason why simple fornication is a sin according to divine law, and that matrimony is natural.

From the foregoing we can see the futility of the argument of certain people who say that simple fornication is not a sin.

SOURCE: From *On the Truth of the Catholic Faith* by St. Thomas Aquinas, Book Three: Providence, Parts I and II, translated by Vernon J. Bourke. Copyright © 1956 by Doubleday & Company, Inc. Reprinted by permission of Doubleday & Company, Inc.

For they say: Suppose there is a woman who is not married, or under the control of any man, either her father or another man. Now, if a man performs the sexual act with her, and she is willing, he does not injure her, because she favors the action and she has control over her own body. Nor does he injure any other person, because she is understood to be under no other person's control. So, this does not seem to be a sin.

Now, to say that he injures God would not seem to be an adequate answer. For we do not offend God except by doing something contrary to our own good, as has been said. But this does not appear contrary to man's good. Hence, on this basis, no injury seems to be done to God.

Likewise, it also would seem an inadequate answer to say that some injury is done to one's neighbor by this action, inasmuch as he may be scandalized. Indeed, it is possible for him to be scandalized by something which is not in itself a sin. In this event, the act would be accidentally sinful. But our problem is not whether simple fornication is accidentally a sin, but whether it is so essentially.

Hence, we must look for a solution in our earlier considerations. We have said that God exercises care over every person on the basis of what is good for him. Now, it is good for each person to attain his end, whereas it is bad for him to serve away from his proper end. Now, this should be considered applicable to the parts, just as it is to the whole being; for instance, each and every part of man, and every one of his acts, should attain the proper end. Now, though the male semen is superfluous in regard to the preservation of the individual, it is nevertheless necessary in regard to the propagation of the species. Other superfluous things, such as excrement, urine, sweat, and such things, are not at all necessary; hence, their emission contributes to man's good. Now, this is not what is sought in the case of semen, but, rather, to emit it for the purpose of generation, to which purpose the sexual act is directed. But man's generative process would be frustrated unless it were followed by proper nutrition, because the offspring would not survive if proper nutrition were withheld. Therefore, the emission of semen ought to be so ordered that it will result in both the production of the proper offspring and in the upbringing of this offspring.

It is evident from this that every emission of semen, in such a way that generation cannot follow, is contrary to the good for man. And if this be done deliberately, it must be a sin. Now, I am speaking of a way from which, *in itself,* generation could not result: such would be any emission of semen apart from the natural union of male and female. For which reason, sins of this type are called *contrary to nature*. But, if by accident generation cannot result from the emission of semen, then this is not a reason for it being against nature, or a sin; as for instance, if the woman happens to be sterile.

Likewise, it must also be contrary to the good for man if the semen be emitted under conditions such that generation could result but the proper upbringing would be prevented. We should take into consideration the fact that, among some animals where the female is able to take care of the upbringing of offspring, male and female do not remain together for any time after the act of generation. This is obviously the case with dogs. But in the case of animals of which the female is not able to provide for the upbringing of offspring, the male and female do stay together after the act of generation as long as is necessary for the upbringing and instruction of the offspring. Examples are found among certain species of birds whose young are not able to seek out food for themselves immediately after hatching. In fact, since a bird does not nourish its young with milk, made available by nature as it were, as occurs in the case of quadrupeds, but the bird must look elsewhere for food for its young, and since besides this it must protect them by sitting on them, the female is not able to do this by herself. So, as a result of divine providence, there is naturally implanted in the male of these animals a tendency to remain with the female in order to bring up the young. Now, it is abundantly evident that the female in the human species is not at all able to take care of the upbringing of offspring by herself, since the needs of human life demand many things which cannot be provided by one person alone. Therefore, it is appropriate to human nature that a man remain together with a woman after the generative act, and not leave her immediately to have such relations with another woman, as is the practice with fornicators.

Nor, indeed, is the fact that a woman may be able by means of her own wealth to care for the child by herself an obstacle to this argument. For natural rectitude in human acts is not dependent on things accidentally possible in the case of one individual, but, rather, on those conditions which accompany the entire species.

Again, we must consider that in the human species offspring require not only nourishment for the body, as in the case of other animals, but also education for the soul. For other animals naturally possess their own kinds of prudence whereby they are enabled to take care of themselves. But a man lives by reason, which he must develop by lengthy, temporal experience so that he may achieve prudence. Hence, children must be instructed by parents who are already experienced people. Nor are they able to receive such instruction as soon as they are born, but after a long time, and especially after they have reached the age of discretion. Moreover, a long time is needed for this instruction. Then, too, because of the impulsion of the passions, through which prudent judgment is vitiated, they require not merely instruction but correction. Now, a woman alone is not adequate to this task; rather, this demands the work of a husband, in whom reason is more developed for giving instruction and strength is more available for giving punishment. Therefore, in the human species, it is not enough, as in the case of birds, to devote a small amount of time to bringing up offspring, for a long period of life is required. Hence, since among all animals it is necessary for male and female to remain together as long as the work of the father is needed by the offspring, it is natural to the human being for the man to establish a lasting association with a designated woman, over no short period of time. Now, we call this society *matrimony*. Therefore, matrimony is natural for man, and promiscuous performance of the sexual act, outside matrimony, is contrary to man's good. For this reason, it must be a sin.

Nor, in fact, should it be deemed a slight sin for a man to arrange for the emission of semen apart from the proper purpose of generating and bringing up children, on the argument that it is either a slight sin, or none at all, for a person to use a part of the body for a different use than that to which it is directed by nature (say, for instance, one chose to walk on his hands, or to use his feet for something usually done with the hands) because man's good is not much opposed by such inordinate use. However, the inordinate emission of semen is incompatible with the natural good; namely, the preservation of the species. Hence, after the sin of homicide whereby a human nature already in existence is destroyed, this type of sin appears to take next place, for by it the generation of human nature is precluded.

Moreover, these views which have just been given have a solid basis in divine authority. That the emission of semen under conditions in which offspring cannot follow is illicit is quite clear. There is the text of Leviticus (18:22-23): "thou shalt not lie with mankind as with womankind . . . and thou shalt not copulate with any beast." And in I Corinthians (6:10): "Nor the effeminate, nor liers with mankind . . . shall possess the kingdom of God."

Also, that fornication and every performance of the act of reproduction with a person other than one's wife are illicit is evident. For it is said: "There shall be no whore among the daughters of Israel, nor whoremonger among the sons of Israel" (Deut. 23:17); and in Tobias (4:13): "Take heed to keep thyself from all fornication, and beside thy wife never endure to know a crime"; and in I Corinthians (6:18): "Fly fornication."

By this conclusion we refute the error of those who say that there is no more sin in the emission of semen than in the emission of any other superfluous matter, and also of those who state that fornication is not a sin.

II

That matrimony should be indivisible.

If one will make a proper consideration, the preceding reasoning will be seen to lead to the conclusion not only that the society of man and woman of the human species, which we call matrimony, should be long lasting, but even that it should endure throughout an entire life.

Indeed, possessions are ordered to the preservation of natural life, and since natural life, which cannot be preserved perpetually in the father, is by a sort of succession preserved in the son in its specific likeness, it is naturally fitting for the son to succeed also to the things which belong to the father. So, it is natural that the father's solicitude for his son should endure until the end of the father's life. Therefore, if even in the case of birds the solicitude of the father gives rise to the cohabitation of male and female, the natural order demands that father and mother in the human species remain together until the end of life.

It also seems to be against equity if the aforesaid society be dissolved. For the female needs the male, not merely for the sake of generation, as in the case of other animals, but also for the sake of government, since the male is both more perfect in reasoning and stronger in his powers. In fact, a woman is taken into man's society for the needs of generation; then, with the disappearance of a woman's fecundity and beauty, she is prevented from association with another man. So, if any man took a woman in the time of her youth, when beauty and fecundity were hers, and then sent her away after she had reached an advanced age, he would damage that woman contrary to natural equity.

Again, it seems obviously inappropriate for a woman to be able to put away her husband, because a wife is naturally subject to her husband as governor, and it is not within the power of a person subject to another to depart from his rule. So, it would be against the natural order if a wife were able to abandon her husband. Therefore, if a husband were permitted to abandon his wife, the society of husband and wife would not be an association of equals, but, instead, a sort of slavery on the part of the wife.

Besides, there is in men a certain natural solicitude to know their offspring. This is necessary for this reason: the child requires the father's direction for a long time. So, whenever there are obstacles to the ascertaining of offspring they are opposed to the natural instinct of the human species. But, if a husband could put away his wife, or a wife her husband, and have sexual relations with another person, certitude as to offspring would be precluded, for the wife would be united first with one man and later with another. So, it is contrary to the natural instinct of the human species for a wife to be separated from her husband. And thus, the union of male and female in the human species must be not only lasting, but also unbroken.

Furthermore, the greater that friendship is, the more solid and long-lasting will it be. Now, there seems to be the greatest friendship between husband and wife, for they are united not only in the act of fleshly union, which produces a certain gentle association even among beasts, but also in the partnership of the whole range of domestic activity. Consequently, as an indication of this, man must even "leave his father and mother" for the sake of his wife, as is said in Genesis (2:24). Therefore, it is fitting for matrimony to be completely indissoluble.

It should be considered, further, that generation is the only natural act that is ordered to the common good, for eating and the emission of waste matters pertain to the individual good, but generation to the preservation of the species. As a result, since law is established for the common good, those matters which pertain to generation must, above all others, be ordered by laws, both divine and human. Now, laws that are established should stem from the prompting of nature, if they are human; just as in the demonstrative sciences, also, every human discovery takes its origin from naturally known principles. But, if they are divine laws, they not only develop the prompting of nature but also supplement the deficiency of natural instinct, as things that are divinely revealed surpass the capacity of human reason. So, since there is a natural prompting within the human species, to the end that the union of man and wife be undivided, and that it be between one man and one woman, it was necessary for this to be ordered by human law. But divine law supplies a supernatural reason, drawn from the symbolism of the inseparable union between Christ and the Church, which is a union of one spouse with another (Eph. 5:24–32). And thus, disorders connected with the act of generation are not only opposed to natural instinct, but are also transgressions of divine and human laws. Hence, a greater sin results from a disorder in this area than in regard to the use of food or other things of that kind.

Moreover, since it is necessary for all other things to be ordered to what is best in man, the union of man and wife is not only ordered in this way because it is important to the generating of offspring, as it is in the case of other animals, but also because it is in agreement with good behavior, which right reason directs either in reference to the individual man in himself, or in regard to man as a member of a family, or of civil society. In fact, the undivided union of husband and wife is pertinent to good behavior. For thus, when they know that they are indivisibly united, the love of one spouse for the other will be more faithful. Also, both will be more solicitous in their care for domestic possessions when they keep in mind that they will remain continually in possession of these same things. As a result of this, the sources of disagreements which would have to come up between a man and his wife's relatives, if he could put away his wife, are removed, and a more solid affection is established among the relatives. Removed, also, are the occasions for adultery which are presented when a man is permitted to send away his wife, or the converse. In fact, by this practice an easier way of arranging marriage with those outside the family circle is provided.

Hence it is said in Matthew 5:31 and in I Corinthians 7:10: "But I say to you . . . that the wife depart not from her husband."

By this conclusion, moreover, we oppose the custom of those who put away their wives, though this was permitted the Jews in the old Law, "by reason of the hardness of their hearts" (Matt. 19:8); that is, because they were ready to kill their wives. So, the lesser evil was permitted them in order to prevent a greater evil.

III

That matrimony should be between one man and one woman.

It seems, too, that we should consider how it is inborn in the minds of all animals accustomed to sexual reproduction to allow no promiscuity; hence, fights occur among animals over the matter of sexual reproduction. And, in fact, among all animals there is one common reason, for every animal desires to enjoy freely the pleasure of the sexual act, as he also does the pleasure of food; but this liberty is restricted by the fact that several males may have access to one female, or the converse. The same situation obtains in the freedom of enjoying food, for one animal is obstructed if the food which he desires to eat is taken over by another animal. And so, animals fight over food and sexual relations in the same way. But among men there is a special reason, for, as we said, man naturally desires to know his offspring, and this knowledge would be completely destroyed if there were several males for one female. Therefore, that one female is for one male is a consequence of natural instinct.

But a difference should be noted on this point. As far as the view that one woman should not have sexual relations with several men is concerned, both the aforementioned reasons apply. But, in regard to the conclusion that one man should not have relations with several females, the second argument does not work, since certainty as to offspring is not precluded if one male has relations with several women. But the first reason works against this practice, for, just as the freedom of associating with a woman at will is taken away from the husband, when the woman has another husband, so, too, the same freedom is taken away from a woman when her husband has several wives. Therefore, since certainty as to offspring is the principal good which is sought in matrimony, no law or human custom has permitted one woman to be a wife for several husbands. This was even deemed unfitting among the ancient Romans, of whom Maximus Valerius reports that they believed that the conjugal bond should not be broken even on account of sterility.

Again, in every species of animal in which the father has some concern for offspring, one male has only one female; this is the case with all birds that feed their young together, for one male would not be able to offer enough assistance to bring up the offspring of several females. But in the case of animals among whom there is no concern on the part of the males for their offspring, the male has promiscuous relations with several females and the female with plural males. This is so among dogs, chickens, and the like. But since, of all animals, the male in the human species has the greatest concern for offspring, it is obviously natural for man that one male should have but one wife, and conversely.

Besides, friendship consists in an equality. So, if it is not lawful for the wife to have several husbands, since this is contrary to certainty as to offspring, it would not be lawful, on the other hand, for a man to have several wives, for the friendship of wife for husband would not be free, but somewhat servile. And this argument is corroborated by experience, for among husbands having plural wives the wives have a status like that of servants.

Furthermore, strong friendship is not possible in regard to many people, as is evident from the Philosopher in *Ethics* VIII. Therefore, if a wife has but one husband, but the husband has several wives, the friendship will not be equal on both sides. So, the friendship will not be free, but servile in some way.

Moreover, as we said, matrimony among humans should be ordered so as to be keeping with good moral customs. Now, it is contrary to good behavior for one man to have several wives, for the result of this is discord in domestic society, as is

evident from experience. So, it is not fitting for one man to
have several wives.

Hence it is said: "They shall be two in one flesh" (Gen.
2:24).

By this, the custom of those having several wives is set
aside, and also the opinion of Plato who maintained that wives
should be common. And in the Christian period he was followed by Nicolaus, one of the seven deacons.

IV

That matrimony should not take place between close relatives.

Moreover, because of reasonable considerations of this kind
it has been ordered by the laws that certain persons, related
by their origin, are excluded from matrimony.

In fact, since there is in matrimony a union of diverse
persons, those persons who should already regard themselves
as one because of having the same origin are properly excluded from matrimony, so that in recognizing themselves as
one in this way they may love each other with greater fervor.

Again, because the acts performed by husband and wife are
associated with a certain natural shame, it is necessary that
those persons to whom respect is due because of the bond of
blood should be prohibited from performing such actions with
each other. Indeed, this reason seems to have been suggested
in the Old Testament law, in the text which states: "Thou shalt
not uncover the nakedness of thy sister" (Lev. 18:9), and also
in other texts.

Besides, for man to be much given to sexual pleasures contributes to the dissolution of good moral behavior; because,
since this pleasure greatly occupies the mind, reason is withdrawn from things which should be done rightly. Now, if a
man were permitted sexual relations with those persons with
whom he must live, such as sisters and other relatives, exces-

sive indulgence in this pleasure would result, for the occasion for sexual relations with such persons could not be removed. Therefore, it was suitable to good moral behavior for such union to be prohibited by laws.

Furthermore, the enjoyment of sexual relations "greatly corrupts the judgment of prudence." So, the multiplication of such pleasure is opposed to good behavior. Now, such enjoyment is increased through the love of the persons who are thus united. Therefore, intermarriage between relatives would be contrary to good behavior, for, in their case, the love which springs from community of origin and upbringing would be added to the love of concupiscence, and, with such an increase of love, the soul would necessarily become more dominated by these pleasures.

Moreover, in human society it is most necessary that there be friendship among many people. But friendship is increased among men when unrelated persons are bound together by matrimony. Therefore, it was proper for it to be prescribed by laws that matrimony should be contracted with persons outside one's family and not with relatives.

Besides, it is unfitting for one to be conjugally united with persons to whom one should naturally be subject. But it is natural to be subject to one's parents. Therefore, it would not be fitting to contract matrimony with one's parents, since in matrimony there is a conjugal union.

Hence it is said: "No man shall approach to her that is near of kin to him" (Lev. 18:6).

By these arguments the custom of those who practice carnal relations with their relatives is refuted.

Moreover, we should note that just as natural inclination tends toward things which happen in most cases, so also positive law depends on what happens in most cases. It is not contrary to the foregoing arguments if in a particular case the outcome might be otherwise, for the good of many should not be sacrificed for the sake of one person's good, because "the good of many is always more divine than the good of one person." However, lest the disadvantage which could occur in the individual case be altogether without remedy, there remains with lawmakers and others of similar function the authority to grant a dispensation from what is generally required by law, in view of what is necessary in any particular case. For, if the law be a human one, it can be dispensed by men who have such power. But, if the law be divinely given, dispensation can be granted by divine authority; as, in the Old Law, permission seems to have been granted by dispensation to have several wives and concubines and to put away one's wife.

V

That not all sexual intercourse is sinful.

Now, just as it is contrary to reason for a man to perform the act of carnal union contrary to what befits the generation and upbringing of offspring, so also is it in keeping with reason for a man to exercise the act of carnal union in a manner which is suited to the generation and upbringing of offspring. But only those things that are opposed to reason are prohibited by divine law, as is evident from what we said above. So, it is not right to say that every act of carnal union is a sin.

Again, since bodily organs are the instruments of the soul, the end of each organ is its use, as is the case with any other instrument. Now, the use of certain bodily organs is carnal union. So, carnal union is the end of certain bodily organs. But that which is the end of certain natural things cannot be evil in itself, because things that exist naturally are ordered to their end by divine providence, as is plain from what was said above. Therefore, it is impossible for carnal union to be evil in itself.

Besides, natural inclinations are present in things from God, Who moves all things. So, it is impossible for the natural inclination of a species to be toward what is evil in itself. But there is in all perfect animals a natural inclination toward carnal union. Therefore, it is impossible for carnal union to be evil in itself.

Moreover, that without which a thing cannot be what is good and best is not evil in itself. But the perpetuation of the species can only be preserved in animals by generation, which is the result of carnal union. So, it is impossible for carnal union to be evil in itself.

Hence it is said in I Corinthians (7:28): "if a virgin marry, she hath not sinned."

Now, this disposes of the error of those who say that every act of carnal union is illicit, as a consequence of which view they entirely condemn matrimony and marriage arrangements. In fact, some of these people say this because they believe that bodily things arise, not from a good, but from an evil, source.

10. LUTHER: The Natural Place of Women

Martin Luther (1483–1546) was born in Eisleben, Saxony. After beginning to study law he underwent a spiritual crisis occasioned by a violent thunderstorm which caused him to enter the Erfurt monastery of the Augustinian Friars. From 1512 until his death he held a professorship in biblical studies at the University of Wittenberg. His statement of ninety-five theses on indulgences in 1517 marks the beginning of the Protestant Reformation. The selection here comprises a number of passages from his writings commenting on women, chasteness and marriage.

Woman's Greatest Honor—The Mother of All the Living:
Through the Holy Spirit Adam called his wife by the excellent

Source: Martin Luther, *What Luther Says,* 3 vols., comp. Ewald M. Plass (St. Louis: Concordia Publishing House, 1959), pp. 132–134, 884–886, 902, 906, 1457–1459. Copyright 1959 by Concordia Publishing House. Used by permission.

name of Eve, that is, mother. He does not say woman, but mother, and adds "of all the living" (Gen. 3:20). Here you have the true distinction (*ornamentum*) of womanhood, to wit, to be the source of all living human beings. The words are brief, yet they are an oration such as neither Demosthenes nor Cicero ever composed. But this oration is by the Holy Spirit, who is most eloquent; and yet it is worthy of our first parent. The Holy Spirit is to deliver the address at this point. If *this* Orator so defines and praises woman, we may in fairness cover up whatever frailties she has. . . .

The Natural Caretaker of Infants: It has often been a great delight and wonder to me to see how the whole body of a woman is adapted and formed for the care of infants. How becomingly even little girls carry infants in their arms! And how appropriate are the gestures with which mothers dandle the little ones when they hush a crying infant or lay it in the cradle! Let a man do these things, and you will say he acts like a dancing camel, so awkward are all his motions if he has only to touch an infant with his finger. I say nothing of all the other duties which only mothers can do for children. . . .

Woman Unexcelled—if She Stays in Her Sphere: Men are commanded to rule and to reign over their wives and families. But if woman, forsaking her position (*officio*), presumes to rule over her husband, she then and there engages in a work for which she was not created, a work which stems from her own failing (*vitio*) and is evil.

For God did not create this sex to rule. For this reason domination by women is never a happy one. The history of the Amazons, celebrated by Greek writers, might be advanced against this view. They are reported to have held the rule and to have conducted wars. But I believe what is told of them to be a fable. To be sure, the Ethiopians choose women to be both queens and princesses, in accordance with their custom, as the Ethiopian queen Candace is mentioned in Acts 9:27; but this is stupid of them. . . . There is no divine permission for ruling by a woman. It may, of course, happen that she is placed in the position of a king and is given the rule; but she always has a senate of prominent men according to whose counsel all is administered. Therefore even though a woman may be put in the place of a king, this does not confirm the rule of woman; for the text is clear: "Thy desire shall be to thy husband, and he shall rule over thee" (Gen. 3:16). Woman was created for the benefit (*usum*) of man, that is, for the prudent and sensible training of children. Everyone does best when he does that for which he was created. "A woman handles a child better with her smallest finger than a man does with both hands (*Fäusten*)." Therefore let everyone stick to that work to which God has called him and for which he was created. . . .

How Women Reveal Their Predetermined Domain: Women speak well and with much grace and elegance on domestic matters, so much so, in fact, that they outdo Cicero. And what they cannot bring about by eloquence they attain by tears, as Cicero has said. Moreover, they are born to this eloquence; for they are far more adept in the domestic area than we men are, who acquire ability by long practice and by effort. But they do not rate when they talk outside the domestic field, about political matters. For while it is granted that they certainly have the words, yet they do not grasp and talk about the matter in hand. This is why they speak so confusedly and absurdly when they talk about politics that nothing could be worse. From this it appears that woman was created for domestic concerns but man for political ones, for wars, and the affairs of the law courts. . . .

Singing the Praise of Woman: The Holy Spirit praises woman, as, for example, Judith, Esther, Sarah. And among the heathen

Lucretia and Artemisia were praised. Without women marriage would be impossible. Taking a wife is a remedy for fornication. A woman is a pleasant life companion. Women bear children and are wont to educate them and to administer domestic affairs. Moreover, they are inclined to be merciful; for they were appointed by God to bear children, to please man, and to be compassionate. . . .

Woman Rather Desires to Be Loved: Women, it is true, have a sort of natural inclination to *be* desired and loved, men *to* desire and to love, although the opposite of both may occur; that a woman may madly desire and love and a man may seek to be desired and loved. . . .

Woman Cannot but Attract Man: Just as we cannot dispense with eating and drinking, we cannot get along without women; for we can in no wise rid ourselves of our natural desire. The reason is this: We have been conceived in the bodies of women, have been nourished in them, borne by them, nursed and reared by them. Therefore our flesh is, for the most part, the flesh of women, and it is impossible for us entirely to separate ourselves from them. . . .

What Is Marriage?: This is a true definition of marriage: Marriage is the God-appointed and legitimate union of man and woman in the hope of having children or at least for the purpose of avoiding fornication and sin and living to the glory of God. The ultimate purpose is to obey God, to find aid and counsel against sin; to call upon God; to seek, love, and educate children for the glory of God; to live with one's wife in the fear of God and to bear the cross; but if there are no children, nevertheless to live with one's wife in contentment; and to avoid all lewdness with others. . . .

Marriage Is Not a Religious Relation: Marriage is a civic matter (*res politica*). It is really not, together with all its circumstances, the business of the church. It is so only when a matter of conscience is involved. . . .

Marriage Is Essentially a Secular Affair: Surely, no one can deny that marriage is an external, a secular, affair, subject to secular government, as are clothing and food, house and home. The many imperial decrees concerning marital matters prove this to be the case. Nor do I find any instance in the New Testament in which Christ or the apostles interested themselves in such matters. They did so only, as St. Paul in 1 Corinthians 7, in exceptional cases, where consciences were involved and particularly where believers and non-Christians were concerned. . . .

The Importance and Seriousness of Marriage: But since this Commandment is directed particularly at the state of matrimony and gives us a reason to speak about it, you should clearly understand and note, first, how gloriously God honors and extols this estate by both confirming and protecting it through His Commandment. He has confirmed it above in the Fourth Commandment: Honor thy father and thy mother; but here He has, as I said, secured and shielded it. He wants it honored, maintained, and conducted by us, too, as a divine, blessed estate, because He instituted it first, before all others; and with it in view, He did not create man and woman alike, as is evident, not for lewdness, but that they should live together, be fruitful, beget children, and nourish and rear them to the glory of God. Therefore God has also most richly blessed this estate above all others and, in addition, has made everything in the world serve it and depend on it that this estate might without fail be well and amply provided for. Hence married life is not a jest or an object for inordinate curiosity but a splendid institution and a matter of divine seriousness. . . .

This Estate a Biological and Moral Necessity: In the second place, you should also know that marriage is not only an honorable but a necessary state. It is earnestly commanded by God that in every condition and station in life men and women, who were created for it, should be found in this estate. Nevertheless, there are some exceptions, although few, whom God has particularly exempted, either because they are unfit for married life or because He has given them the freedom, by the bestowal of a high, supernatural gift, to maintain chastity outside this estate. For where nature, as God has implanted it in man, runs its course, it is not possible to remain chaste without marriage. Flesh and blood remain flesh and blood, and the natural inclination and attraction run their course without let or hindrance, as everyone sees and feels. In order, therefore, that it may be easier to some degree to avoid unchasteness, God has commanded marriage so that everyone may have his moderate portion and be satisfied with it, although God's grace is still required to have a pure heart in addition. . . .

Try Reconciliation before Divorce: Accordingly, if a spouse has committed adultery and the fact can be publicly proved, I may and dare not keep the other person from being free, from permission to obtain a divorce, and from marrying someone else. But if it can be done, it is very much better to reconcile the two and keep them together. But if the innocent spouse so desires, he or she may in the name of God make use of his or her right and get a divorce. . . . .

But in order to reduce the number of such divorces as much as possible the innocent person should not be permitted to change his or her status in haste but should wait at least a year or a half year. Otherwise the offensive impression is created that he or she finds pleasure and delight in the fact that his or her spouse has disrupted the marriage and gladly embraces the opportunity to get rid of him or her and promptly take another, thus indulging wantonness under the cloak of legality. . . .

Give Penitent Another Chance: We neither commend nor forbid such divorces but leave it to the government to act here, and we submit to whatever the secular law prescribes in this matter. To those who really want to be Christians we would give this advice: The two partners should be admonished and urged to stay together. If the guilty person is humbled and reformed, the innocent person should let himself be reconciled and should forgive him in Christian love. Sometimes there is no hope for improvement, or the reconciliation of the guilty one and his restoration to good graces is followed only by his abuse of this kindness. He persists in his flagrant and loose behavior and takes it for granted that he is entitled to be spared and forgiven. I would not advise or prescribe mercy for a person like that; rather I would help to have such a person flogged or jailed. For one oversight is still pardonable, but a sin that takes mercy and forgiveness for granted is intolerable. . . .

The Woman Should Love, Honor, and Obey: A woman should either be subjected to her husband or should not marry. If she does not want a master, then let her keep from taking a man; for this is the order God has prescribed and ordained through His apostles and Scripture. . . .

Beware of "Sowing Wild Oats" before Marriage: Many intend to escape marriage by deliberately sowing wild oats for a while and promising to become good later on. But, my friend, hardly one out of a thousand turns out well. He who is to live a chaste life must begin betimes and must not achieve it by fornication, but without it, by the grace of God, or through marriage. Moreover, we daily see how such folk turn out. I refer to those mentioned above. They can be said to have become adept at sowing wild oats rather than being through with it (*mehr eingebubet denn ausgebubet*). The devil has trumped up this matter and has composed accursed proverbs, such as: A fellow must be a fool some time; again: He who does not do it in his youth does it in his old age; again: A young angel, an old devil. The poet Terence and other heathen speak to the same effect. Heathen they are; like heathen, nay, like devils, they speak. . . .

Scripture Plainly Condemns Fornication: Since Paul says (1 Cor. 6:9) that fornicators and adulterers will not possess the kingdom of God, it is astounding to find people to this day who ask whether simple fornication is a mortal sin. To such inquirers I say that they should themselves read what has been written. If they want me to be the judge, I certainly cannot judge any differently from what Scripture says. . . .

Legalized Prostitution—Opposed: Those who want to reintroduce such houses of prostitution should first deny the name of Christ and confess that they are not Christians but heathen, who know nothing of God. If we want to be Christians, we have a clear directive in God's Word when St. Paul says: "Whoremongers and adulterers God will judge" (Heb. 13:4). He will punish those much more who further, protect, and help these folk with word and deed. How can one publicly teach against fornication and censure it if one is expected to praise the government which tolerates and permits it? But, they say and boast, after all, the people in N. [Nürnberg] permit it and do not speak as if we are doing nothing but wrong in this matter; for if such houses were not permitted, the country would be full of fornication. Answer: By the grace of God a good remedy for fornication is marriage or the prospect of marriage. But why would marriage or the prospect of marriage be required as a remedy if we were to permit fornication to go unpunished? When such common houses were still standing in full bloom and were nurtured under the regime of the devil, we certainly found out that matters are not improved in this way. On the contrary, by the example of publicly permitted fornication the raping of girls and women and the practice of fornication were increased and also publicly and shamelessly confessed. But since by the grace of God fornication is now forbidden, there is also less fornication and adultery, particularly in the open. Let the government, if, indeed, it wants to be Christian, severely punish both fornication, the violation of women and girls, and adultery, at least the cases that are public. If it has done its duty in this respect, the government is excused from responsibility for what is done in secret. In short, we cannot do, permit, or tolerate anything against God. *Fiat iustitia et pereat mundus,* Let the right prevail though the would go to ruin. . . .

Brothels Do Not Remedy Immoral Conditions: Finally, is it not a miserable thing that we Christians should maintain open and common houses of prostitution among us, though all of us are baptized unto chastity? I know well what some are saying about this scandal. We are being told that the evil is not the custom of any one people, that it is hard to abolish, that, besides, it is better to tolerate such houses than to have married women or virgins or those of more honorable estate ravished. But should not civil and religious authorities consider that the evil is not to be controlled in this pagan manner? If the people of Israel could exist without such an abomination, why should Christian people not be able to do as much? Nay, how do many cities, towns, hamlets, and villages exist without such houses? Why should not great cities also exist without them? . . .

Homosexuality Is Inhuman, Satanic: The vice of the Sodomites is an unparalleled enormity. It departs from the natural passion and desire, planted into nature by God, according to which the male has a passionate desire for the female. Sodomy craves what is entirely contrary to nature. Whence comes this perversion? Without a doubt it comes from the devil. After a man has once turned aside from the fear of God, the devil puts such great pressure upon his nature that he extinguishes the fire of natural desire and stirs up another, which is contrary to nature. . . .

Beware in a World of Unchasteness: The world is a veritable brothel and is completely steeped in this vice. We, too, must live in the world, and its examples and allurements influence us. Therefore we are in great danger and must carefully watch that we do not let the devil ride us. . . .

Maintaining Purity Is a Constant Struggle: If no other work were commanded than chasteness, we would all have enough to do, so dangerous and raging a vice is unchasteness. It is furiously active in all our members: in the thinking of our heart, in the seeing of our eyes, in the hearing of our ears, in the speaking of our mouth, in the acting of our hands, our feet, and our entire body. To keep all of these under control calls for labor and exertion. . . . St. Augustine says that among all the conflicts of Christians the struggle for chasteness is the hardest for the sole reason that it continues daily, without ceasing; and chasteness seldom wins out.

11. HUME: The Advantages of Monogamous Marriage

David Hume (1711–1776) was born in Edinburgh, and although his family wished him to study law, he devoted himself to being a man of letters. He wrote widely in philosophy and history, living for several years in France where he wrote his famous work, **A Treatise of Human Nature,** which was received by the public virtually without comment. He became a well-known and liked literary figure of the period. The Earl of Charlemont recalls him as physically looking more like "a turtle-eating Alderman than a refined philosopher," a comment that would not have affected Hume's good humor.

As marriage is an engagement entered into by mutual consent, and has for its end the propagation of the species, it is

Source: David Hume, "Of Polygamy and Divorces," in *Essays Moral, Political, and Literary,* ed. T. H. Green and T. H. Grose (London: Longmans, Green, 1875), 2:231–239.

evident, that it must be susceptible of all the variety of conditions, which consent establishes, provided they be not contrary to this end.

A man, in conjoining himself to a woman, is bound to her according to the terms of his engagement: In begetting children, he is bound, by all the ties of nature and humanity, to provide for their subsistence and education. When he has performed these two parts of duty, no one can reproach him with injustice or injury. And as the terms of his engagement, as well as the methods of subsisting his offspring, may be various, it is mere superstition to imagine, that marriage can be entirely uniform, and will admit only of one mode or form. Did not human laws restrain the natural liberty of men, every particular marraige would be as different as contracts or bargains of any other kind or species.

As circumstances vary, and the laws propose different advantages, we find, that, in different times and places, they impose different conditions on this important contract. In Tonquin, it is usual for the sailors, when the ships come into harbor, to marry for the season; and notwithstanding this precarious engagement, they are assured, it is said, of the strictest fidelity to their bed, as well as in the whole management of their affairs, from those temporary spouses.

I cannot, at present, recollect my authorities; but I have somewhere read, that the republic of Athens, having lost many of its citizens by war and pestilence, allowed every man to marry two wives, in order the sooner to repair the waste which had been made by these calamities. The poet Euripides happened to be coupled to two noisy Vixens who so plagued him with their jealousies and quarrels, that he became ever after a professed *woman-hater;* and is the only theatrical writer, perhaps the only poet, that ever entertained an aversion to the sex.

In that agreeable romance, called *the History of the*

Sevarambians, where a great many men and a few women are supposed to be shipwrecked on a desert coast; the captain of the troop, in order to obviate those endless quarrels which arose, regulates their marriages after the following manner: He takes a handsome female to himself alone; assigns one to every couple of inferior officers; and to five of the lowest rank he gives one wife in common.

The ancient Britons had a singular kind of marriage, to be met with among no other people. Any number of them, as ten or a dozen, joined in a society together, which was perhaps requisite for mutual defence in those barbarous times. In order to link this society the closer, they took an equal number of wives in common; and whatever children were born, were reputed to belong to all of them, and were accordingly provided for by the whole community.

Among the inferior creatures, nature herself, being the supreme legislator, prescribes all the laws which regulate their marriages, and varies those laws according to the different circumstances of the creature. Where she furnishes, with ease, food and defence to the newborn animal, the present embrace terminates the marriage; and the care of the offspring is committed entirely to the female. Where the food is of more difficult purchase, the marriage continues for one season, till the common progeny can provide for itself; and the union immediately dissolves, and leaves each of the parties free to enter into a new engagement at the ensuing season. But nature, having endowed man with reason, has not so exactly regulated every article of his marriage contract, but has left him to adjust them, by his own prudence, according to his particular circumstances and situation. Municipal laws are a supply to the wisdom of each individual; and, at the same time, by restraining the natural liberty of men, make private interest submit to the interest of the public. All regulations, therefore, on this head are equally lawful, and equally conformable to the principles of nature; though they are not all equally convenient, or equally useful to society. The laws may allow of polygamy, as among the *Eastern* nations; or of voluntary divorces, as among the Greeks and Romans; or they may confine one man to one woman, during the whole course of their lives, as among the modern Europeans. It may not be disagreeable to consider the advantages and disadvantages, which result from each of these institutions.

The advocates for polygamy may recommend it as the only effectual remedy for the disorders of love, and the only expedient for freeing men from that slavery to the females, which the natural violence of our passions has imposed upon us. By this means alone can we regain our right of sovereignty; and, sating our appetite, re-establish the authority of reason in our minds, and, of consequence, our own authority in our families. Man, like a weak sovereign, being unable to support himself against the wiles and intrigues of his subjects, must play one faction against another, and become absolute by the mutual jealousy of the females. *To divide and to govern* is an universal maxim; and by neglecting it, the Europeans undergo a more grievous and a more ignominious slavery than the Turks or Persians, who are subjected indeed to a sovereign, that lies at a distance from them, but in their domestic affairs rule with an uncontrollable sway.

On the other hand, it may be urged with better reason, that this sovereignty of the male is a real usurpation, and destroys that nearness of rank, not to say equality, which nature has established between the sexes. We are, by nature, their lovers, their friends, their patrons: Would we willingly exchange such endearing appellations, for the barbarous title of master and tyrant?

In what capacity shall we gain by this inhuman proceeding? As lovers, or as husbands? The *lover,* is totally annihilated; and courtship, the most agreeable scene in life, can no longer have place, where women have not the free disposal of themselves, but are bought and sold, like the meanest animal. The *husband* is as little a gainer, having found the admirable secret of extinguishing every part of love, except its jealousy. No rose without its thorn; but he must be a foolish wretch indeed, that throws away the rose and preserves only the thorn.

But the Asiatic manners are as destructive to friendship as to love. Jealousy excludes men from all intimacies and familiarities with each other. No one dares bring his friend to his house or table, lest he bring a lover to his numerous wives. Hence all over the east, each family is as much separate from another, as if they were so many distinct kingdoms. No wonder then, that Solomon, living like an eastern prince, with his seven hundred wives, and three hundred concubines, without one friend, could write so pathetically concerning the vanity of the world. Had he tried the secret of one wife or mistress, a few friends, and a great many companions, he might have found life somewhat more agreeable. Destroy love and friendship; what remains in the world worth accepting?

The bad education of children, especially children of condition, is another unavoidable consequence of these eastern institutions. Those who pass the early part of life among slaves, are only qualified to be, themselves, slaves and tyrants; and in every future intercourse, either with their inferiors or superiors, are apt to forget the natural equality of mankind. What attention, too, can it be supposed a parent, whose seraglio affords him fifty sons, will give to instilling principles of morality or science into a progeny, with whom he himself is scarcely acquainted, and whom he loves with so divided an affection? Barbarism, therefore, appears, from reason as well as experience, to be the inseparable attendant of polygamy.

To render polygamy more odious, I need not recount the frightful effects of jealousy, and the constraint in which it holds the fair-sex all over the east. In those countries men are not allowed to have any commerce with the females, not even physicians, when sickness may be supposed to have extinguished all wanton passions in the bosoms of the fair, and, at the same time, has rendered them unfit objects of desire. Tournefort tells us, that, when he was brought into the *grand signor's* seraglio as a physician, he was not a little surprised, in looking along a gallery, to see a great number of naked arms, standing out from the sides of the room. He could not imagine what this could mean; till he was told, that those arms belonged to bodies, which he must cure, without knowing any more about them, than what he could learn from the arms. He was not allowed to ask a question of the patient, or even of her attendants, lest he might find it necessary to inquire concerning circumstances, which the delicacy of the seraglio allows not to be revealed. Hence physicians in the east pretend to know all diseases from the pulse; as our quacks in Europe undertake to cure a person merely from seeing his water. I suppose, had *Monsieur* Tournefort been of this latter kind, he would not, in Constantinople, have been allowed by the jealous Turks to be furnished with materials requisite for exercising his art.

In another country, where polygamy is also allowed, they render their wives cripples, and make their feet of no use to them, in order to confine them to their own houses. But it will, perhaps, appear strange, that, in a European country, jealousy can yet be carried to such a height, that it is indecent so much as to suppose that a woman of rank can have feet or legs. Witness the following story, which we have from very good authority. When the mother of the late king of Spain was on her road towards Madrid, she passed through a little town in Spain, famous for its manufactory of gloves and stockings. The magistrates of the place thought they could not better express their joy for the reception of their new queen, than by presenting her with a sample of those commodities, for which

alone their town was remarkable. The *major domo,* who conducted the princess, received the gloves very graciously: But
when the stockings were presented, he flung them away with
great indignation, and severely reprimanded the magistrates
for this egregious piece of indecency. *Know,* says he, *that a
queen of* Spain *has no legs.* The young queen, who, at that
time, understood the language but imperfectly, and had often
been frightened with stories of Spanish jealousy, imagined
that they were to cut off her legs. Upon which she fell a crying,
and begged them to conduct her back to Germany; for that
she never could endure the operation: And it was with some
difficulty they could appease her. Philip IV is said never in his
life to have laughed heartily, but at the recital of this story.

Having rejected polygamy, and matched one man with one
woman, let us now consider what duration we shall assign to
their union, and whether we shall admit of those voluntary
divorces, which were customary among the Greeks and
Romans. Those who would defend this practice may employ
the following reasons.

How often does disgust and aversion arise after marriage,
from the most trivial accidents, or from an incompatibility of
humor; where time, instead of curing the wounds, proceeding
from mutual injuries, festers them every day the more, by new
quarrels and reproaches? Let us separate hearts, which were
not made to associate together. Each of them may, perhaps,
find another for which it is better fitted. At least, nothing can
be more cruel than to preserve, by violence, an union, which,
at first, was made by mutual love, and is now, in effect, dissolved by mutual hatred.

But the liberty of divorces is not only a cure to hatred and
domestic quarrels: It is also an admirable preservative against
them, and the only secret for keeping alive that love, which
first united the married couple. The heart of man delights in
liberty: The very image of constraint is grievous to it: When

you would confine it by violence, to what would otherwise have been its choice, the inclination immediately changes, and desire is turned into aversion. If the public interest will not allow us to enjoy in polygamy that *variety*, which is so agreeable in love: at least, deprive us not of that liberty, which is so essentially requisite. In vain you tell me, that I had my choice of the person, with whom I would conjoin myself. I had my choice, it is true, of my prison; but this is but a small comfort, since it must still be a prison.

Such are the arguments which may be urged in favor of divorces: But there seem to be these three unanswerable objections against them. *First*, what must become of the children, upon the separation of the parents? Must they be committed to the care of a step-mother; and instead of the fond attention and concern of a parent, feel all the indifference or hatred of a stranger or an enemy? These inconveniences are sufficiently felt, where nature has made the divorce by the doom inevitable to all mortals: And shall we seek to multiply those inconveniences, by multiplying divorces, and putting it in the power of parents, upon every caprice, to render their posterity miserable?

Secondly, if it be true, on the one hand, that the heart of man naturally delights in liberty, and hates every thing to which it is confined; it is also true, on the other, that the heart of man naturally submits to necessity, and soon loses an inclination, when there appears an absolute impossibility of gratifying it. These principles of human nature, you'll say, are contradictory: But what is man but a heap of contradictions! Though it is remarkable, that, where principles are, after this manner, contrary in their operation, they do not always destroy each other; but the one or the other may predominate on any particular occasion, according as circumstances are more or less favorable to it. For instance, love is a restless and impatient passion, full of caprices and variations: arising in a moment from a feature, from an air, from nothing, and suddenly extinguishing after the same manner. Such a passion requires liberty above all things; and therefore Eloisa had reason, when, in order to preserve this passion, she refused to marry her beloved Abelard.

> *How oft, when prest to marriage, have I said,*
> *Curse on all laws but those which love has made;*
> *Love, free as air, at sight of human ties,*
> *Spreads his light wings, and in a moment flies.*

But *friendship* is a calm and sedate affection, conducted by reason and cemented by habit; springing from long acquaintance and mutual obligations; without jealousies or fears, and without those feverish fits of heat and cold, which cause such an agreeable torment in the amorous passion. So sober an affection, therefore, as friendship, rather thrives under constraint, and never rises to such a height, as when any strong interest or necessity binds two persons together, and gives them some common object of pursuit. We need not, therefore, be afraid of drawing the marriage-knot, which chiefly subsists by friendship, the closest possible. The amity between the persons, where it is solid and sincere, will rather gain by it: And where it is wavering and uncertain, this is the best expedient for fixing it. How many frivolous quarrels and disgusts are there, which people of common prudence endeavor to forget, when they lie under a necessity of passing their lives together; but which would soon be inflamed into the most deadly hatred, were they pursued to the utmost, under the prospect of an easy separation?

In the *third* place, we must consider, that nothing is more dangerous than to unite two persons so closely in all their interests and concerns, as man and wife, without rendering the union entire and total. The least possibility of a separate interest must be the source of endless quarrels and suspicions. The wife, not secure of her establishment, will still be driving some separate end or project; and the husband's selfishness, being accompanied with more power, may be still more dangerous.

Should these reasons against voluntary divorces be deemed insufficient, I hope no body will pretend to refuse the testimony of experience. At the time when divorces were most frequent among the Romans, marriages were most rare; and Augustus was obliged, by penal laws, to force men of fashion into the married state: A circumstance which is scarcely to be found in any other age or nation. The more ancient laws of Rome, which prohibited divorces, are extremely praised by Dionysius Halycarnassaeus. Wonderful was the harmony, says the historian, which this inseparable union of interests produced between married persons; while each of them considered the inevitable necessity by which they were linked together, and abandoned all prospect of any other choice or establishment.

The exclusion of polygamy and divorces sufficiently recommends our present European practice with regard to marriage.

12. KANT: Duties to the Body and Crimes against Nature

Immanuel Kant (1724–1804) was born in Königsberg in East Prussia. He was educated in Königsberg and taught at the university there, and except for an early employment as tutor to two families, never traveled outside his birthplace. He was of delicate health and lived an extraordinarily self-regulated life which passed, as one of his biographers says, like the most regular of regular verbs. His three **Critiques** are among the most important works of human thought.

Amongst our inclinations there is one which is directed towards other human beings. They themselves, and not their work and services, are its Objects of enjoyment. It is true that man has no inclination to enjoy the flesh of another—except,

Source: Immanuel Kant, *Lectures on Ethics*, trans. Louis Infield (London: Methuen & Co. Ltd., 1930), pp. 162–171. Reprinted by permission of Methuen & Co. Ltd.

perhaps, in the vengeance of war, and then it is hardly a desire—but none the less there does exist an inclination which we may call an appetite for enjoying another human being. We refer to sexual impulse. Man can, of course, use another human being as an instrument for his service; he can use his hands, his feet, and even all his powers; he can use him for his own purposes with the other's consent. But there is no way in which a human being can be made an Object of indulgence for another except through sexual impulse. This is in the nature of a sense, which we can call the sixth sense; it is an appetite for another human being. We say that a man loves someone when he has an inclination towards another person. If by this love we mean true human love, then it admits of no distinction between types of persons, or between young and old. But a love that springs merely from sexual impulse cannot be love at all, but only appetite. Human love is good-will, affection, promoting the happiness of others and finding joy in their happiness. But it is clear that, when a person loves another purely from sexual desire, none of these factors enter into the love. Far from there being any concern for the happiness of the loved one, the lover, in order to satisfy his desire and still his appetite, may even plunge the loved one into the depths of misery. Sexual love makes of the loved person an Object of appetite; as soon as that appetite has been stilled, the person is cast aside as one casts away a lemon which has been sucked dry. Sexual love can, of course, be combined with human love and so carry with it the characteristics of the latter, but taken by itself and for itself, it is nothing more than appetite. Taken by itself it is a degradation of human nature; for as soon as a person becomes an Object of appetite for another, all motives of moral relationship cease to function, because as an Object of appetite for another a person becomes a thing and can be treated and used as such by every one. This is the only case in which a human being is designed by nature as the Object of another's enjoyment. Sexual desire is at the root of it; and that is why we are ashamed of it, and why all strict moralists, and those who had pretensions to be regarded as saints, sought to suppress and extirpate it. It is true that without it a man would be incomplete; he would rightly believe that he lacked the necessary organs, and this would make him imperfect as a human being; none the less men made pretense of this question and sought to suppress these inclinations because they degraded mankind.

Because sexuality is not an inclination which one human being has for another as such, but is an inclination for the sex of another, it is a principle of the degradation of human nature, in that it gives rise to the preference of one sex to the other, and to the dishonoring of that sex through the satisfaction of desire. The desire which a man has for a woman is not directed towards her because she is a human being, but because she is a woman; that she is a human being is of no concern to the man; only her sex is the object of his desires. Human nature is thus subordinated. Hence it comes that all men and women do their best to make not their human nature but their sex more alluring and direct their activities and lusts entirely towards sex. Human nature is thereby sacrificed to sex. If then a man wishes to satisfy his desire, and a woman hers, they stimulate each other's desire; their inclinations meet, but their object is not human nature but sex, and each of them dishonors the human nature of the other. They make of humanity an instrument for the satisfaction of their lusts and inclinations, and dishonor it by placing it on a level with animal nature. Sexuality, therefore, exposes mankind to the danger of equality with the beasts. But as man has this desire from nature, the question arises how far he can properly make use of it without injury to his manhood. How far may persons allow one of the opposite sex to satisfy his or her desire upon them? Can they sell themselves, or let themselves out on hire, or by some other contract allow use to be made of their sexual faculties? Philosophers generally point out the harm done by this inclination and the ruin it brings to the body or to the commonwealth, and they believe that, except for the harm it does, there would be nothing contemptible in such conduct in itself. But if this were so, and if giving vent to this desire was not in itself abominable and did not involve immorality, then any one who could avoid being harmed by them could make whatever use he wanted of his sexual propensities. For the prohibitions of prudence are never unconditional; and the conduct would in itself be unobjectionable, and would only be harmful under certain conditions. But in point of fact, there is in the conduct itself something which is contemptible and contrary to the dictates of morality. It follows, therefore, that there must be certain conditions under which alone the use of the *facultates sexuales* would be in keeping with morality. There must be a basis for restraining our freedom in the use we make of our inclinations so that they conform to the principles of morality. We shall endeavor to discover these conditions and this basis. Man cannot dispose over himself because he is not a thing; he is not his own property; to say that he is would be self-contradictory; for in so far as he is a person he is a Subject in whom the ownership of things can be vested, and if he were his own property, he would be a thing over which he could have ownership. But a person cannot be a property and so cannot be a thing which can be owned, for it is impossible to be a person and a thing, the proprietor and the property.

Accordingly, a man is not at his own disposal. He is not entitled to sell a limb, not even one of his teeth. But to allow one's person for profit to be used by another for the satisfaction of sexual desire, to make of oneself an Object of demand, is to dispose over oneself as over a thing and to make of oneself a thing on which another satisfies his appetite, just

as he satisfies his hunger upon a steak. But since the inclination is directed towards one's sex and not towards one's
humanity, it is clear that one thus partially sacrifices one's
humanity and thereby runs a moral risk. Human beings are,
therefore, not entitled to offer themselves, for profit, as things
for the use of others in the satisfaction of their sexual propensities. In so doing they would run the risk of having their
person used by all and sundry as an instrument for the satisfaction of inclination. This way of satisfying sexuality is *vaga
libido*, in which one satisfies the inclinations of others for gain.
It is possible for either sex. To let one's person out on hire and
to surrender it to another for the satisfaction of his sexual
desire in return for money is the depth of infamy. The underlying moral principle is that man is not his own property and
cannot do with his body what he will. The body is part of the
self; in its togetherness with the self it constitutes the person; a
man cannot make of his person a thing, and this is exactly
what happens in *vaga libido*. This manner of satisfying sexual
desire is, therefore, not permitted by the rules of morality. But
what of the second method, namely *concubinatus*? Is this
also inadmissible? In this case both persons satisfy their desire
mutually and there is no idea of gain, but they serve each
other only for the satisfaction of sexuality. There appears to be
nothing unsuitable in this arrangement, but there is nevertheless one consideration which rules it out. Concubinage consists
in one person surrendering to another only for the satisfaction
of their sexual desire whilst retaining freedom and rights in
other personal respects affecting welfare and happiness. But
the person who so surrenders is used as a thing; the desire is
still directed only towards sex and not towards the person as a
human being. But it is obvious that to surrender part of oneself is to surrender the whole, because a human being is a
unity. It is not possible to have the disposal of a part only of a
person without having at the same time a right of disposal

over the whole person, for each part of a person is integrally bound up with the whole. But concubinage does not give me a right of disposal over the whole person but only over a part, namely the *organa sexualia*. It presupposes a contract. This contract deals only with the enjoyment of a part of the person and not with the entire circumstances of the person. Concubinage is certainly a contract, but it is one-sided; the rights of the two parties are not equal. But if in concubinage I enjoy a part of a person, I thereby enjoy the whole person; yet by the terms of the arrangement I have not the rights over the whole person, but only over a part; I, therefore, make the person into a thing. For that reason this method of satisfying sexual desire is also not permitted by the rules of morality. The sole condition on which we are free to make use of our sexual desire depends upon the right to dispose over the person as a whole —over the welfare and happiness and generally over all the circumstances of that person. If I have the right over the whole person, I have also the right over the part and so I have the right to use that person's *organa sexualia* for the satisfaction of sexual desire. But how am I to obtain these rights over the whole person? Only by giving that person the same rights over the whole of myself. This happens only in marriage. Matrimony is an agreement between two persons by which they grant each other equal reciprocal rights, each of them undertaking to surrender the whole of their person to the other with a complete right of disposal over it. We can now apprehend by reason how a *commercium sexuale* is possible without degrading humanity and breaking the moral laws. Matrimony is the only condition in which use can be made of one's sexuality. If one devotes one's person to another, one devotes not only sex but the whole person; the two cannot be separated. If, then, one yields one's person, body and soul, for good and ill and in every respect, so that the other has complete rights over it, and if the other does not similarly yield himself in return and does not extend in return the same rights and privileges, the arrangement is one-sided. But if I yield myself completely to another and obtain the person of the other in return, I win myself back; I have given myself up as the property of another, but in turn I take that other as my property, and so win myself back again in winning the person whose property I have become. In this way the two persons become a unity of will. Whatever good or ill, joy or sorrow befall either of them, the other will share in it. Thus sexuality leads to a union of human beings, and in that union alone its exercise is possible. This condition of the use of sexuality, which is only fulfilled in marriage, is a moral condition. But let us pursue this aspect further and examine the case of a man who takes two wives. In such a case each wife would have but half a man, although she would be giving herself wholly and ought in consequence to be entitled to the whole man. To sum up: *vaga libido* is ruled out on moral grounds; the same applies to concubinage; there only remains matrimony, and in matrimony polygamy is ruled out also for moral reasons; we, therefore, reach the conclusion that the only feasible arrangement is that of monogamous marriage. Only under that condition can I indulge my *facultas sexualis*. We cannot here pursue the subject further.

But one other question arises, that of incest. Incest consists in intercourse between the sexes in a form which, by reason of consanguinity, must be ruled out; but are there moral grounds on which incest, in all forms of sexual intercourse, must be ruled out? They are grounds which apply conditionally, except in one case, in which they have absolute validity. The sole case in which the moral grounds against incest apply absolutely is that of intercourse between parents and children. Between parents and children there must be a respect which should continue throughout life, and this rules out of court any question of equality. Moreover, in sexual intercourse each person submits to the other in the highest degree, whereas between parents and their children subjection is one-sided; the children must submit to the parents only; there can, therefore, be no equal union. This is the only case in which incest is absolutely forbidden by nature. In other cases incest forbids itself, but is not incest in the order of nature. The state prohibits incest, but at the beginning there must have been intermarriage between brothers and sisters. At the same time nature has implanted in our breasts a natural opposition to incest. She intended us to combine with other races and so to prevent too great a sameness in one society. Too close a connection, too intimate an acquaintance produces sexual indifference and repugnance. But this propensity must be restrained by modesty; otherwise it becomes commonplace, reduces the object of the desire to the commonplace and results in indifference. Sexual desire is very fastidious; nature has given it strength, but it must be restrained by modesty. It is on that account that savages, who go about stark-naked, are cold towards each other; for that reason, too, a person whom we have known from youth evokes no desire within us, but a strange person attracts us much more strongly. Thus nature has herself provided restraints upon any desire between brother and sister.

Crimina carnis are contrary to self-regarding duty because they are against the ends of humanity. They consist in abuse of one's sexuality. Every form of sexual indulgence, except in marriage, is a misuse of sexuality, and so a *crimen carnis*. All *crimina carnis* are either *secundum naturam* or *contra naturam*. *Crimina carnis secundum naturam* are contrary to sound reason; *crimina carnis contra naturam* are contrary to our animal nature. Among the former we reckon *vaga libido*, which is the opposite of matrimony and of which there are two kinds: *scortatio* and *concubinatus*. *Concubinatus* is indeed a *pactum*, but a *pactum inaequale*, in which the rights are not reciprocal. In this pact the woman surrenders her sex completely to the man, but the man does not completely surrender his sex to the woman. The second *crimen carnis secundum naturam* is *adulterium*. Adultery cannot take place except in marriage; it signifies a breach of marriage. Just as the engagement to marry is the most serious and the most inviolable engagement between two persons and binds them for life, so also is adultery the greatest breach of faith that there can be, because it is disloyalty to an engagement than which there can be none more important. For this reason adultery is cause for divorce. Another cause is incompatibility and inability to be at one, whereby unity and concord of will between the two persons is impossible. Next comes the question whether incest is incest *per se*, or whether it is by the civil law that it is made a *crimen carnis*, natural or unnatural. The question might be answered either by natural instinct or by reason. From the point of view of natural instinct incest is a *crimen carnis secundum naturam*, for it is after all a union of the sexes; it is not *contra naturam animalium*, because animals do not differentiate in this respect in their practices. But on the judgment of the understanding incest is *contra naturam*.

Uses of sexuality which are contrary to natural instinct and to animal nature are *crimina carnis contra naturam*. First amongst them we have onanism. This is abuse of the sexual faculty without any object, the exercise of the faculty in the complete absence of any object of sexuality. The practice is contrary to the ends of humanity and even opposed to animal nature. By it man sets aside his person and degrades himself below the level of animals. A second *crimen carnis contra naturam* is intercourse between *sexus homogenii*, in which the object of sexual impulse is a human being but there is homogeneity instead of heterogeneity of sex, as when a woman satisfies her desire on a woman, or a man on a man. This practice too is contrary to the ends of humanity; for the end of humanity in respect of sexuality is to preserve the species without debasing the person; but in this instance the species is not being preserved (as it can be by a *crimen carnis secundum naturam*), but the person is set aside, the self is degraded below the level of the animals, and humanity is dishonored. The third *crimen carnis contra naturam* occurs when the object of the desire is in fact of the opposite sex but is not human. Such is sodomy, or intercourse with animals. This, too, is contrary to the ends of humanity and against our natural instinct. It degrades mankind below the level of animals, for no animal turns in this way from its own species. All *crimina carnis contra naturam* degrade human nature to a level below that of animal nature and make man unworthy of his humanity. He no longer deserves to be a person. From the point of view of duties towards himself such conduct is the most disgraceful and the most degrading of which man is capable. Suicide is the most dreadful, but it is not as dishonorable and base as the *crimina carnis contra naturam*. It is the most abominable conduct of which man can be guilty. So abominable are these *crimina carnis contra naturam* that they are unmentionable, for the very mention of them is nauseating, as is not the case with suicide. We all fight shy of mentioning these vices; teachers refrain from mentioning them, even when their intention is unobjectionable and they only wish to warn their charges against them. But as they are of frequent occurrence, we are in a dilemma: are we to name them in order that people should know and prevent their frequent occurrence, or are we to keep them dark in order that people should not learn of them and so not have the opportunity of transgressing? Frequent mention would familiarize people with them and the vices might as a result cease to disgust us and come to appear more tolerable. Hence our modesty in not referring to them. On the other hand, if we mention them only circumspectly and with disinclination, our aversion from them is still apparent. There is also another reason for our modesty. Each sex is ashamed of the vices of which its members are capable. Human beings feel, therefore, ashamed to mention those things of which it is shameful for humanity to be capable. These vices make us ashamed that we are human beings and, therefore, capable of them, for an animal is incapable of all such *crimina carnis contra naturam.*

III

The Modern Age:
The Attack on the Tradition

The Christian tradition is the source for what today can be called conventional sexual morality. The philosophical views on sexual morality that are part of the thought of such figures as Augustine, Thomas Aquinas and Martin Luther, as well as David Hume and Immanuel Kant, are quite close to our commonly held attitudes toward sex. Many of these views and views subsequently derived from them have been written into laws that govern present sexual behavior, e.g., laws against adultery, fornication, "unnatural acts," and "crimes against nature." However, contemporary attitudes toward sex are changing as are attitudes toward laws that regulate or attempt to regulate personal sexual behavior. Set off against the Christian sexual ethic of marriage, fidelity, chastity and self-denial of sexual pleasure are liberal and experimental views which advocate premarital sexual relations, the right to homosexual and heterosexual relations between consenting adults, group marriage, group sex, etc. There are attempts to redefine the role of women in marriage as well as in society. Sexual behavior that was thought to be sinful, perverse and dangerous is seen from these contemporary perspectives as simply the fulfillment of natural human inclinations.

Contemporary liberal and experimental views on sex have their basis in the reconceptions of man and nature that are part of the rise of modern science and philosophy from the Renaissance onward. In this development of thought philosophy and intellectual thought in general is freed from its secondary position to religious doctrine and scripture. In modern thought man comes to see himself as something he can understand directly through the powers of his own reason and through the observation of his own activities in the customs and institutions of the social world. The secular world, the world in which we now live, was built throughout the seventeenth, eighteenth and nineteenth centuries. The contemporary changes in man's attitude toward his sexual nature can only be understood against the background of the intellectual and historical development of the modern age; only a full history of man's sexual development could make this relationship clear. These changes, however, are most clearly seen against the background of thinkers of the last half of the nineteenth century and early years of the twentieth century such as Arthur Schopenhauer, Friedrich Nietzsche, Karl Marx, Friedrich Engels and Sigmund Freud. They voice general criticism and attack on traditional views of man, rationality and society.

Three ideas lie behind their general outlook and contribute to the development of the modern age: (1) the idea that the principles of human knowledge and conduct can be grasped through reason reflecting on its own activity; (2) the awareness of the existence of other societies with religions and customs that function on principles different from those of the Christian tradition; and (3) the idea that the human world is connected to the animal world and that the animal world provides a basis for understanding some aspects of man's nature.

The first of these challenges the classic Christian view in that it makes man understandable directly through himself whereas the Christian tradition regards man as understandable primarily through his relation to God. This first idea enables man to scrutinize any and all of his activities and arrive at their meaning directly through the power of rational reflection: man is free to alter the conditions of his social existence solely on the basis of the conclusions he comes to through this rational assessment.

The second acts to provide a basis for a critical response to the Christian tradition and Western European culture generally. The reliance on reason is coupled, particularly in the eighteenth century, with the awareness of other social customs. The awareness of other societies and religions which arises in the modern age originally through exploration and travelers' reports provides a basis for raising questions about the history and foundations of Western social institutions. Western society comes to be seen as made up of institutions and customs which have a history and which have political and economic, rather than divine, origins.

The third idea enables man to see his connections with the animal world and allows him to make positive, rather than negative, sense of his own animal nature. In the classic Christian view man's bodily passions are seen as a negative aspect of his existence, e.g., the Augustinian view that sexual lust is connected with original sin. In modern thought man comes to see a continuity between the human and the animal world and thus sees his own passions as natural instincts and not as permanent temptations to sin. The animal world becomes the subject of scientific and philosophical inquiry which yields knowledge of the natural conditions of life and has implications for man's understanding of himself.

The development of these three, as well as other notions and subnotions related to them, lies behind many fundamental questions which can be found in the thought of the late nineteenth and early twentieth centuries. What is the extent to which human affairs are directed by reason? To what extent is human reason dependent upon processes of life that are in themselves instinctual and blind to reason? Is civilization natural to man or artificial? Does it contain restrictions which frustrate the natural sensibilities of human life? Behind such questions is the view that man is a being whose activities are in large part directed by instincts and self-interests. Sex is seen as a powerful instinct which has a central role in determining human behavior. The institutions of marriage and the family are seen not as divinely ordained institutions but as instruments serving particular economic and social interests. Conventional Christian morality is seen as creating essentially unhealthy conditions for man's psychic life. Traditional sexual morality is called into question from many directions and on many counts.

Schopenhauer's philosophy is based on a general theory of the Will which has within it a theory of human sexuality. The selection is taken from one of the supplementary essays to his major work *The World as Will and Idea* titled, "The Metaphysics of Sexual Love." Generally speaking Schopenhauer sees a connection between animal and human mentality. Human mentality differs from animal mentality because man possesses abstract concepts of things. Reason, Schopenhauer argues, is primarily a biological function. With the development of the organism to human form there is a corresponding increase in needs and wants, and higher mental abilities are required to satisfy them. Reason exists primarily in man as an instrument to fulfill physical needs. Throughout nature is the one single Will. The Will according to Schopenhauer, is a blind impulse or endless striving which can also be termed the "Will to live." The Will to live can be seen throughout the natural world directing the activity of its various species through the phenomena of animal instincts. Each individual thing is an objectification of the one Will and strives to assert its existence over other things.

Schopenhauer's theory of sexuality is based on these general notions of his thought. Sexual love, for Schopenhauer, is an instinct embedded in each human individual's existence that is in actuality a drive by the species to perpetuate itself. Nature deludes the individual into thinking that its particular urge toward sexual love is part of its own particular being and under its control. In reality the sexual instinct is a manifestation of the universal Will. The panorama of human love affairs is simply a surface activity of the Will to live. The end of all love affairs is sexual union and sexual union is the necessary condition for the continuance of the species. In all love affairs, even those we pursue most consciously for our own particular ends and pleasures, the species is at work. There are similarities between Schopenhauer's view and that of such thinkers of the Christian tradition as Thomas Aquinas, e.g., both urge that the purpose of sexual relations is the continuance of the species. But according to Schopenhauer, man's urge is not part of a divine plan. It is an instinct which serves blindly the endless activity of Will. Perhaps the single aspect of Schopenhauer's metaphysical analysis of sexual love most important for an understanding of the psychological theories of sex which follow him is his insistence on the notion that sex is an instinct and an instinct that profoundly affects human behavior.

Nietzsche's thought was influenced by Schopenhauer. It deals with many subjects, is complicated, goes through several stages of development and is personal and existential in style. Two subjects on which Nietzsche has much to say throughout his works are morality and psychology. The selection is from the *Twilight of the Idols* and capsulizes much of Nietzsche's criticism of conventional European Christian morality. In his earlier work, *Beyond Good and Evil,* Nietzsche distinguishes between two types of morality: "master-morality" and "slave-morality." Slave-morality is a morality which extols qualities that are exemplified in the lives of the weak and powerless such as humility and kindness. Slave-morality is thus herd-morality, the morality of the mass of men. Master-morality is exhibited by those individuals who rise above the herd. Because such individuals forge a moral perspective that goes beyond the mass of men, they are regarded as immoral, evil, and dangerous. Nietzsche sees Christianity as an agency of the slave-morality and herd-instinct.

For Nietzsche Christianity fosters a morality that deprecates the body, human passions and instincts. Through the pursuit of such morality man becomes weak and powerless. A higher type of man is required who can transcend conventional herd-notions of good and evil and create a new stance on values. In many ways Nietzsche's view of morality can be seen as a translation into ethical terms of Schopenhauer's metaphysics of the Will. One of the ways that Christianity and conventional morality cut man off from his bodily instincts is through its attitude toward sex and sexual pleasure. It should be noted, however, that although Nietzsche argues for the transcendence of conventional morality, he also maintains the most conventional view of women and marriage throughout his works.[1] Women appear in Nietzsche's works as figures to be dominated and to find their place in marriage. Women, for

1. See "Human, All-too-Human," chap. 7; "Beyond Good and Evil," chap. 7, sec. 231 ff.; "The Joyful Wisdom," sec. 363 in *The Complete Works of Friedrich Nietzsche,* ed., Oscar Levy, 18 vols. (New York: Russell and Russell, 1964).

Nietzsche, are quite evidently not beings who can participate in the master-morality and achieve transcendence and transvaluation of values.

Karl Marx and Friedrich Engels advance ideas about marriage and the family that are based on their analysis of property and the economic basis of class structure in society. Marx and Engels, the founders of the philosophy of dialectical materialism and the communistic theory of the state, regard philosophy as more than the intellectual criticism of ideas. Philosophy must engage in criticism of the social and political contexts in which these ideas arise and live. In so doing philosophy raises problems that cannot be solved by intellectual processes. Thus philosophy itself, for Marx and Engels, must be overcome. It must leave the level of theorizing and alter the consciousness of the masses. In this way the activity of philosophizing finds its true fulfillment in becoming the instrument of the working class. Philosophy is conceived by Marx and Engels not only as an instrument of social understanding, but also as an instrument of social change.

The selection contains both a passage from the *Communist Manifesto*, which the Communist League commissioned Marx and Engels to draw up in 1847, and part of Engel's work on *The Origin of the Family, Private Property and the State*, a study which is directed to showing that class divisions in the state originate from the institution of private property. Marx and Engels see the conventional or bourgeois notion of marriage and life in individual family units as having their basis in capitalist economics and as frameworks through which persons exploit each other in a way necessary to the continuance of the capitalist system. Engels argues that the practice of monogamous marriage is rooted in the concern to concentrate wealth and property in a single figure, the man, and provide for the transference of it by inheritance to his children. Monogamous marriage originates as a way of maintaining wealth and furthering class interests. It follows, for Engels, that marriage as a spiritual or love relationship can only occur if property is held collectively, and it only will when the proletarian working class has overthrown the bourgeois capitalist class. Women within the bourgeois practice of monogamy can never become equals with men because they are part of the property relation and are themselves treated as property, subject to the class interest of men which are tied to the class interests of capitalist society. Women can only become the equals of men through the abolishment of private property and the establishment of the collective care of children and other collective modes of life.

Freud more than any other figure has called attention to the importance of the sexual instinct in understanding human affairs and the development of human personality. The selection is from a paper by Freud, " 'Civilized' Sexual Morality and Modern Nervous Illness," which appeared in 1908. Freud's discussion is a clear and penetrating analysis of the conventional concept and practice of marriage that was dominant at the turn of the century and which is still under attack today, although some aspects of it have undergone successful modification. Freud's central question is whether the classic Christian concept of marriage, with its principles of sexual abstinence before marriage and sexual relations for child bearing and not pleasure after marriage, can in any way be justified as promoting human happiness or healthy human personality. Considered beside Freud's analysis, the discussions of the sex instinct of Schopenhauer and Nietzsche and the unnaturalness of Christian morality seem quite broad and preliminary. For Freud the sex instinct becomes the central thing to be understood in developing a theory of man and society as well as the central factor in the clinical treatment of psychic disorder.

In the selection Freud argues that the sexual instinct can place at our disposal an extraordinary amount of energy for cultural activity. This is because "it possesses, namely, the ability to displace its aim without materially losing its intensity." In this sense it is of great value to civilization as a creative force. But it can also tend to fixate and produce unrewarding and unhappy abnormalities. Our conventional system of sexual morality fosters the latter. Freud sees a connection between the exercise of sexual power and the forceful and creative man. The doctrine of sexual abstinence when followed in practice, Freud argues, tends to produce, although not in all individuals, a loss of personal power and pyschic strength. Once individuals who have followed premarital abstinence marry and engage in legitimate sexual relations, their sexual activity tends to be antiseptic and pleasureless and lasts only through the first few years of marriage. This takes a psychic toll on their relations with each other which is in turn communicated to their children. Freud's criticisms of marriage and conventional sexual morality and his analysis of the sex instinct have more than any other set of ideas shaped our twentieth century attitudes toward sex.

13. SCHOPENHAUER: Love Affairs and the Aim of the Species

Arthur Schopenhauer (1788–1860) was born in the Free City of Danzig, the son of a wealthy merchant who intended that he also enter business. Instead he entered the University of Göttingen first as a student in medicine and then philosophy. Throughout his life he had no interest in, nor sympathy for, political affairs or revolution. On lecturing at the University of Berlin he scheduled his lectures at the same hour as Hegel, but it was such a complete failure that he left off lecturing at the end of the term. In the last decade of his life, however, his work was widely recognized and brought him considerable fame.

For all amorousness is rooted in the sexual impulse alone, is in fact absolutely only a more closely determined, special-

SOURCE: Arthur Schopenhauer, "The Metaphysics of Sexual Love," in *The World as Will and Representation* (New York: Dover Publications, Inc., 1958), 2:533–540. Reprinted by permission of the publisher.

ized, and indeed, in the strictest sense, individualized sexual impulse, however ethereally it may deport itself. Now, keeping this in mind, we consider the important role played by sexual love in all its degrees and nuances, not merely in theatrical performances and works of fiction, but also in the world of reality. Next to the love of life, it shows itself here as the strongest and most active of all motives, and incessantly lays claim to half the powers and thoughts of the younger portion of mankind. It is the ultimate goal of almost all human effort; it has an unfavorable influence on the most important affairs, interrupts every hour the most serious occupations, and sometimes perplexes for a while even the greatest minds. It does not hesitate to intrude with its trash, and to interfere with the negotiations of statesmen and the investigations of the learned. It knows how to slip its love-notes and ringlets even into ministerial portfolios and philosophical manuscripts. Every day it brews and hatches the worst and most perplexing quarrels and disputes, destroys the most valuable relationships, and breaks the strongest bonds. It demands the sacrifice sometimes of life or health, sometimes of wealth, position, and happiness. Indeed, it robs of all conscience those who were previously honorable and upright, and makes traitors of those who have hitherto been loyal and faithful. Accordingly, it appears on the whole as a malevolent demon, striving to pervert, to confuse, and to overthrow everything. If we consider all this, we are induced to exclaim: Why all this noise and fuss? Why all the urgency, uproar, anguish, and exertion? It is merely a question of every Jack finding his Jill.[1] Why should such a trifle play so important a role, and constantly introduce disturbance and confusion into the well-regulated life of man? To the earnest investigator, however, the spirit of truth gradu-

---

1. I have not dared to express myself precisely here; the patient and gracious reader must therefore translate the phrase into Aristophanic language.

ally reveals the answer. It is no trifle that is here in question; on the contrary, the importance of the matter is perfectly in keeping with the earnestness and ardor of the effort. The ultimate aim of all love-affairs, whether played in sock or in buskin, is actually more important than all other aims in man's life; and therefore it is quite worthy of the profound seriousness with which everyone pursues it. What is decided by it is nothing less than the *composition of the next generation*. The *dramatis personae* who will appear when we have retired from the scene are determined, according to their existence and their disposition, by these very frivolous love-affairs. Just as the being, the *existentia*, of these future persons is absolutely conditioned by our sexual impulse in general, so is their true nature, their *essentia*, by the individual selection in the satisfaction of this impulse, i.e., by sexual love; and by this it is in every respect irrevocably fixed. This is the key to the problem; we shall become more accurately acquainted with it in its application when we go through the degrees of amorousness from the most casual inclination up to the most intense passion. Then we shall recognize that the variety of these degrees springs from the degree of individualization of the choice.

The collected *love-affairs* of the present generation, taken together, are accordingly the human race's serious *meditatio compositionis generationis futurae, e qua iterum pendent innumerae generationes.*[2] This high importance of the matter is not a question of *individual* weal and woe, as in all other matters, but of the existence and special constitution of the human race in times to come; therefore the will of the individual appears at an enhanced power as the will of the species. It is this high importance on which the pathetic and sublime elements of love-affairs, the transcendent element of their

2. "Meditation on the composition of the future generation on which in their turn innumerable generations depend." [Tr.]

ecstasies and pains, rest. For thousands of years poets have never wearied of presenting these in innumerable examples, for no theme can equal this in interest. As it concerns the weal and woe of the species, it is related to all the rest, which concern only the weal of the individual, as a solid body is to a surface. This is the reason why it is so hard to impart interest to a drama without love-affairs; on the other hand, this theme is never worn out even by daily use.

That which makes itself known to the individual consciousness as sexual impulse in general, and without direction to a definite individual of the other sex, is in itself, and apart from the phenomenon, simply the will-to-live. But what appears in consciousness as sexual impulse, directed to a definite individual, is in itself the will-to-live as a precisely determined individual. Now in this case the sexual impulse, though in itself a subjective need, knows how to assume very skilfully the mask of an objective admiration, and thus to deceive consciousness; for nature requires this stratagem in order to attain her ends. But in every case of being in love, however objective and touched with the sublime that admiration may appear to be, what alone is aimed at is the generation of an individual of a definite disposition. This is confirmed first of all by the fact that the essential thing is not perhaps mutual affection, but possession, in other words, physical enjoyment. The certainty of the former, therefore, cannot in any way console us for the want of the latter; on the contrary, in such a situation many a man has shot himself. On the other hand, when those who are deeply in love cannot obtain mutual affection, they are easily satisfied with possession, i.e., with physical enjoyment. This is proved by all forced marriages, and likewise by a woman's favor, so often purchased, in spite of her dislike, with large presents or other sacrifices, and also by cases of rape. The true end of the whole love-story, though the parties concerned are unaware of it, is that this particular child may be begotten; the method and manner by which this end is attained is of secondary importance. However loudly those persons of a lofty and sentimental soul, especially those in love, may raise an outcry over the gross realism of my view, they are nevertheless mistaken. For is not the precise determination of the individualities of the next generation a much higher and worthier aim than those exuberant feelings and immaterial soap-bubbles of theirs? Indeed, of earthly aims can there be one that is more important and greater? It alone corresponds to the depth with which we feel passionate love, to the seriousness with which it appears, and to the importance attached by it even to the trifling details of its sphere and occasion. Only in so far as *this* end is assumed to be the true one do the intricacies and difficulties, the endless exertions and annoyances, encountered for the attainment of the beloved object, appear appropriate to the matter. For it is the future generation in the whole of its individual definiteness which is pressing into existence by means of these efforts and exertions. In fact, it is itself already astir in that far-sighted, definite, and capricious selection for the satisfaction of the sexual impulse which is called love. The growing attachment of two lovers is in itself in reality the will-to-live of the new individual, an individual they can and want to produce. Its new life, indeed, is already kindled in the meeting of their longing glances, and it announces itself as a future individuality, harmonious and well constituted. They feel the longing for an actual union and fusion into a single being, in order then to go on living only as this being; and this longing receives its fulfillment in the child they produce. In the child the qualities transmitted by both parents continue to live, fused and united into one being. Conversely, the mutual, decided, and persistent dislike between a man and a girl is the announcement that what they might produce would only be a badly organized, unhappy being, wanting in harmony in itself. Therefore a deeper meaning lies in the fact that, although Calderón calls the atrocious Semiramis the daughter of the air, yet he introduces her as the daughter of a rape followed by the murder of the husband.

But what ultimately draws two individuals of different sex exclusively to each other with such power is the will-to-live which manifests itself in the whole species, and here anticipates, in the individual that these two can produce, an objectification of its true nature corresponding to its aims. Hence this individual will have the will or character from the father, the intellect from the mother, and the corporization from both. But the form will depend more on the father, the size more on the mother, in accordance with the law which comes to light in the breeding of hybrids among animals, and rests mainly on the fact that the size of the fetus must conform to that of the uterus. The quite special and individual passion of two lovers is just as inexplicable as is the quite special individuality of any person, which is exclusively peculiar to him; indeed at bottom the two are one and the same; the latter is *explicite* what the former was *implicite*. The moment when the parents begin to love each other—*to fancy each other,* as a very apposite English expression has it—is actually to be regarded as the very first formation of a new individual, and the true *punctum saliens* of its life; and, as I have said, in the meeting and fixation of their longing glances there arises the first germ of the new being, which of course, like all germs, is often crushed out. To a certain extent this new individual is a new (Platonic) Idea; and, just as all the Ideas strive to enter into the phenomenon with the greatest vehemence, avidly seizing for this purpose the matter which the law of causality divides among them all, so does this particular Idea of a human individuality strive with the greatest eagerness and vehemence for its realization in the phenomenon. This eagerness and vehemence is precisely the two future parents' passion for each other. It has innumerable degrees, the two extremes of which at any rate may be described as Ἀφροδίτη πάνδημος and οὐρανία[3]; but essentially it is everywhere the same. On the other hand, it will be the more powerful in degree the more *individualized* it is, in other words, the more the beloved individual is exclusively suited, by virtue of all his or her parts and qualities, to satisfy the desire of the lover and the need established through his or her own individuality. The point here in question will become clear to us in the further course of our discussion. Primarily and essentially, the amorous inclination is directed to health, strength, and beauty, and consequently to youth as well, since the will strives first of all to exhibit the specific character of the human species as the basis of all individuality; ordinary flirtation (Ἀφροδίτη πάνδημος) does not go much farther. Connected with these, then, are the more special demands which we shall investigate in detail later, and with which the passion rises, where they see satisfaction before them. The highest degrees of this passion, however, spring from that suitability of the two individualities to each other. By virtue of this, the will, i.e., the character, of the father and the intellect of the mother bring about in their union precisely that individual for which the will-to-live in general, exhibiting itself in the whole species, feels a longing. This longing is in keeping with the magnitude of the will, and therefore exceeds the measure of a mortal heart; in just the same way, its motives lie beyond the sphere of the individual intellect. This, therefore, is the soul of a true and great passion. Now the more perfect the mutual suitability to each other of two individuals in each of the many different respects to be considered later, the stronger will their mutual passion prove to be. As there are no two individuals exactly alike, one particular woman must correspond most perfectly to each particular man—always with regard to what is to be produced. Really passionate love is as rare as is the accident of

3. "Vulgar and celestial love." [Tr.]

these two meeting. Since, however, the possibility of such a love is present in everyone, the descriptions of it in the works of the poets are intelligible to us. Just because the passion of being in love really turns on what is to be produced and on its qualities, and because the kernel of this passion lies in this, a friendship without any admixture of sexual love can exist between two young and comely persons of different sex by virtue of the harmony of their disposition, their character, and their mental tendency; in fact, as regards sexual love, there may even exist between them a certain aversion. The reason for this is to be found in the fact that a child produced by them would have unharmonious bodily or mental qualities; in short, the child's existence and nature would not be in keeping with the aims of the will-to-live as it exhibits itself in the species. In the opposite case, in spite of difference of disposition, character, and mental tendency, and of the dislike and even hostility resulting therefrom, sexual love can nevertheless arise and exist; if it then blinds us to all that, and leads to marriage, such a marriage will be very unhappy.

Now to the more thorough investigation of the matter. Egoism is so deep-rooted a quality of all individuality in general that, in order to rouse the activity of an individual being, egotistical ends are the only ones on which we can count with certainty. It is true that the species has a prior, closer, and greater claim to the individual than has the perishable individuality itself. Yet when the individual is to be active, and even to make sacrifices for the sake of the continuance and constitution of the species, the importance of the matter cannot be made so comprehensible to his intellect, calculated as this is merely for individual ends, that its effect would be in accordance with the matter. Therefore in such a case, nature can attain her end only by implanting in the individual a certain *delusion*, and by virtue of this, that which in truth is merely a good thing for the species seems to him to be a good thing for himself, so that he serves the species, whereas he is under the delusion that he is serving himself. In this process a mere chimera, which vanishes immediately afterwards, floats before him, and, as motive, takes the place of a reality. This *delusion* is *instinct*. In the great majority of cases, instinct is to be regarded as the sense of the *species* which presents to the will what is useful to *it*. Since, however, the will has here become individual, it must be deceived in such a way that it perceives through the sense of the *individual* what the sense of the *species* presents to it. Thus it imagines it is pursuing individual ends, whereas in truth it is pursuing merely general ends (taking this word in the most literal sense). We observe the external phenomenon of instinct best in animals, where its role is most important; but only in ourselves can we become acquainted with the internal process, as with everything internal. Now it is supposed of course that man has hardly any instinct at all, at any rate only the instinct by which the new-born baby seeks and seizes its mother's breast. But we have in fact a very definite, distinct, and indeed complicated instinct, namely that to select the other individual for sexual satisfaction, a selection that is so fine, so serious, and so capricious. The beauty or ugliness of the other individual has absolutely nothing to do with this satisfaction in itself, that is to say, in so far as this satisfaction is a sensual pleasure resting on the individual's pressing need. Therefore the regard for this beauty or ugliness which is nevertheless pursued with such ardor, together with the careful selection that springs therefrom, evidently refers not to the chooser himself, although he imagines it does so, but to the true end and purpose, namely that which is to be produced; for this is to receive the type of the species as purely and correctly as possible. Thus through a thousand physical accidents and moral misfortunes there arises a very great variety of deteriorations of the human form; yet its true type in all its parts is always re-established. This takes place under the guidance of that sense of beauty which generally directs the sexual impulse, and without which this impulse sinks to the level of a disgusting need. Accordingly, in the first place, everyone will decidedly prefer and ardently desire the most beautiful individuals; in other words, those in whom the character of the species is most purely and strongly marked. But in the second place he will specially desire in the other individual *those* perfections that he himself lacks; in fact, he will even find beautiful those imperfections that are the opposite of his own. Hence, for example, short men look for tall women, persons with fair hair like those with dark, and so on. The delusive ecstasy that seizes a man at the sight of a woman whose beauty is suited to him, and pictures to him a union with her as the highest good, is just the *sense of the species*. Recognizing the distinctly expressed stamp of the species, this sense would like to perpetuate the species with this man. The maintenance of the type of the species rests on this decided inclination to beauty; hence it acts with such great power. Later on, we shall specially examine the considerations that it follows. Therefore, what here guides man is really an instinct directed to what is best for the species, whereas man himself imagines he is seeking merely a heightening of his own pleasure. In fact, we have in this an instructive explanation of the inner nature of *all* instinct, which, as here, almost always sets the individual in motion for the good of the species. For obviously the care with which an insect hunts for a particular flower, or fruit, or dung, or meat, or, like the ichneumon, for the larva of another insect, in order to lay its eggs only *there,* and to attain this does not shrink from trouble or danger, is very analogous to the care with which a man specially selects for sexual satisfaction a woman with qualities that appeal to him individually. He strives after her so eagerly that, to attain this end, he often, in defiance of all reason, sacrifices his own

happiness in life by a foolish marriage, by love-affairs that cost
him his fortune, his honor, and his life, even by crimes, such as
adultery or rape; all merely in order to serve the species in the
most appropriate way, in accordance with the will of nature
that is everywhere supreme, although at the expense of the
individual. Thus instinct is everywhere an action as if in
accordance with the conception of an end or purpose, and yet
entirely without such a conception. Nature implants it, wherever the acting individual would be incapable of understanding the end, or unwilling to pursue it. Therefore, as a rule,
instinct is given only to the animals, especially indeed to the
lowest of them, as having the least understanding; but almost
only in the case here considered is it given also to man, who, it
is true, might understand the end, but would not pursue it
with the necessary ardor, that is to say, even at the cost of his
individual welfare. Here then, as in the case of all instinct,
truth assumes the form of delusion, in order to act on the will.
It is a voluptuous delusion which leads a man to believe that
he will find a greater pleasure in the arms of a woman whose
beauty appeals to him than in those of any other, or which,
exclusively directed to a *particular* individual, firmly convinces
him that her possession will afford him boundless happiness.
Accordingly, he imagines he is making efforts and sacrifices for
his own enjoyment, whereas he is doing so merely for the
maintenance of the regular and correct type of the species; or
there is to attain to existence a quite special and definite individuality that can come only from these parents. The character
of instinct is here so completely present, namely an action as
though in accordance with the conception of an end and yet
entirely without such a conception, that whoever is urged by
the delusion often abhors and would like to prevent the end,
procreation, which alone guides it; this is the case with almost
all illicit love-affairs. According to the character of the matter
expounded, everyone who is in love will experience an extraor-

dinary disillusionment after the pleasure he finally attains; and he will be astonished that what was desired with such longing achieves nothing more than what every other sexual satisfaction achieves, so that he does not see himself very much benefited by it. That desire was related to all his other desires as the species is to the individual, hence as the infinite to something finite. On the other hand, the satisfaction is really for the benefit only of the species, and so does not enter into the consciousness of the individual, who, inspired by the will of the species, here served with every kind of sacrifice a purpose that was not his own at all. Therefore, after the consummation of the great work, everyone who is in love finds himself duped; for the delusion by means of which the individual was the dupe of the species has disappeared.

14. NIETZSCHE: The Morality of the Passions

Friedrich Wilhelm Nietzsche (1844–1900) was born in Röcken in Prussian Saxony, the son of a Lutheran pastor who died several years later leaving him to be raised by his mother, his sister, grandmother, and two aunts. He was given a chair at the University of Basel before he had taken the doctorate. Shortly thereafter he joined the ambulance corps of the German army at the beginning of the Franco-Prussian War. Throughout his life he had uneven health, but he wrote widely and intensely, and his work goes through several phases. In the last year of his life he was clinically insane.

I

There is a time when all passions are simply fatal in their action, when they wreck their victims with the weight of their

SOURCE: Friedrich Nietzsche, "Morality as the Enemy of Nature," in *The Twilight of the Idols,* trans. Anthony M. Ludovici, pp. 26–32, vol. 16

folly,—and there is a later period, a very much later period, when they marry with the spirit, when they "spiritualize" themselves. Formerly, owing to the stupidity inherent in passion, men waged war against passion itself: men pledged themselves to annihilate it,—all ancient moral-mongers were unanimous on this point, *"il faut tuer les passions."* The most famous formula for this stands in the New Testament, in that Sermon on the Mount, where, let it be said incidentally, things are by no means regarded *from a height*. It is said there, for instance, with an application to sexuality: "if thy eye offend thee, pluck it out": fortunately no Christian acts in obedience to this precept. To annihilate the passions and desires, simply on account of their stupidity, and to obviate the unpleasant consequences of their stupidity, seems to us today merely an aggravated form of stupidity. We no longer admire those dentists who extract teeth simply in order that they may not ache again. On the other hand, it will be admitted with some reason, that on the soil from which Christianity grew, the idea of the "spiritualization of passion" could not possibly have been conceived. The early Church, as everyone knows, certainly did wage war against the "intelligent," in favor of the "poor in spirit." In these circumstances how could the passions be combated intelligently? The Church combats passion by means of excision of all kinds: its practice, its "remedy," is *castration*. It never inquires "how can a desire be spiritualized, beautified, deified?"—In all ages it has laid the weight of discipline in the process of extirpation (the extirpation of sensuality, pride, lust of dominion, lust of property, and revenge).—But to attack the passions at their roots, means

of *The Complete Works of Friedrich Nietzsche,* translated under the general editorship of Oscar Levy [1909–1911] (New York: Russell & Russell, 1964). Reprinted by permission of Russell & Russell and George Allen & Unwin, Ltd.

attacking life itself at its source: the method of the Church is
hostile to life.

II

The same means, castration and extirpation, are instinctively
chosen for waging war against a passion, by those who are too
weak of will, too degenerate, to impose some sort of modera-
tion upon it; by those natures who, to speak in metaphor
(—and without metaphor), need *la Trappe,* or some kind of
ultimatum of war, a *gulf* set between themselves and a passion. Only degenerates find radical methods indispensable:
weakness of will, or more strictly speaking, the inability not to
react to a stimulus, is in itself simply another form of degen-
eracy. Radical and mortal hostility to sensuality, remains a
suspicious symptom: it justifies one in being suspicious of the
general state of one who goes to such extremes. Moreover, that
hostility and hatred reach their height only when such natures
no longer possess enough strength of character to adopt the
radical remedy, to renounce their inner "Satan." Look at the
whole history of the priests, the philosophers, and the artists as
well: the most poisonous diatribes against the senses have not
been said by the impotent, nor by the ascetics; but by those
impossible ascetics, by those who found it necessary to be
ascetics.

III

The spiritualization of sensuality is called *love:* it is a great
triumph over Christianity. Another triumph is our spiritualization of hostility. It consists in the fact that we are beginning to
realize very profoundly the value of having enemies: in short
that with them we are forced to do and to conclude precisely
the reverse of what we previously did and concluded. In all
ages the Church wished to annihilate its enemies: we, the

immoralists and Antichrists, see our advantage in the survival
of the Church. Even in political life, hostility has now become
more spiritual,—much more cautious, much more thoughtful,
and much more moderate. Almost every party sees its self-
preservative interests in preventing the Opposition from going
to pieces; and the same applies to politics on a grand scale. A
new creation, more particularly, like the new Empire, has
more need of enemies than friends: only as a contrast does it
begin to feel necessary, only as a contrast does it *become*
necessary. And we behave in precisely the same way to the
"inner enemy": in this quarter too we have spiritualized en-
mity, in this quarter too we have understood its value. A man
is productive only in so far as he is rich in contrasted instincts;
he can remain young only on condition that his soul does not
begin to take things easy and to yearn for peace. Nothing has
grown more alien to us than that old desire—the "peace of the
soul," which is the aim of Christianity. Nothing could make us
less envious than the moral cow and the plump happiness of a
clean conscience. The man who has renounced war has renounced a grand life. In many cases, of course, "peace of the
soul" is merely a misunderstanding,—it is something *very
different* which has failed to find a more honest name for itself.
Without either circumlocution or prejudice I will suggest a
few cases. "Peace of the soul" may for instance be the sweet
effulgence of rich animality in the realm of morality (or religion). Or the first presage of weariness, the first shadow that
evening, every kind of evening, is wont to cast. Or a sign that
the air is moist, and that winds are blowing up from the south.
Or unconscious gratitude for a good digestion (sometimes
called "brotherly love"). Or the serenity of the convalescent,
on whose lips all things have a new taste, and who bides his
time. Or the condition which follows upon a thorough gratification of our strongest passion, the well-being of unaccus-
tomed satiety. Or the senility of our will, of our desires, and of

our vices. Or laziness, coaxed by vanity into togging itself out in a moral garb. Or the ending of a state of long suspense and of agonizing uncertainty, by a state of certainty, of even terrible certainty. Or the expression or ripeness and mastery in the midst of a task, of a creative work, of a production, of a thing willed, the calm breathing that denotes that "freedom of will" has been attained. Who knows?—maybe *The Twilight of the Idols* is only a sort of "peace of the soul."

IV

I will formulate a principle. All naturalism in morality—that is to say, every sound morality is ruled by a life instinct,—any one of the laws of life is fulfilled by the definite canon "thou shalt," "thou shalt not," and any sort of obstacle or hostile element in the road of life is thus cleared away. Conversely, the morality which is antagonistic to nature—that is to say, almost every morality that has been taught, honored and preached hitherto, is directed precisely against the life-instincts,—it is a condemnation, now secret, now blatant and impudent, of these very instincts. Inasmuch as it says "God sees into the heart of man," it says Nay to the profoundest and most superior desires of life and takes God as the enemy of life. The saint in whom God is well pleased, is the ideal eunuch. Life terminates where the "Kingdom of God" begins.

V

Admitting that you have understood the villainy of such a mutiny against life as that which has become almost sacrosanct in Christian morality, you have fortunately understood something besides; and that is the futility, the fictitiousness, the absurdity and the falseness of such a mutiny. For the condemnation of life by a living creature is after all but the symptom of a definite kind of life: the question as to whether the condemnation is justified or the reverse is not even raised. In order even to approach the problem of the value of life, a man would need to be placed outside life, and moreover know it as well as one, as many, as all in fact, who have lived it. These are reasons enough to prove to us that this problem is an inaccessible one to us. When we speak of values, we speak under the inspiration, and through the optics of life: life itself urges us to determine values: life itself values through us when we determine values. From which it follows that even that morality which is antagonistic to life, and which conceives God as the opposite and the condemnation of life, is only a valuation of life—of what life? of what kind of life? But I have already answered this question: it is the valuation of declining, of enfeebled, of exhausted and of condemned life. Morality, as it has been understood hitherto—as it was finally formulated by Schopenhauer in the words "The Denial of the Will to Life," is the instinct of degeneration itself, which converts itself into an imperative: it says: "Perish!" It is the death sentence of men who are already doomed.

VI

Let us at last consider how exceedingly simple it is on our part to say: "Man should be thus and thus!" Reality shows us a marvelous wealth of types, and a luxuriant variety of forms and changes: and yet the first wretch of a moral loafer that comes along cries "No! Man should be different!" He even knows what man should be like, does this sanctimonious prig: he draws his own face on the wall and declares: "*ecce homo!*" But even when the moralist addresses himself only to the individual and says "thus and thus shouldst thou be!" he still makes an ass of himself. The individual in his past and future is a piece of fate, one law the more, one necessity the more for all that is to come and is to be. To say to him "change thyself," is tantamount to saying that everything should change, even backwards as well. Truly these have been consistent moralists, they wished man to be different, *i.e.*, virtuous; they wished him to be after their own image,—that is to say sanctimonious humbugs. And to this end they denied the world! No slight form of insanity! No modest form of immodesty! Morality, in so far it condemns *per se,* and *not* out of any aim, consideration or motive of life, is a specific error, for which no one should feel any mercy, a degenerate idiosyncrasy, that has done an unutterable amount of harm. We others, we immoralists, on the contrary, have opened our hearts wide to all kinds of comprehension, understanding and approbation. We do not deny readily, we glory in saying yea to things. Our eyes have opened ever wider and wider to that economy which still employs and knows how to use to its own advantage all that which the sacred craziness of priests and the morbid reason in priests, rejects; to that economy in the law of life which draws its own advantage even out of the repulsive race of bigots, the priests and the virtuous,—what advantage?—But we ourselves, we immoralists, are the reply to this question.

15. MARX AND ENGELS:
Women in the Capitalist Society

Karl Marx (1818–1883) and Friedrich Engels (1820–1895) are
the founders of the philosophy of dialectical materialism and the
theory of communist society. Marx was raised as a Protestant in an
atmosphere of political liberalism and Kantian thought. Engels was
the son of a wealthy industrialist and held a position in his father's
firm. The friendship of Marx and Engels dates from their meeting
in Paris in 1844, although they had met several years before. They
were commissioned by the Communist League in 1847 to write the
Communist Manifesto. The first section of the selection presented
here is the passage on women and the bourgeois family from the
Communist Manifesto.

I

Abolition of the family! Even the most radical flare up at this
infamous proposal of the Communists.

Source: Friedrich Engels and Karl Marx, *Communist Manifesto*, ed.
Frederick Engels, trans. (Chicago: Charles H. Kerr & Co., 1906),
pp. 107–109.

On what foundation is the present family, the bourgeois family, based? On capital, on private gain. In its completely developed form this family exists only among the bourgeoisie. But this state of things finds its complement in the practical absence of the family among the proletarians, and in public prostitution.

The bourgeois family will vanish as a matter of course when its complement vanishes, and both will vanish with the vanishing of capital.

Do you charge us with wanting to stop the exploitation of children by their parents? To this crime we plead guilty.

But, you will say, we destroy the most hallowed of relations when we replace home education by social.

And your education! Is not that also social, and determined by the social conditions under which you educate, by the intervention, direct or indirect, of society, by means of schools, etc.? The Communists have not invented the intervention of society in education; they do but seek to alter the character of that intervention, and to rescue education from the influence of the ruling class.

The bourgeois clap-trap about the family and education, about the hallowed correlation of parent and child, becomes all the more disgusting, the more, by the action of Modern Industry, all family ties among the proletarians are torn asunder and their children transformed into simple articles of commerce and instruments of labor.

But you Communists would introduce community of women, screams the whole bourgeoisie in chorus.

The bourgeois sees in his wife a mere instrument of production. He hears that the instruments of production are to be exploited in common, and, naturally, can come to no other conclusion, than that the lot of being common to all will likewise fall to the women.

He has not even a suspicion that the real point aimed at is to do away with the status of women as mere instruments of production.

For the rest, nothing is more ridiculous than the virtuous indignation of our bourgeois at the community of women which, they pretend, is to be openly and officially established by the Communists. The Communists have no need to introduce community of women; it has existed almost from time immemorial.

Our bourgeois, not content with having the wives and daughters of their proletarians at their disposal, not to speak of common prostitutes, take the greatest pleasure in seducing each other's wives.

Bourgeois marriage is in reality a system of wives in common and thus, at the most, what the Communists might possibly be reproached with, is that they desire to introduce, in substitution for a hypocritically concealed, an openly legalized community of women. For the rest, it is self-evident that the abolition of the present system of production must bring with it the abolition of the community of women springing from that system, i.e., of prostitution both public and private. . . .

II

We have, then, three main forms of the family, corresponding in general to the three main stages of human development. For savagery group marriage, for barbarism the pairing family, for civilization monogamy supplemented by adultery and prostitution. Between the pairing family and monogamy, in the higher stage of barbarism, the rule of men over female slaves and polygamy is inserted.

As we proved by our whole argument, the progress visible in this chain of phenomena is connected with the peculiarity of

SOURCE: Friedrich Engels, *The Origin of the Family, Private Property and the State,* trans. Ernest Untermann (Chicago: Charles H. Kerr & Co., 1902), pp. 90–100.

more and more curtailing the sexual freedom of the group marriage for women, but not for men. And group marriage is actually practiced by men to this day. What is considered a crime for women and entails grave legal and social consequences for them, is considered honorable for men or in the worst case a slight moral blemish born with pleasure. But the more traditional hetaerism is changed in our day by capitalistic production and conforms to it, the more hetaerism is transformed into undisguised prostitution, the more demoralizing are its effects. And it demoralizes men far more than women. Prostitution does not degrade the whole female sex, but only the luckless women that become its victims, and even those not to the extent generally assumed. But it degrades the character of the entire male world. Especially a long engagement is in nine cases out of ten a perfect training school of adultery.

We are now approaching a social revolution, in which the old economic foundations of monogamy will disappear just as surely as those of its complement, prostitution. Monogamy arose through the concentration of considerable wealth in one hand—a man's hand—and from the endeavor to bequeath this wealth to the children of this man to the exclusion of all others. This necessitated monogamy on the woman's, but not on the man's part. Hence this monogamy of women in no way hindered open or secret polygamy of men. Now, the impending social revolution will reduce this whole care of inheritance to a minimum by changing at least the overwhelming part of permanent and inheritable wealth—the means of production—into social property. Since monogamy was caused by economic conditions, will it disappear when these causes are abolished?

One might reply, not without reason: not only will it not disappear, but it will rather be perfectly realized. For with the transformation of the means of production into collective property, wagelabor will also disappear, and with it the proletariat and the necessity for a certain, statistically ascertainable number of women to surrender for money. Prostitution disappears and monogamy, instead of going out of existence, at last becomes a reality—for men also.

At all events, the situation will be very much changed for men. But also that of women, and of all women, will be considerably altered. With the transformation of the means of production into collective property the monogamous family ceases to be the economic unit of society. The private household changes to a social industry. The care and education of children becomes a public matter. Society cares equally well for all children, legal or illegal. This removes the care about the "consequences" which now forms the essential social factor—moral and economic—hindering a girl to surrender unconditionally to the beloved man. Will not this be sufficient cause for a gradual rise of a more unconventional intercourse of the sexes and a more lenient public opinion regarding virgin honor and female shame? And finally, did we not see that in the modern world monogamy and prostitution, though antitheses, are inseparable and poles of the same social condition? Can prostitution disappear without engulfing at the same time monogamy?

Here a new element becomes active, an element which at best existed only in the germ at the time when monogamy developed: individual sexlove.

Before the middle ages we cannot speak of individual sexlove. It goes without saying that personal beauty, intimate intercourse, harmony of inclinations, etc., awakened a longing for sexual intercourse in persons of different sex, and that it was not absolutely immaterial to men and women, with whom they entered into such most intimate intercourse. But from such a relation to our sexlove there is a long way yet. All

through antiquity marriages were arranged for the partici-
pants by the parents, and the former quietly submitted. What
little matrimonial love was known to antiquity was not subjective inclination, but objective duty; not cause, but corollary of
marriage. Love affairs in a modern sense occurred in classical
times only outside of official society. The shepherds whose
happiness and woe in love is sung by Theocritos and Moschus,
such as Daphnis and Chloë of Longos, all these were slaves
who had no share in the state and in the daily sphere of the
free citizen. Outside of slave circles we find love affairs only as
products of disintegration of the sinking old world. Their
objects are women who also are standing outside of official
society, hetaerae that are either foreigners or liberated slaves:
in Athens since the beginning of its decline, in Rome at the
time of the emperors. If love affairs really occurred between
free male and female citizens, it was only in the form of
adultery. And to the classical love poet of antiquity, the old
Anakreon, sexlove in our sense was so immaterial, that he did
not even care a fig for the sex of the beloved being.

Our sexlove is essentially different from the simple sexual
craving, the Eros, of the ancients. In the first place it presupposes mutual love. In this respect woman is the equal of man,
while in the antique Eros her permission is by no means
always asked. In the second place our sexlove has such a
degree of intensity and duration that in the eyes of both
parties lack of possession and separation appear as a great, if
not the greatest, calamity. In order to possess one another they
play for high stakes, even to the point of risking their lives, a
thing heard of only in adultery during the classical age. And
finally a new moral standard is introduced for judging sexual
intercourse. We not only ask: "Was it legal or illegal?" but
also: "Was it caused by mutual love or not?" Of course, this
new standard meets with no better fate in feudal or bourgeois

practice than all other moral standards—it is simply ignored. But neither does it fare worse. It is recognized just as much as the others—in theory, on paper. And that is all we can expect at present.

Where antiquity left off with its attempts at sexual love, there the middle ages resumed the thread: with adultery. We have already described the love of the knights that invented the day songs. From this love endeavoring to break through the bonds of marriage to the love destined to found marriage, there is a long distance which was never fully traversed by the knights. Even in passing on from the frivolous Romanic race to the virtuous Germans, we find in the Nibelungen song Kriemhild, who secretly is no less in love with Siegfried than he with her, meekly replying to Gunther's announcement that he has pledged her in troth to a certain knight whom he does not name: "You need not beg for my consent; as you will demand, so I shall ever be; whomever you, sir, will select for my husband, I shall willingly take in troth." It does not enter her head at all that her love could find any consideration. Gunther asks for Brunhild, Etzel for Kriemhild without ever having seen one another. The same is true of the suit of Gutrun Sigebant of Ireland for the Norwegian Ute and of Hetel of Hegelingen for Hilda of Ireland. When Siegfried of Morland, Hartmut of Oranien and Herwig of Sealand court Gutrun, then it happens for the first time that the lady voluntarily decides, favoring the last named knight. As a rule the bride of the young prince is selected by his parents. Only when the latter are no longer alive, he chooses his own bride with the advice of the great feudal lords who in all cases of this kind have a decisive voice. Nor could it be otherwise. For the knight and the baron as well as for the ruler of the realm himself, marriage is a political act, an opportunity for increasing their power by new federations. The interest of the house must decide, not the arbitrary inclination of the individual. How could love have a chance to decide the question of marriage in the last instance under such conditions?

The same held good for the bourgeois of the medieval towns, the members of the guilds. Precisely the privileges protecting them, the clauses and restrictions of the guild charters, the artificial lines of division separating them legally, here from the other guilds, there from their journeymen and apprentices, drew a sufficiently narrow circle for the selection of a fitting bourgeois spouse. Under such a complicated system, the question of fitness was unconditionally decided, not by individual inclination, but by family interests.

In the overwhelming majority of cases the marriage contract thus remained to the end of the middle ages what it had been from the outset: a matter that was not decided by the parties most interested. In the beginning one was already married from his birth—married to a whole group of the other sex. In the later forms of group marriage, a similar relation was probably maintained, only under a continual narrowing of the group. In the pairing family it is the rule for mothers to exchange mutual pledges for the marriage of their children. Here also the main consideration is given to new ties of relationship that will strengthen the position of the young couple in the gens and the tribe. And when with the preponderance of private property over collective property and with the interest for inheritance paternal law and monogamy assumed the supremacy, then marriage became still more dependent on economic considerations. The form of purchase marriage disappears, but the essence of the transaction is more and more intensified, so that not only the woman, but also the man have a fixed price—not according to his qualities, but to his wealth. That mutual fondness of the marrying parties should be the one factor dominating all others had always been unheard of in the practice of the ruling classes. Such a thing occurred at best in romances or—among the oppressed classes that were not counted.

This was the situation encountered by capitalist production when it began to prepare, since the epoch of geographical discoveries, for the conquest of the world by international trade and manufacture. One would think that this mode of making the marriage contract would have been extremely acceptable to capitalism, and it was. And yet—the irony of fate is inexplicable—capitalist production had to make the decisive breach through this mode. By changing all things into commodities, it dissolved all inherited and traditional relations and replaced time hallowed custom and historical right by purchase and sale, by the "free contract." And the English jurist, H. S. Maine, thought he had made a stupendous discovery by saying that our whole progress over former epochs consisted in arriving from status to contract, from inherited to voluntarily contracted conditions. So far as this is correct, it had already been mentioned in the Communist Manifesto.

But in order to make contracts, people must have full freedom over their persons, actions and possessions. They must furthermore be on terms of mutual equality. The creation of these "free" and "equal" people was precisely one of the main functions of capitalistic production. What though this was done at first in a half-conscious way and, moreover, in a religious disguise? Since the Lutheran and Calvinist reformation the thesis was accepted that a human being is fully responsible for his actions only then, when these actions were due to full freedom of will. And it was held to be a moral duty to resist any compulsion for an immoral action. How did this agree with the prevailing practice of match-making? Marriage according to bourgeois conception was a contract, a legal business affair, and the most important one at that, because it decided the weal and woe of body and spirit of two beings for life. At that time the agreement was formally voluntary;

without the consent of the contracting parties nothing could
be done. But it was only too well known how this consent was
obtained and who were really the contracting parties. If, however, perfect freedom of decision is demanded for all other
contracts, why not for this one? Did not the two young people
who were to be coupled together have the right freely to dispose of themselves, of their bodies and the organs of these?
Had not sexual love become the custom through the knights
and was not, in opposition to knightly adultery, the love of
married couples its proper bourgeois form? And if it was the
duty of married couples to love one another, was it not just as
much the duty of lovers to marry each other and nobody else?
Stood not the right of lovers higher than the right of parents,
relatives and other customary marriage brokers and matrimonial agents? If the right of free personal investigation made
its way unchecked into the church and religion, how could it
bear with the insupportable claims of the older generation on
the body, soul, property, happiness and misfortune of the
younger generation?

These questions had to be raised at a time when all the old
ties of society were loosened and all traditional conceptions
tottering. The size of the world had increased tenfold at a
bound. Instead of one quadrant of one hemisphere, the whole
globe now spread before the eyes of West Europeans who
hastened to take possession of the other seven quadrants. And
the thousand-year-old barriers of conventional medieval
thought fell like the old narrow obstacles to marriage. An infinitely wider horizon opened out before the outer and inner
eyes of humanity. What mattered the well-meaning propriety,
what the honorable privilege of the guild overcome through
generations to the young man tempted by the gold and silver
mines of Mexico and Potosi?

It was the knight errant time of the bourgeoisie. It had its own romances and love dreams, but on a bourgeois footing and, in the last instance, with bourgeois aims.

Thus it came about that the rising bourgeoisie more and more recognized the freedom of contracting in marriage and carried it through in the manner described above, especially in Protestant countries, where existing institutions were most strongly shaken. Marriage remained class marriage, but within the class a certain freedom of choice was accorded to the contracting parties. And on paper, in moral theory as in poetical description, nothing was more unalterably established than the idea that every marriage was immoral unless founded on mutual sexlove, and perfectly free agreement of husband and wife. In short, the love match was proclaimed as a human right, not only as droit de l'homme—man's right—but also for once as droit de femme—woman's right.

However, this human right differed from all other so-called human rights in one respect. While in practice other rights remained the privileges of the ruling class, the bourgeoisie, and were directly or indirectly curtailed for proletarians, the irony of history once more asserted itself in this case. The ruling class remains subject to well-known economic influences and, therefore, shows marriage by free selection only in exceptional cases. But among the oppressed class, love matches are the rule, as we have seen.

Hence the full freedom of marriage can become general only after all minor economic considerations, that still exert such a powerful influence on the choice of a mate for life, have been removed by the abolition of capitalistic production and of the property relations created by it. Then no other motive will remain but mutual fondness.

Since sexlove is exclusive by its very nature—although this exclusiveness is at present realized for women alone—marriage founded on sexlove must be monogamous. We have seen that Bachofen was perfectly right in regarding the progress from group marriage to monogamy mainly as the work of women. Only the advance from the pairing family to monogamy must be charged to the account of men. This advance implied, historically, a deterioration in the position of women and a greater opportunity for men to be faithless. Remove the economic considerations that now force women to submit to the customary disloyalty of men, and you will place women on an equal footing with men. All present experiences prove that this will tend much more strongly to make men truly monogamous, than to make women polyandrous.

However, those peculiarities that were stamped upon the face of monogamy by its rise through property relations, will decidedly vanish, namely the supremacy of men and the indissolubility of marriage. The supremacy of man in marriage is simply the consequence of his economic superiority and will fall with the abolition of the latter.

The indissolubility of marriage is partly the consequence of economic conditions, under which monogamy arose, partly tradition from the time where the connection between this economic situation and monogamy, not yet clearly understood, was carried to extremes by religion. Today, it has been perforated a thousand times. If marriage founded on love is alone moral, then it follows that marriage is moral only as long as love lasts. The duration of an attack of individual sexlove varies considerably according to individual disposition, especially in men. A positive cessation of fondness or its replacement by a new passionate love makes a separation a blessing for both parties and for society. But humanity will be spared the useless wading through the mire of a divorce case.

What we may anticipate about the adjustment of sexual relations after the impending downfall of capitalist production is mainly of a negative nature and mostly confined to elements that will disappear. But what will be added? That will be decided after a new generation has come to maturity: a race of men who never in their lives have had any occasion for buying with money or other economic means of power the surrender of a woman; a race of women who have never had any occasion for surrendering to any man for any other reason but love, or for refusing to surrender to their lover from fear of economic consequences. Once such people are in the world, they will not give a moment's thought to what we today believe should be their course. They will follow their own practice and fashion their own public opinion about the individual practice of every person—only this and nothing more.

16. FREUD: The Sex Instinct and Human Happiness

Sigmund Freud (1856–1939) was born in Freiburg, Moravia (now Czechoslovakia), and when he was three his family moved to Vienna. Freud entered the University of Vienna in 1873 and studied medicine with a specialty in neurology. Because of his ideas Freud had to endure considerable loneliness and conflicts. Not until 1971 did the Viennese create a museum out of his flat which was the birthplace of psychoanalysis. The selection is taken from a paper " 'Civilized' Sexual Morality and Modern Nervous Illness," published in 1908, the same year as the first International Psychoanalytical Congress was held at Salzburg, which marked the beginning of psychoanalysis as a movement.

Generally speaking, our civilization is built up on the suppression of instincts. Each individual has surrendered some

SOURCE: Sigmund Freud, " 'Civilized' Sexual Morality and Modern Nervous Illness," in *The Standard Edition of the Complete Psychological*

part of his possessions—some part of the sense of omnipotence or of the aggressive or vindictive inclinations in his personality. From these contributions has grown civilization's common possession of material and ideal property. Besides the exigencies of life, no doubt it has been family feelings, derived from erotism, that have induced the separate individuals to make this renunciation. The renunciation has been a progressive one in the course of the evolution of civilization. The single steps in it were sanctioned by religion; the piece of instinctual satisfaction which each person had renounced was offered to the Deity as a sacrifice, and the communal property thus acquired was declared "sacred." The man who, in consequence of his unyielding constitution, cannot fall in with this suppression of instinct, becomes a "criminal," an "outlaw," in the face of society—unless his social position or his exceptional capacities enable him to impose himself upon it as a great man, a "hero."

The sexual instinct—or, more correctly, the sexual instincts, for analytic investigation teaches us that the sexual instinct is made up of many separate constituents or component instincts—is probably more strongly developed in man than in most of the higher animals; it is certainly more constant, since it has almost entirely overcome the periodicity to which it is tied in animals. It places extraordinarily large amounts of force at the disposal of civlized activity, and it does this in virtue of its especially marked characteristic of being able to displace its aim without materially diminishing in intensity. This capacity to exchange its originally sexual aim for another one, which is no longer sexual but which is psychically related to the first aim, is called the capacity for *sublimation.* In contrast to this

Works of Sigmund Freud, ed. James Strachey, rev. ed. (London: Hogarth Press, 1959), 9:187–204. Reprinted by permission of Basic Books, Inc., Sigmund Freud Copyrights Ltd., The Institute of Psycho-Analysis, and the Hogarth Press.

displaceability, in which its value for civilization lies, the sexual instinct may also exhibit a particularly obstinate fixation which renders it unserviceable and which sometimes causes it to degenerate into what are described as abnormalities. The original strength of the sexual instinct probably varies in each individual; certainly the proportion of it which is suitable for sublimation varies. It seems to us that it is the innate constitution of each individual which decides in the first instance how large a part of his sexual instinct it will be possible to sublimate and make use of. In addition to this, the effects of experience and the intellectual influences upon his mental apparatus succeed in bringing about the sublimation of a further portion of it. To extend this process of displacement indefinitely is, however, certainly not possible, any more than is the case with the transformation of heat into mechanical energy in our machines. A certain amount of direct sexual satisfaction seems to be indispensable for most organizations, and a deficiency in this amount, which varies from individual to individual, is visited by phenomena which, on account of their detrimental effects on functioning and their subjective quality of unpleasure, must be regarded as an illness.

Further prospects are opened up when we take into consideration the fact that in man the sexual instinct does not originally serve the purposes of reproduction at all, but has as its aim the gaining of particular kinds of pleasure. It manifests itself in this way in human infancy, during which it attains its aim of gaining pleasure not only from the genitals but from other parts of the body (the erotogenic zones), and can therefore disregard any objects other than these convenient ones. We call this stage the stage of *auto-erotism,* and the child's upbringing has, in our view, the task of restricting it, because to linger in it would make the sexual instinct uncontrollable and unserviceable later on. The development of the sexual instinct then proceeds from auto-erotism to object-love and from the autonomy of the erotogenic zones to their subordination under the primacy of the genitals, which are put at the service of reproduction. During this development a part of the sexual excitation which is provided by the subject's own body is inhibited as being unserviceable for the reproductive function and in favorable cases is brought to sublimation. The forces that can be employed for cultural activities are thus to a great extent obtained through the suppression of what are known as the *perverse* elements of sexual excitation.

If this evolution of the sexual instinct is borne in mind, three stages of civilization can be distinguished: a first one, in which the sexual instinct may be freely exercised without regard to the aims of reproduction; a second, in which all of the sexual instinct is suppressed except what serves the aims of reproduction; and a third, in which only *legitimate* reproduction is allowed as a sexual aim. This third stage is reflected in our present-day "civilized" sexual morality.

If we take the second of these stages as an average, we must point out that a number of people are, on account of their organization, not equal to meeting its demands. In whole classes of individuals the development of the sexual instinct, as we have described it above, from auto-erotism to object-love with its aim of uniting the genitals, has not been carried out correctly and sufficiently fully. As a result of these disturbances of development two kinds of harmful deviation from normal sexuality—that is, sexuality which is serviceable to civilization—come about; and the relation between these two is almost that of positive and negative.

In the first place (disregarding people whose sexual instinct is altogether excessive and uninhibitable) there are the different varieties of *perverts*, in whom an infantile fixation to a preliminary sexual aim has prevented the primacy of the reproductive function from being established, and the *homosexuals* or *inverts*, in whom, in a manner that is not yet quite understood, the sexual aim has been deflected away from the opposite sex. If the injurious effects of these two kinds of developmental disturbance are less than might be expected, this mitigation can be ascribed precisely to the complex way in which the sexual instinct is put together, which makes it possible for a person's sexual life to reach a serviceable final form even if one or more components of the instinct have been shut off from development. The constitution of people suffering from inversion—the homosexuals—is, indeed, often distinguished by their sexual instinct's possessing a special aptitude for cultural sublimation.

More pronounced forms of the perversions and of homosexuality, especially if they are exclusive, do, it is true, make those subject to them socially useless and unhappy, so that it must be recognized that the cultural requirements even of the second stage are a source of suffering for a certain proportion of mankind. The fate of these people who differ constitutionally from the rest varies, and depends on whether they have been born with a sexual instinct which by absolute standards is strong or comparatively weak. In the latter case—where the sexual instinct is in general weak—perverts succeed in totally suppressing the inclinations which bring them into conflict with the moral demands of their stage of civilization. But this, from the ideal point of view, is also the only thing they succeed in achieving; for, in order to effect this suppression of their sexual instinct, they use up the forces which they would otherwise employ in cultural activities. They are, as it were, inwardly inhibited and outwardly paralyzed. What we shall be saying again later on about the abstinence demanded of men and women in the third stage of civilization applies to them too.

Where the sexual instinct is fairly intense, but perverse, there are two possible outcomes. The first, which we shall not discuss further, is that the person affected remains a pervert and has to put up with the consequences of his deviation from the standard of civilization. The second is far more interesting. It is that, under the influence of education and social demands, a suppression of the perverse instincts is indeed achieved, but it is a kind of suppression which is really no suppression at all. It can better be described as a suppression that has failed. The inhibited sexual instincts are, it is true, no longer expressed as such—and this constitutes the success of the process—but they find expression in other ways, which are quite as injurious to the subject and make him quite as useless for society as satisfaction of the suppressed instincts in an unmodified form would have done. This constitutes the failure of the process, which in the long run more than counterbalances its success. The substitutive phenomena which emerge in consequence of the suppression of the instinct amount to what we call nervous illness, or, more precisely, the psychoneuroses. Neurotics are the class of people who, since they possess a recalcitrant organization, only succeed, under the influence of cultural requirements, in achieving a suppression of their instincts which is *apparent* and which becomes increasingly unsuccessful. They therefore only carry on their collaboration with cultural activities by a great expenditure of force and at the cost of an internal impoverishment, or are obliged at times to interrupt it and fall ill. I have described the neuroses as the "negative" of the perversions because in the neuroses the perverse impulses, after being repressed, manifest themselves from the unconscious part of the mind—because the neuroses contain the same tendencies, though in a state of "repression," as do the positive perversions.

Experience teaches us that for most people there is a limit beyond which their constitution cannot comply with the demands of civilization. All who wish to be more noble-minded than their constitution allows fall victims to neurosis; they would have been more healthy if it could have been possible for them to be less good. The discovery that perversions and neuroses stand in the relation of positive and negative is often unmistakably confirmed by observations made on the members of one generation of a family. Quite frequently a brother is a sexual pervert, while his sister, who, being a woman, possesses a weaker sexual instinct, is a neurotic whose symptoms express the same inclinations as the perversions of her sexually more active brother. And correspondingly, in many families the men are healthy, but from a social point of view immoral to an undesirable degree, while the women are high-minded and over-refined, but severely neurotic.

It is one of the obvious social injustices that the standard of civilization should demand from everyone the same conduct of sexual life—conduct which can be followed without any difficulty by some people, thanks to their organization, but which imposes the heaviest psychical sacrifices on others; though, indeed, the injustice is as a rule wiped out by disobedience to the injunctions of morality.

These considerations have been based so far on the requirement laid down by the second of the stages of civilization which we have postulated, the requirement that every sexual activity of the kind described as perverse is prohibited, while what is called normal sexual intercourse is freely permitted. We have found that even when the line between sexual freedom and restriction is drawn at this point, a number of individuals are ruled out as perverts, and a number of others, who make efforts not to be perverts whilst constitutionally they should be so, are forced into nervous illness. It is easy to predict the result that will follow if sexual freedom is still further circumscribed and the requirements of civilization are raised to the level of the third stage, which bans all sexual activity outside legal marriage. The number of strong natures who openly oppose the demands of civilization will increase enormously, and so will the number of weaker ones who, faced with the conflict between the pressure of cultural influences and the resistance of their constitution, take flight into neurotic illness.

Let us now try to answer three questions that arise here:

1. What is the task that is set to the individual by the requirements of the third stage of civilization?

2. Can the legitimate sexual satisfaction that is permissible offer acceptable compensation for the renunciation of all other satisfactions?

3. In what relation do the possible injurious effects of this renunciation stand to its exploitation in the cultural field?

The answer to the first question touches on a problem which has often been discussed and cannot be exhaustively treated here—that of sexual abstinence. Our third stage of civilization demands of individuals of both sexes that they shall practice abstinence until they are married and that all who do not contract a legal marriage shall remain abstinent throughout their lives. The position, agreeable to all the authorities, that sexual abstinence is not harmful and not difficult to maintain, has also been widely supported by the medical profession. It may be asserted, however, that the task of mastering such a powerful impulse as that of the sexual instinct by any other means than satisfying it is one which can call for the whole of a man's forces. Mastering it by sublimation, by deflecting the sexual instinctual forces away from their sexual aim to higher cultural aims, can be achieved by a minority and then only intermittently, and least easily during the period of ardent and vigorous youth. Most of the rest become neurotic or are harmed in one way or another. Experience shows that the majority of the people who make up our society are constitutionally unfit to face the task of abstinence. Those who would have fallen ill under milder sexual restrictions fall ill all the more readily and more severely before the demands of our cultural sexual morality of today; for we know no better safeguard against the threat to normal sexual life offered by defective innate dispositions or disturbances of development than sexual satisfaction itself. The more a person is disposed to neurosis, the less can he tolerate abstinence; instincts which have been withdrawn from normal development, in the sense in which it has been described above, become at the same time all the more uninhibitable. But even those people who would have retained their health under the requirements of the second stage of civilization will now succumb to neurosis in great numbers. For the psychical value of sexual satisfaction increases with its frustration. The dammed-up libido is now put in a position to detect one or other of the weaker spots which are seldom absent in the structure of sexual life, and there to break through and obtain substitutive satisfaction of a neurotic kind in the form of pathological symptoms. Anyone who is able to penetrate the determinants of nervous illness will soon become convinced that its increase in our society arises from the intensification of sexual restrictions.

This brings us to the question whether sexual intercourse in legal marriage can offer full compensation for the restrictions imposed before marriage. There is such an abundance of material supporting a reply in the negative that we can give only the briefest summary of it. It must above all be borne in mind that our cultural sexual morality restricts sexual intercourse even in marriage itself, since it imposes on married couples the necessity of contenting themselves, as a rule, with a very few procreative acts. As a consequence of this consideration, satisfying sexual intercourse in marriage takes place only for a few years; and we must subtract from this, of course, the intervals of abstention necessitated by regard for the wife's health. After these three, four or five years, the marriage becomes a failure in so far as it has promised the satisfaction of sexual needs. For all the devices hitherto invented for preventing conception impair sexual enjoyment, hurt the fine susceptibiliites of both partners and even actually cause illness. Fear of the consequences of sexual intercourse first brings the married couple's physical affection to an end; and then, as a remoter result, it usually puts a stop as well to the mental sympathy between them, which should have been the successor to their original passionate love. The spiritual disillusionment and bodily deprivation to which most marriages are thus doomed puts both partners back in the state they were in before their marriage, except for being the poorer by the loss of an illusion, and they must once more have recourse to their fortitude in mastering and deflecting their sexual instinct. We need not inquire how far men, by then in their maturer years, succeed in this task. Experience shows that they very frequently avail themselves of the degree of sexual freedom which is allowed them—although only with reluctance and under a veil of silence—by even the strictest sexual code. The "double" sexual morality which is valid for men in our society is the plainest admission that society itself does not believe in the possibility of enforcing the precepts which it itself has laid down. But experience shows as well that women, who, as being the actual vehicle of the sexual interests of mankind, are only endowed in a small measure with the gift of sublimating their instincts, and who, though they may find a sufficient substitute for the sexual object in an infant at the breast, do not find one in a growing child—experience shows, I repeat, that women, when they are subjected to the disillusionments of marriage, fall ill of severe neuroses which permanently darken their lives. Under the cultural conditions of today, marriage has long ceased to be a panacea for the nervous troubles of women; and if we doctors still advise marriage in such cases, we are nevertheless aware that, on the contrary, a girl must be very healthy if she is to be able to tolerate it, and we urgently advise our male patients not to marry any girl who has had nervous trouble before marriage. On the contrary, the cure for nervous illness arising from marriage would be marital unfaithfulness. But the more strictly a woman has been brought up and the more sternly she has submitted to the demands of civilization, the more she is afraid of taking this way out; and in the conflict between her desires and her sense of duty, she once more seeks refuge in a neurosis. Nothing protects her virtue as securely as an illness. Thus the married state, which is held out as a consolation to the sexual instinct of the civilized person in his youth, proves to be inadequate even to the demands of the actual period of life covered by it. There is no question of its being able to compensate for the deprivation which precedes it.

But even if the damage done by civilized sexual morality is admitted, it may be argued in reply to our third question that the cultural gain derived from such an extensive restriction of sexuality probably more than balances these sufferings, which, after all, only affect a minority in any severe form. I must confess that I am unable to balance gain against loss correctly on this point, but I could advance a great many more considerations on the side of the loss. Going back to the subject of abstinence, which I have already touched on, I must insist that it brings in its train other noxae besides those involved in the neuroses and that the importance of the neuroses has for the most part not been fully appreciated.

The retardation of sexual development and sexual activity at which our education and civilization aim is certainly not injurious to begin with. It is seen to be a necessity, when one considers the late age at which young people of the educated classes reach independence and are able to earn a living. (This reminds one, incidentally, of the intimate interconnection between all our cultural institutions and of the difficulty of altering any part of them without regard to the whole.) But abstinence continued long after the age of twenty is no longer unobjectionable for a young man; and it leads to other damage even when it does not lead to neurosis. People say, to be sure, that the struggle against such a powerful instinct, and the strengthening of all the ethical and aesthetic forces which are necessary for this struggle, "steel" the character; and this is true for a few specially favorably organized natures. It must also be admitted that the differentiation of individual character, which is so marked in our day, has only become possible with the existence of sexual restriction. But in the vast majority of cases the struggle against sexuality eats up the energy available in a character and this at the very time when a young man is in need of all his forces in order to win his share and place in society. The relationship between the amount of sublimation possible and the amount of sexual activity necessary naturally varies very much from person to person and even from one calling to another. An abstinent artist is hardly conceivable; but an abstinent young *savant* is certainly no rarity. The latter can, by his self-restraint, liberate forces for his studies; while the former probably finds his artistic achievements powerfully stimulated by his sexual experience. In general I have not gained the impression that sexual abstinence helps to bring about energetic and self-reliant men of action or original thinkers or bold emancipators and reformers. Far more often it goes to produce well-behaved weaklings who later become lost in the great mass of people that tends to follow, unwillingly, the leads given by strong individuals.

The fact that the sexual instinct behaves in general in a self-willed and inflexible fashion is also seen in the results produced by efforts at abstinence. Civilized education may only attempt to suppress the instinct temporarily, till marriage, intending to give it free rein afterwards with the idea of then making use of it. But extreme measures are more successful against it than attempts at moderating it; thus the suppression often goes too far, with the unwished-for result that when the instinct is set free it turns out to be permanently impaired. For this reason complete abstinence in youth is often not the best preparation for marriage for a young man. Women sense this, and prefer among their suitors those who have already proved their masculinity with other women. The harmful results which the strict demand for abstinence before marriage produces in women's natures are quite especially apparent. It is clear that education is far from underestimating the task of suppressing a girl's sensuality till her marriage, for it makes use of the most drastic measures. Not only does it forbid sexual intercourse and set a high premium on the preservation of female chastity, but it also protects the young woman from temptation as she grows up, by keeping her ignorant of all the facts of the part she is to play and by not tolerating any impulse of love in her which cannot lead to marriage. The result is that when the girl's parental authorities suddenly allow her to fall in love, she is unequal to this psychical achievement and enters marriage uncertain of her own feelings. In consequence of this artificial retardation in her function of love, she has nothing but disappointments to offer the man who has saved up all his desire for her. In her mental feelings she is still attached to her parents, whose authority has brought about the suppression of her sexuality; and in her physical behavior she shows herself frigid, which deprives the man of any high degree of sexual enjoyment. I do not know whether the anesthetic type of woman exists apart from civilized education, though I consider it probable. But in any case such education actually breeds it, and these women who conceive without pleasure show little willingness afterwards to face the pains of frequent childbirth. In this way, the preparation for marriage frustrates the aims of marriage itself. When later on the retardation in the wife's development has been overcome and her capacity to love is awakened at the climax of her life as a woman, her relations to her husband have long since been ruined; and, as a reward for her previous docility, she is left with the choice between unappeased desire, unfaithfulness or a neurosis.

The sexual behavior of a human being often *lays down the pattern* for all his other modes of reacting to life. If a man is energetic in winning the object of his love, we are confident that he will pursue his other aims with an equally unswerving energy; but if, for all sorts of reasons, he refrains from satisfying his strong sexual instincts, his behavior will be conciliatory and resigned rather than vigorous in other spheres of life as well. A special application of this proposition that sexual life lays down the pattern for the exercise of other functions can easily be recognized in the female sex as a whole. Their upbringing forbids their concerning themselves intellectually with sexual problems though they nevertheless feel extremely curious about them, and frightens them by condemning such curiosity as unwomanly and a sign of a sinful disposition. In this way they are scared away from *any* form of thinking, and knowledge loses its value for them. The prohibition of thought extends beyond the sexual field, partly through unavoidable association, partly automatically, like the prohibition of thought about religion among men, or the prohibition of thought about loyalty among faithful subjects. I do not believe that women's "physiological feeble-mindedness" is to be explained by a biological opposition between intellectual work and sexual activity, as Moebius has asserted in a work which has been widely disputed. I think that the undoubted intellectual inferiority of so many women can rather be traced back to the inhibition of thought necessitated by sexual suppression.

In considering the question of abstinence, the distinction is not nearly strictly enough made between two forms of it—namely abstention from any sexual activity whatever and abstention from sexual intercourse with the opposite sex.

Many people who boast of succeeding in being abstinent have only been able to do so with the help of masturbation and similar satisfactions which are linked with the autoerotic sexual activities of early childhood. But precisely because of this connection such substitutive means of sexual satisfaction are by no means harmless; they predispose to the numerous varieties of neuroses and psychoses which are conditional on an involution of sexual life to its infantile forms. Masturbation, moreover, is far from meeting the ideal demands of civilized sexual morality, and consequently drives young people into the same conflicts with the ideals of education which they hoped to escape by abstinence. Furthermore, it vitiates the character through *indulgence,* and this in more than one way. In the first place, it teaches people to achieve important aims without taking trouble and by easy paths instead of through an energetic exertion of force—that is, it follows the principle that *sexuality lays down the pattern* of behavior; secondly, in the fantasies that accompany satisfaction the sexual object is raised to a degree of excellence which is not easily found again in reality. A witty writer (Karl Kraus in the Vienna paper *Die Fackel*) once expressed this truth in reverse by cynically remarking: "Copulation is no more than an unsatisfying substitute for masturbation."

The sternness of the demands of civilization and difficulty of the task of abstinence have combined to make avoidance of the union of the genitals of the two opposite sexes into the central point of abstinence and to favor other kinds of sexual activity, which, it might be said, are equivalent to semi-obedience. Since normal intercourse has been so relentlessly persecuted by morality—and also, on account of the possibilities of infection, by hygiene—what are known as the perverse forms of intercourse between the two sexes, in which other parts of the body take over the role of the genitals, have undoubtedly increased in social importance. These activities cannot, however, be regarded as being as harmless as analogous extensions [of the sexual aim] in love-relationships. They are ethically objectionable, for they degrade the relationships of love between two human beings from a serious matter to a convenient game, attended by no risk and no spiritual participation. A further consequence of the aggravation of the difficulties of normal sexual life is to be found in the spread of homosexual satisfaction; in addition to all those who are homosexuals in virtue of their organization, or who became so in their childhood, there must be reckoned the great number of those in whom, in their maturer years, a blocking of the main stream of their libido has caused a widening in the side-channel of homosexuality.

All these unavoidable and unintended consequences of the requirement for abstinence converge in the one common result of completely ruining the preparation for marriage—marriage, which civilized sexual morality thinks should be the sole heir to the sexual impulsions. Every man whose libido, as a result of masturbatory or perverse sexual practices, has become habituated to situations and conditions of satisfaction which are not normal, develops diminished potency in marriage. Women, too, who have been able to preserve their virginity with the help of similar measures, show themselves anesthetic to normal intercourse in marriage. A marriage begun with a reduced capacity to love on both sides succumbs to the process of dissolution even more quickly than others. As a result of the man's weak potency, the woman is not satisfied, and she remains anesthetic even in cases where her disposition to frigidity, derived from her education, could have been overcome by a powerful sexual experience. A couple like this finds more difficulties, too, in the prevention of children than a healthy one, since the husband's diminished potency tolerates the use of contraceptives badly. In this perplexity, sexual intercourse, as being the source of all their embarrassments, is soon given up, and with this the basis of married life is abandoned.

I ask any well-informed person to bear witness to the fact that I am not exaggerating but that I am describing a state of affairs of which equally bad instances can be observed over and over again. To the uninitiated it is hardly credible how seldom normal potency is to be found in a husband and how often a wife is frigid among married couples who live under the dominance of our civilized sexual morality, what a degree of renunciation, often on both sides, is entailed by marriage, and to what narrow limits married life—the happiness that is so ardently desired—is narrowed down. I have already explained that in these circumstances the most obvious outcome is nervous illness; but I must further point out the way in which a marriage of this kind continues to exercise its influence on the few children, or the only child born of it. At a first glance, it seems to be a case of transmission by inheritance; but closer inspection shows that it is really a question of the effect of powerful infantile impressions. A neurotic wife who is unsatisfied by her husband is, as a mother, over-tender and over-anxious towards her child, on to whom she transfers her need for love; and she awakens it to sexual precocity. The bad relations between its parents, moreover, excite its emotional life and cause it to feel love and hatred to an intense degree while it is still at a very tender age. Its strict upbringing, which tolerates no activity of the sexual life that has been aroused so early, lends support to the suppressing force and this conflict at such an age contains everything necessary for bringing about lifelong nervous illness.

I return now to my earlier assertion that, in judging the neuroses, their full importance is not as a rule taken into account. I do not mean by this the undervaluation of these states shown in their frivolous dismissal by relatives and in the boasting assurances by doctors that a few weeks of cold water treatment or a few months of rest and convalescence will cure the condition. These are merely the opinions of quite ignorant doctors and laymen and are mostly no more than words intended to give the sufferer a short-lived consolation. It is, on the contrary, a well-known fact that a chronic neurosis, even if it does not totally put an end to the subject's capacity for existence, represents a severe handicap in his life, of the same order, perhaps, as tuberculosis or a cardiac defect. The situation would even be tolerable if neurotic illness were to exclude from civilized activities only a number of individuals who were in any case of the weaker sort, and allowed the rest to play their part in it at the cost of troubles that were merely subjective. But, far from this being so, I must insist upon the view that neuroses, whatever their extent and wherever they occur, always succeed in frustrating the purposes of civilization, and in that way actually perform the work of the suppressed mental forces that are hostile to civilization. Thus, when society pays for obedience to its far-reaching regulations by an increase in nervous illness, it cannot claim to have purchased a gain at the price of sacrifices; it cannot claim a gain at all. Let us, for instance, consider the very common case of a woman who does not love her husband, because, owing to the conditions under which she entered marriage, she has no reason to love him, but who very much wants to love him, because that alone corresponds to the ideal of marriage to which she has been brought up. She will in that case suppress every impulse which would express the truth and contradict her endeavors to fulfill her ideal, and she will make special efforts to play the part of a loving, affectionate and attentive wife. The outcome of this self-suppression will be a neurotic illness; and this neurosis will in a short time have taken revenge on the unloved husband and have caused him just as much lack of satisfaction and worry as would have resulted from an acknowledgment of the true state of affairs. This example is completely typical of what a neurosis achieves. A similar failure to obtain compensation is to be seen after the suppression of impulses inimical to civilization which are not directly sexual. If a man, for example, has become over-kind as a result of a violent suppression of a constitutional inclination to harshness and cruelty, he often loses so much energy in doing this that he fails to carry out all that his compensatory impulses require, and he may, after all, do less good on the whole than he would have done without the suppression.

Let us add that a restriction of sexual activity in a community is quite generally accompanied by an increase of anxiety about life and of fear of death which interferes with the individual's capacity for enjoyment and does away with his readiness to face death for any purpose. A diminished inclination to beget children is the result, and the community or group of people in question is thus excluded from any share in the future. In view of this, we may well raise the question whether our "civilized" sexual morality is worth the sacrifice which it imposes on us, especially if we are still so much enslaved to hedonism, as to include among the aims of our cultural development a certain amount of satisfaction of individual happiness. It is certainly not a physician's business to come forward with proposals for reform; but it seemed to me that I might support the urgency of such proposals if I were to amplify Von Ehrenfels's description of the injurious effects of our "civilized" sexual morality by pointing to the important bearing of that morality upon the spread of modern nervous illness.

IV

Toward a Theory of Love

Theories of sex and the nature of the sexes cannot ultimately be separated from theories of love. Analysis of human sexuality, if done in more than medical and physiological terms, involves references to human love. Both humans and animals have sexual natures, but love is a distinctly human phenomenon. Love is an aspect of human relationships and is one of the primary ideas whereby man makes sense of his ethical and cultural world. When we speak of sex, we usually mean, more precisely, sexual love, that is, a particular network of emotions, attractions and unions that exists between persons and not just the physiology of their genital and reproductive systems. In the term "sexual love," love is the broader idea. Sexual love is one of the forms of love. Thus it is not possible to understand sexual love fully unless we have some grasp of the larger role of love itself in human affairs. Love, however, is a difficult idea in that it is of the broadest terms through which we attempt to make sense of the positive side of human affairs. It, like justice, hope, good, beauty, etc., is one of the ultimate ideas whereby we attempt to capture the ethical aspect of the human world.

Love, as a subject, can be viewed from a number of perspectives. It can be considered in terms of the types of love which exist. In this sense it is viewed as an aspect of human relationships and the human condition which can take on various ethical and psychological forms. Love can also be regarded from the standpoint of the forms in which it occurs in literature and various historical periods. In this sense we speak of courtly love, passionate love, romantic love and sentimental love. Love is often used in another sense to express a profound attraction for or orientation of one's being toward some value. Thus we speak of the "love of" something—the love of country, love of life or love of family, etc. One of the problems surrounding any analysis of love is the almost indefinite number of ways in which the topic can be considered. The fundamental interest for the philosophical analysis of love lies primarily in its role in human relationships and society. Philosophical theories of love tend to approach love as a form of human consciousness, sometimes as the ultimate form of human consciousness or awareness. Before considering the selections of this section, it may be useful to consider some of the general distinctions between types of love.[1]

1. *Brotherly love* is that type of relationship that holds between friends. The persons involved regard each other as

1. There are a number of ways that love can be divided into types. My comments sketch only some of the distinctions involved. See Erich Fromm, *The Art of Loving* (New York: Harper & Row, 1956), chap. 2 and Rollo May, *Love and Will* (New York: Norton & Co., Inc., 1969), pt. 1. In particular, see May's initial comment in the final selection in this volume in which he capsulizes the types of love in terms of a fourfold distinction.

equals. They regard each other as companions, mutually, but nonsexually, sharing experience and spiritual outlook. The first and classic analyses of the love of friendship are to be found in Plato's *Lysis* and Aristotle's *Ethics* (see Section I above). Brotherly love is usually thought of as a relationship between members of the same sex, but it can also exist between man and woman. When brotherly love is expanded to a love for all persons, that is, when all persons are seen as brothers or friends, it becomes humanistic love. In this generalized form it is the common element of humanity that is loved.

2. *Erotic or sexual love* in its ordinary sense involves genital relations between the persons involved or interest in such relations. Erotic love can occur between persons of either the same or opposite sex and can exist between many individuals at once. The tradition of monogamy tends to make us overlook the fact that erotic love relationships can involve more than two persons and frequently do both within and without our own culture. The feelings on which erotic love is based can be extended to wider contexts than other persons. Since erotic love has its basis in the body, erotic feeling can be extended toward the bodily or sensual aspects of the world generally. For some peoples and individuals the whole environment is experienced as having erotic qualities much in the same way one person experiences another for whom he has erotic feeling. Something of this generalized erotic love is portrayed in novels such as those of Henry Miller and D. H. Lawrence.

3. *Compassionate love* is love for persons who are not re-garded as companions or equals. It involves feeling for those more helpless than oneself. It is love based on the ability to feel the world through the other's perspective. The doing of good for others when it is seen as an act of love is love of a compassionate type. Compassionate love when it is general-ized to a feeling for the universal suffering of all creatures is that which is attributed to founders of religions, such as

Buddha and Jesus and to saints. Compassionate love differs from the brotherly love of humanity in that the latter is a feeling for the unity of all men, whereas the former involves the suffering of all men and the metaphysical awareness of the finitude of all creatures. Parental love can be seen as a special type of compassionate love in the sense that it is between unequals, involves the need of the child, and when it functions creatively, it requires full empathy for the child's perspective by the parent. The complexities of this relationship and the differences between the child's relation to the father and to the mother have comprised much of the subject matter of psychiatry and clinical psychology since their beginnings.

4. *Self-love* raises immediately the question whether it is a genuine form of love. Self-love is the idea of love extended to the relationship of the individual to his own psyche or soul. Aristotle discusses it as a genuine type of love in his *Ethics* (see Section I above). It can assume the negative form of narcissism. But in being capable of passing into a negative form it is no different than other forms of love. Compassionate love can turn to its opposite and be nothing more than disguised superiority; erotic love can be just the mask of sexual aggression; and brotherly love can be used as a cover for indifference and ease in human relationships. Self-love is involved with the notion of self-respect or that relationship I have to myself such that I experience myself as a whole being. Self-love in this sense is a basis for other love relationships between persons. It is necessary that I have a positive apprehension of myself as a being so that my love for another is not simply masochism in which I regard myself as nothing and the other as all.

5. *Intellectual or philosophical love* is the love of ideas. In the literal meaning of "philosophy," it is the love of wisdom. It is a form of love which is often overlooked in psychological and psychoanalytic discussions of love. It has its roots in the

alleged response of Pythagoras when asked whether he was wise. Pythagoras is reported to have replied that only the gods were wise and that he was a lover of wisdom. Plato uses the notion of love to explain the relationship between the philosopher and the truth he seeks (see Section I above). This relationship has similarities with erotic love, for Plato, and also involves brotherly love, as the inquiry, which is the way to truth, takes place through conversations between friends. For Plato and for many philosophers and thinkers since Plato, the exercise of man's rational and speculative powers is seen as a kind of love.

6. *Religious and divine love* is like intellectual or philosophical love in that it is directed to an object other than another person. This is true even for the theistic religions; for, although they regard God as a person, He is a person in a different sense than a human being, who has a body and is finite. Religious love is generally regarded as the love of God. God is viewed as the ultimate object of love. All other love relationships between persons involve approximations to this central and primary love. In turn, once God is experienced as the object of love, all other human relationships are transformed and enlivened in a way that they were not before. A further aspect of this type of love is divine love or God's love for man and the world. Traditionally in metaphysics and theology God is portrayed as relating to the world through divine love. Related to religious and divine love are the claims mystics make to attain unity with all things through an act of love. Generally, religious and divine love calls attention to the fact that love is regarded as a force wherein all of the things of the world can be brought together as one.

The selections which follow are from G. W. F. Hegel, Vladimir Solovyov, Jean-Paul Sartre and Erich Fromm and can be generally thought of as part of the broad tradition of idealistic and existentialist thought which runs from the nineteenth century to the present time. If their analyses of love are viewed against the various types of love, such as those distinguished above, they appear as analyses that do not concentrate on any one type of love but attempt to discover the function of love itself in human consciousness. That is, they do not argue for one type of love relationship over another but attempt to identify and describe that function of consciousness upon which all love, including sexual love, is based. The types of love which we can observe and classify have their roots deep in the processes of consciousness wherein man comes to recognize himself as a particular sort of being and wherein the individual consciousness builds its relationship to itself and to other selves.

The selection from Hegel is his fragment on "Love," which is part of what is known as his *Early Theological Writings* and which was written in 1797 or 1798. In it, however, is captured in quite clear language much of the whole perspective of Hegel's thought. This short writing is Hegel's most direct comment on love, yet his whole philosophy sets the stage for contemporary theories of love. In the *Phenomenology of Mind* (1807), Hegel's first major work and one of the most difficult and important works in the history of philosophy, Hegel shows how human consciousness can be understood as a process which sets up oppositions within itself. The human spirit is portrayed as coming to understand itself through its own oppositions. In the act of love, as Hegel states in the selection, living beings overcome their oppositions, and "life is present as a duplicate of itself and as a single and unified self." Hegel's comments on love suggest that behind the dialectical progression of the states of human consciousness that he describes in his *Phenomenology* is the notion of love as a force bringing each state into unity with itself. Love is the force which holds human consciousness together and our particular experience of love between persons is our guarantee that consciousness itself is a unity.

The selection from Solovyov is from *The Meaning of Love,* which is a work that restates in more concrete terms the leading ideas of Solovyov's major work of metaphysics—the *Lectures on Godmanhood.* Solovyov's notion of "Godmanhood," the central principle of his philosophy, embodies the aim of his system as a philosophy of total unity that brings together all aspects of thought and experience. In this way, and in other ways. Solovyov's philosophy has similarities with that of Hegel. Solovyov writes that man can have a direct intuition of God, a direct grasp of absolute reality which involves him in a union with God. Much of Solovyov's metaphysics involves the interpretation of Christian imagery in terms of his notion of the intuitive union of man with God. This notion is the general framework within which he develops his theory of love and toward which it leads.

Solovyov argues that the theory of sexual love, which regards it as an instinct or an instrument of the species (such as Schopenhauer's theory), is unable to account for the fact that reproduction can take place in nature without sexual attraction and for the fact that human love occurs through completely individualized feelings for the person loved. It is not necessary that love exists simply to guide the biological processes of reproduction and child rearing. Love, and sexual love in particular, for Solovyov is important as "the transfer of all our interests in life from ourselves to another, as the shifting of the very center of our personal life." Love is seen by Solovyov as a power through which we can bring together things which are separate. The isolation of individual existence is overcome initially through sexual love between persons. The power of love that is achieved in this union is connected to love in the larger sense which takes us beyond the unions of separate

things to a union with reality which is itself all-oneness. As a
particular theory of love Solovyov's view shows connections
between sexual love, philosophical love and religious and
divine love. Approached simply as a theory of sexual love, it
contains important criticisms of the theory of sex as an instinct,
at least when held as part of a philosophical theory of man.

Sartre's metaphysics is concerned in large part with the
existential and phenomenological analysis of the human world.
The selection is from his major work, *Being and Nothingness*.
Sartre sees love as part of the way in which one makes his own
being. To make myself into my own being involves a struggle
with the conditions of my own human existence in an effort to
grasp and realize my own freedom. In so doing my encounter
with other beings or "the Other" is of crucial significance, for
the way I deal with the other determines what I am. Sartre's
philosophy is complex, employs a special terminology and
cannot be easily summarized. The selection which follows, like
all parts of *Being and Nothingness*, employs Sartre's own
terminology which cannot readily be defined apart from his
philosophy as a whole. The reader who is not familiar with
Sartre's thought should attempt to largely read past his un-
familiar terms and look to the outlines of his analysis.

Sartre takes us inside the lover-loved relationship and shows
the movement of consciousness whereby the self as lover
attempts to achieve its own freedom. Sartre's question is:
"Why does the lover want to be loved?" His answer is that the
lover wants to guarantee his own reality—experience himself
as real—by being the reality of the other who is loved. But he
knows that this cannot be achieved by the simple enslavement
or possession of the other. He cannot destroy the other's
freedom, for the person who is loved must freely give of
himself in return or it would be merely a relationship of
ownership and not love. The realization of my freedom
through the relationship of the lover is constrained by the fact

that to be a successful lover I must be loved in return. The limit on my freedom as lover is that in no way through my role as lover can I produce the condition that is necessary to make me truly a lover—the condition of being loved. Love for Sartre is part of the concrete relations between individuals, and it involves all of the paradoxical character of human relationships. Love for Sartre is not, as it is for Solovyov and most Christian theorists, an act wherein the ultimate union between beings is achieved.

The selection by Fromm contains a discussion of the relationship of love and the state of contemporary society. Fromm approaches love from a psychoanalytic and therapeutic perspective and regards the practice of the "art of loving" as a positive good in human affairs. He does not regard love as simply a natural feeling or sensation operating in its own way in human affairs. He regards it, rather, as something of which we can acquire a knowledge and consciously encourage, foster and cultivate. Fromm sees love as "a capacity of the mature, productive character" and as the basis for living a creative life and for creativity in human affairs. Regarding love as the key to desirable relationships between persons, Fromm raises the question of whether it is possible for persons living in contemporary Western society to actually engage in such relationships or engage in them completely. Fromm maintains that the relationships that exist in the society at large, which are necessary to make capitalism work as a structure, run counter to love relationships between persons. Love is in the end incompatible with normal life in the capitalist society. Fromm, however, does not offer a solution of proposal to change the social structure but expresses the hope that it will change because of its inability to generate satisfactory human relationships.

17. HEGEL: The Idea of Love

Georg Wilhelm Friedrich Hegel (1770–1831) was born at Stutt-gart and studied theology at the University of Tübingen. He first taught at the University of Jena, leaving after Napoleon's victory at the Battle of Jena. He edited a newspaper in Bramberg and taught in the **Gymnasium** at Nuremberg. He later held a chair of philos-ophy at Heidelberg and then Berlin where he became a kind of official philosopher of Germany. Hegel is the great philosopher of German Idealism and among the most important minds of Western thought. The selection presented here is from the fragment on "Love," which is part of his **Early Theological Writings** which pre-ceded his first major work, **Phenomenology of Mind** (1807).

True union, or love proper, exists only between living be-ings who are alike in power and thus in one another's eyes

Source: Georg Wilhelm Friedrich Hegel, *On Christianity: Early Theologi-cal Writings*, trans. T. M. Knox (New York: Harper & Row, Torch-books, 1961), pp. 304–308. Reprinted by permission of the publisher.

living beings from every point of view; in no respect is either dead for the other. This genuine love excludes all oppositions. It is not the understanding, whose relations always leave the manifold of related terms as a manifold and whose unity is always a unity of opposites [left as opposites]. It is not reason either, because reason sharply opposes its determining power to what is determined. Love neither restricts nor is restricted; it is not finite at all. It is a feeling, yet not a single feeling [among other single feelings]. A single feeling is only a part and not the whole of life; the life present in a single feeling dissolves its barriers and drives on till it disperses itself in the manifold of feelings with a view to finding itself in the entirety of this manifold. This whole life is not contained in love in the same way as it is in this sum of many particular and isolated feelings; in love, life is present as a duplicate of itself and as a single and unified self. Here life has run through the circle of development from an immature to a completely mature unity: when the unity was immature, there still stood over against it the world and the possibility of a cleavage between itself and the world; as development proceeded, reflection produced more and more oppositions (unified by satisfied impulses) until it set the whole of man's life in opposition [to objectivity]; finally, love completely destroys objectivity and thereby annuls and transcends reflection, deprives man's opposite of all foreign character, and discovers life itself without any further defect. In love the separate does still remain, but as something united and no longer as something separate; life [in the subject] senses life [in the object].

Since love is a sensing of something living, lovers can be distinct only in so far as they are mortal and do not look upon this possibility of separation as if there were really a separation or as if reality were a sort of conjunction between possibility and existence. In the lovers there is no matter; they are a living whole. To say that the lovers have an independence and a living principle peculiar to each of themselves means only that they may die [and may be separated by death]. To say that salt and other minerals are part of the makeup of a plant and that these carry in themselves their own laws governing their operation is the judgment of external reflection and means no more than that the plant may rot. But love strives to annul even this distinction [between the lover as lover and the lover as physical organism], to annul this possibility [of separation] as a mere abstract possibility, to unite [with itself] even the mortal element [within the lover] and to make it immortal.

If the separable element persists in either of the lovers as something peculiarly his own before their union is complete, it creates a difficulty for them. There is a sort of antagonism between complete surrender or the only possible cancellation of opposition (i.e., its cancellation in complete union) and a still subsisting independence. Union feels the latter as a hindrance; love is indignant if part of the individual is severed and held back as a private property. This raging of love against [exclusive] individuality is shame. Shame is not a reaction of the mortal body, nor an expression of the freedom to maintain one's life, to subsist. The hostility in a loveless assault does injury to the loving heart itself, and the shame of this now injured heart becomes the rage which defends only its right, its property. If shame, instead of being an effect of love, an effect which only takes an indignant form after encountering something hostile, were something itself by nature hostile which wanted to defend an assailable property of its own, then we would have to say that shame is most of all characteristic of tyrants, or of girls who will not yield their charms except for money, or of vain women who want to fascinate. None of these love; their defense of their mortal body is the opposite of indignation about it; they ascribe an intrinsic worth to it and are shameless.

A pure heart is not ashamed of love; but it is ashamed if its love is incomplete; it upbraids itself if there is some hostile power which hinders love's culmination. Shame enters only through the recollection of the body, through the presence of an [exclusive] personality or the sensing of an [exclusive] individuality. It is not a fear *for* what is mortal, for what is merely one's own, but rather a fear *of* it, a fear which vanishes as the separable element in the lover is diminished by his love. Love is stronger than fear. It has no fear of its fear, but, led by its fear, it cancels separation, apprehensive as it is of finding opposition which may resist it or be a fixed barrier against it. It is a mutual giving and taking; through shyness its gifts may be disdained; through shyness an opponent may not yield to its receiving; but it still tries whether hope has not deceived it, whether it still finds itself everywhere. The lover who takes is not thereby made richer than the other; he is enriched indeed, but only so much as the other is. So too the giver does not make himself poorer; by giving to the other he has at the same time and to the same extent enhanced his own treasure (compare Juliet in *Romeo and Juliet* [2. 1. 175–77]: "My bounty is as boundless as the sea, My love as deep;] the more I give to thee, The more I have"). This wealth of life love acquires in the exchange of every thought, every variety of inner experience, for it seeks out differences and devises unifications ad infinitum; it turns to the whole manifold of nature in order to drink love out of every life. What in the first instance is most the individual's own is united into the whole in the lovers' touch and contact; consciousness of a separate self disappears, and all distinction between the lovers is annulled. The mortal element, the body, has lost the character of separability, and a living child, a seed of immortality, of the eternally self-developing and self-generating [race], has come into existence. What has been united [in the child] is not divided again; [in love and through love] God has acted and created.

This unity [the child], however, is only a point, [an un-differentiated unity,] a seed; the lovers cannot so contribute to it as to give it a manifold in itself at the start. Their union is free from all inner division; in it there is no working on an opposite. Everything which gives the newly begotten child a manifold life and a specific existence, it must draw into itself, set over against itself, and unify with itself. The seed breaks free from its original unity, turns ever more and more to opposition, and begins to develop. Each stage of its development is a separation, and its aim in each is to regain for itself the full riches of life [enjoyed by the parents]. Thus the process is: unity, separated opposites, reunion. After their union the lovers separate again, but in the child their union has become unseparated.

This union in love is complete; but it can remain so only as long as the separate lovers are opposed solely in the sense that the one loves and the other is loved, i.e., that each separate lover is one organ in a living whole. Yet the lovers are in connection with much that is dead; external objects belong to each of them. This means that a lover stands in relation to things opposed to him in his own eyes as objects and opposites; this is why lovers are capable of a multiplex opposition in the course of their multiplex acquisition and possession of property and rights. The dead object in the power of one of the lovers is opposed to both of them, and a union in respect of it seems to be possible only if it comes under the dominion of both. The one who sees the other in possession of a property must sense in the other the separate individuality which has willed this possession. He cannot himself annul the exclusive dominion of the other, for this once again would be an opposition to the other's power, since no relation to an object is possible except mastery over it; he would be opposing a mastery to the other's dominion and would be canceling one of the other's relationships, namely, his exclusion of others from his property. Since possession and property make up such an important part of men's life, cares, and thoughts, even lovers cannot refrain from reflection on this aspect of their relations. Even if the use of the property is common to both, the right to its possession would remain undecided, and the thought of this right would never be forgotten, because everything which men possess has the legal form of property. But if the possessor gives the other the same right of possession as he has himself, community of goods is still only the right of one or other of the two to the thing.

18. SOLOVYOV: Sexual Love and the Intuition of Absolute Reality

Vladimir Sergeyevich Solovyov (1853–1900) is regarded as the most influential and original Russian philosopher of the nineteenth century. At the age of nine he had a vision of a beautiful woman whom he came to refer to as Sophia, and who appeared to him on two later occasions in his life, once directing him to go to Egypt which he immediately did. He lived in an eccentric fashion and had a grasp of almost every philosophical and religious system of thought. While teaching at Moscow University, he met Dostoevsky, and the character of Alyosha in **The Brothers Karamazov** may have been based on him.

I

Ordinarily the significance of sex love is supposed to lie in the increase of the race, to which it serves as a means. I

SOURCE: Vladimir Sergeyevich Solovyov, *The Meaning of Love*, trans. Jane Marshall (London: Geoffrey Bles, 1945), pp. 5–11, 30–34, 58–61. Reprinted by permission of Geoffrey Bles.

consider this view unsound—not merely on the ground of any ideal considerations, but above all on the ground of facts of natural history. That the multiplication of living creatures may take place without sexual love, is already clear from the fact that it does take place without the same division into sexes. An important section of organisms both of the vegetable and of the animal kingdom multiply in a nonsexual fashion: by segmentation, budding, spores and grafting. The truth is, the higher forms of both organic kingdoms multiply by sexual methods. But, in the first place the organisms which multiply in this fashion, vegetable as well as animal in part, *may* likewise multiply in nonsexual fashion (grafting in the vegetable world, parthenogenesis in the higher insects). And secondly, setting this aside, and taking it as a general rule, that the higher organisms multiply by means of sexual union, we are bound to conclude, that this sexual factor is connected not with multiplication in general (which may take place also apart from it), but with the multiplication of *higher* organisms. Consequently, it does not follow by any means that the significance of sexual differentiation (*and* of sexual love) is to be sought in the idea of the life of the race and its multiplication, but only in the idea of the higher organism.

A striking confirmation of this we find in the following important fact. In the animals on the border line, which multiply exclusively in the sexual mode, (the division of vertebrates), in proportion as we ascend higher in the hierarchy of organisms, the smaller the ratio of increase becomes, but the greater on the other hand is the strength of the sexual impulse. In the lowest class of this division—among fish—multiplication takes place on a colossal scale: the embryos produced every year by each female are counted by millions; these embryos are fertilized by the male *outside* the body of the female, and the method, in which this is done, does not admit of the supposition of any strong sexual impulse. Of all the vertebrate animals this cold-blooded class undoubtedly multiplies faster than any, and exhibits the passion of love less. In the next stage—that of the amphibians and reptiles—the rate of increase is far less notable than among the fish, though in some of its kind this class, not without grounds, is assigned in the Bible to the number of those creatures that swarm in great quantities, but, together with a smaller rate of increase, we already find in these animals more intimate sexual relations. . . . Among birds the rate of increase is far less, not only in comparison with fishes, but in comparison for instance with frogs, yet the sexual impulse and the mutual attachment between male and female reaches a development unheard of in the two lower classes. Among mammals—they are already viviparous—the rate of increase is considerably slower than among birds, and the sexual impulse, in the majority at any rate, less constant; but, to balance that, it is far more intensive. Lastly, in man, in comparison with the whole animal kingdom, the increase is effected on the smallest scale, but sex love attains its utmost significance and its highest strength, uniting in the superior grades, constancy in the relation, (as in birds) and intensity of passion, (as in mammals). So then, sex love and multiplication of the species are found to be *in inverse ratio* to each other: the stronger the one, the weaker the other. Speaking generally, on the sides which are being examined, the whole animal kingdom develops in the following order. In the lower grades enormous strength of increase, with complete absence of anything resembling sex love, (owing to the absence even of division into sexes). Farther on, among the more perfect organisms, sexual differentiation makes its appearance, and in conformity with it a certain sexual impulse at first extremely weak, later it gradually extends to more remote stages of organic growth. And in proportion to this the rate of increase diminishes, (i.e., the impulse is in a direct ratio to the perfectness of the organization and in an inverse ratio to the magnitude of the increase), until finally, at the very peak—in man, the strongest possible sex love makes its appearance, with even a complete exclusion of increase. So, if in this way, at the two extremes of animal existence we find on the one hand increase without any sex love, and on the other hand sex love without any increase, then it is perfectly clear, that these two phenomena cannot be ordered in indissoluble connection with one another,—it is clear, that each of them possesses its own independent significance, and that the meaning of the one cannot consist in its being a means to the other. The result is the same, if we examine sex love exclusively in the world of man, where it is incomparably greater, than in the animal world, and assumes that individual character, in virtue of which *just this* person of the other sex possesses for the lover unconditional importance, as unique and irreplaceable, as a very end in itself.

II

At this point we encounter the popular theory, which, while generally acknowledging sex love as the expedient of an inborn instinct, or as an instrument of the multiplication of the race, endeavors partially to account for the individualization of the feeling of love in man as a sort of artifice or allurement, employed by Nature or the will of the universe for the attainment of its own private ends. In the world of mankind, where individual peculiarities receive far greater significance than in the animal and vegetable kingdoms, Nature—otherwise the will of the universe, the will to existence, (or call it the unconscious or supraconscious spirit of the universe), has in view not merely the preservation of the race, but also the realization, within the limits of the race, of an innumerable multitude of possible particulars, or specific types and individual characters. But besides these general aims—the exhibiting of as complete a diversity of forms as possible—human existence, understood as a historical process, has the task of elevating and perfecting human nature. For this it is required not only that there should be the greatest possible diversity of specimens of mankind, but that there should be exhibited in the world *the best* samples of it, which are valuable not only in themselves, as individual types, but also for their elevating and ameliorating influence upon the rest. So, then, besides the increase of the human race, that force—as we should also term it—which sets in motion the process of the universe and of history, is interested not only that there should continually be born into the world human persons in accordance with their race, but also that there should be born *these* definite individualities of the greatest possible significance. But for this, simple increase by way of the fortuitous and indifferent union of persons of the opposite sex is insufficient; for the production of determinate individuals there is necessary the union of individually *determinate* producers, and consequently sex impulse in general, as it achieves the reproduction of the species among animals, appears insufficient. Seeing that in mankind the matter is concerned not only with the production of posterity in general, but with the production of *that* posterity which is most suitable for the aims of the world, and seeing that a given person can produce this desired posterity, not with every person of the opposite sex, but only with a determinate one, then this one must also possess for his person an attractive power, must appear to him something exceptional, irreplaceable, unique and capable of affording the highest felicity. Here then is that individualization and exaltation of the sexual instinct, by which human love is distinguished from animal. Yet it, like the latter, is awakened in us by a power unknown, though it may also be of the highest strength for its own avowed aims foreign to our person,—is awakened as an irrational fateful passion, taking possession of us and vanishing like a mirage at the passing of the need for it.[1]

If this theory were correct, it means that the individualization and elevation of the feeling of love would possess the whole of its meaning, its sole ground and aim outside this feeling, just in the qualities demanded of posterity for the designs of the universe. Then it would logically follow from this, that the degree of this individualization and elevation of affection, or the strength of love, would be found to be in direct ratio with the degree in which the posterity resulting from it is typical and significant. The more eminent the posterity the stronger would have to be the love of the progenitors, and conversely, the stronger the love binding together the two given persons the more remarkable the posterity we should have to anticipate from them in accordance with this theory. If, speaking generally, the feeling of love is awakened by the will of the universe for the sake of the posterity required and is only *the means* for the production of it, then it is intelligible that in each given case the strength of the means employed by the mover of the cosmos should be in proportion to the importance for him of the ends attained. The more the will of the universe shows itself interested in possessing its fruits on earth, the more strongly must it attract to each other and bind together the two persons indispensable to produce them. Let us suppose that the matter concerns the birth of an earthly genius possessing enormous significance for the historical process. The higher power directing this process is obviously as many times more interested in this birth compared with the others, as this earthly genius is a more rare phenomenon in comparison with ordinary mortals. Consequently so

1. I have stated a general view of the theory I am rejecting, not delaying over the secondary aspects, which it presents Schopenhauer, Hartmann and others. In his pamphlet, "The fundamental motives of heredity," Walter attempts to prove, by the facts of history, that great men are born as the fruit of a strong mutual love.

much stronger than the ordinary one must be the sexual impulse by which the will of the universe (according to this theory), assures for itself in this case the attainment of an end so important for its designs. Of course, the defenders of this theory may repudiate the idea of any exact quantitative relation between the importance of the given person and the strength of passion in its progenitors, seeing that these objects do not admit of exact measurement. But it is quite indisputable (from the point of view of this theory), that if the will of the universe is *extremely interested* in the birth of some particular man, it must take *extraordinary measures* to ensure the desired result, i.e., in accordance with the terms of the theory, it must awaken in the parents an *extraordinary strength* of passion, capable of overcoming all obstacles to their union.

As a matter of fact, however, we do not find anything of the kind nor any such correlation between the strong passion of love and the importance of the posterity. Above all we come up against the fact, quite inexplicable on this theory, that the strongest love very frequently is not merely great but unshared, and does not produce any posterity whatsoever. If, as the result of such love, people go into monasteries, or end by committing suicide, then why did the will of the universe interested in posterity take so much trouble on this point? But even if the passionate Werther did not kill himself, his ill-starred passion none the less remains an inexplicable problem for the theory of the qualifications of posterity. The excessively individualized and elevated love of Werther for Charlotte showed (from the point of view of this theory) that it was precisely with Charlotte that he was destined to produce posterity specially important and necessary for mankind, for the sake of which the will of the universe also awakened in him this extraordinary passion. But why was it that this omniscient and omnipotent Will did not think out, or was unable to effect, its desired idea also about Charlotte, without the unhappiness for which Werther's passion was entirely purposeless and unnecessary? For a substance, which functions teleologically, love's labor lost is a downright absurdity. . . .

III

The meaning and worth of love, as a feeling, consists in this, that it effectually constrains us, in all our nature, to acknowledge for *another* the unconditional central significance, of which, in virtue of our egoism, we are conscious only in our own selves. Love is of importance; not only as one of our feelings, but as the transfer of all our interest in life from ourselves to another, as the shifting of the very center of our personal life. This is characteristic of every kind of love, but *par excellence* of sex-love;[2] it is distinguished from other kinds of love by greater intensity, by a more engrossing character, and by the possibility of more complete all-round reciprocity. Only this love can lead to the effective and indissoluble fusion of two existences into one; only of it is it also said in the words of Holy Writ: "They twain shall be one flesh," i.e., shall become one real being.

Feeling demands such a complete union, inward and definitive, but further than this subjective demand and aspiration the affair does not ordinarily go, since this alone is acknowledged as indispensable. As a matter of fact, instead of eternal poetry and central union, there grows up only a more or less lasting, but for all that temporal, more or less close, but for all that external, superficial *rapprochement* of two finite creatures

2. I call *sex love,* for want of a better term, "the exclusive attachment (one-sided as well as mutual), between persons of different sexes, which renders possible the relation between them of husband and wife," but in no wise do I prejudge by this the question of the importance of the physical side of the matter.

within the narrow framework of the prose of every day existence. The object of love does not as a matter of fact preserve
the unconditional significance, which is attached to it by the
lover's enamoured vision. For the outsider's glance this is clear
from the very beginning; but the faint tinge of mockery, which
inevitably accompanies the outsider's relation to the man in
love, turns out to be only the anticipation of his own disen-
chantment. At one stroke, or little by little, the keen emotion of
the enthusiasm of love passes away, and yet all is well, if
having manifested itself in such love, the energy of altruistic
feeling is not wasted and purposeless, but only having lost its
concentration and spirit of high emprise, is transferred in a
divided and weakened form to the children, who are begotten
and reared for a repetition of this same illusion. I say illusion—from the point of view of *individual* existence and of the
unconditional significance of human personality—though I
fully acknowledge the necessity and usefulness of the procreation of children and the succession of generations for the
progress of humanity in its collective existence. But of love in
the strict sense of the word there is here no question. The
coincidence of a strong passion of love with the successful
begetting of children is merely fortuitous and even so is sufficiently rare; historical and every day experience proves beyond doubt that children may be successfully begotten,
ardently loved, and excellently brought up by their parents,
though these latter should never had been in love with each
other. Consequently, the collective and universal interests of
mankind, combined with the shift of the generations, do not at
all demand any lofty and keen emotion of love. And in the
meantime in the life of the individual this supreme flowering
of it proves to be a barren blossom. The primordial power of
love here loses all its meaning, when the object of it, from the
height of the absolute center of immortal individuality, is
degraded to the level of an incidental and easily replaced

means for the production of a fresh generation of human beings, a generation, it may be a little better, or it may be a little worse, but in any case relative and transitory.

If therefore we look only upon what ordinarily exists as the actual outcome of love, then we are bound to acknowledge it as an illusion, which for the time being takes possession of our nature and then disappears, but has no farther influence in that affair (seeing that the begetting of children is not the business proper of love). But recognizing from its conspicuous strength, that the ideal meaning of love is not realized in its actual achievements, are we bound to acknowledge that it is *unrealizable?*

By the very nature of man, who in his rational consciousness, moral freedom and capacities for self-perfecting, possesses infinite potentialities , we have no right to reckon beforehand that any task whatsoever would be beyond his power to realize, unless it comprises in itself internal logical contradictions, or want of conformity with the general meaning of the universe and the harmonious course of cosmic and historical development.

It would be entirely wrong to deny the possibility of realizing love merely on the ground that hitherto it never has been realized: you must know that many another thing was once found in the same position, for instance, all science and art, the civic community, our control of the forces of Nature. Even the rational consciousness itself, before becoming a fact in man, was only a perplexed and unsuccessful aspiration in the world of animals. How many geological and biological epochs passed away in unsuccessful endeavors to construct a brain qualified to become the organ for the embodiment of rational meaning. Love is as yet for man the same as reason was for the animal world: it exists in its beginnings, or as an earnest of what it will be, but not as yet in actual fact. And if enormous world-periods—testifying to the yet unrealized intellect—did

not hinder it from being realized in the end, still less does the
nonrealization of love, in the course of the comparatively few
thousands of years lived through by historical mankind, in any
way give us the right to infer anything whatever against the
future realization of it. All we can say is that it is well to
remember that, if the actuality of rational consciousness has
manifested itself in man but not through man, the realization
of love, as the loftiest stage towards the true life of that same
humanity, must issue not only in mankind but *through it*.

The problem of love consists in *justifying in reality* that
meaning of love which at first is given only in feeling. There is
demanded such a union of two given finite natures as would
create out of them one absolute ideal personality. This problem not only does not comprise in itself any kind of inward
contradiction or any kind of nonconformity with the meaning
of the universe, but is directly posed by our spiritual nature.
The peculiar character of this consists just in a man's being
able, while remaining the self-same man, in his own proper
form to find room for absolute contents, to become an absolute
personality. But in order to be full-fraught with an absolute
content (which in the language of religion is termed eternal
life or the kingdom of God), that same human form must be
restored in its entirety (reintegrated). In the empirical reality
of man, as such, this is by no means so—he exists only in a
determinate onesidedness and finitude, as a male or female
individuality (and just on this basis all other distinctions are
developed). But the authentic man in the fulness of his ideal
personality, obviously, cannot be merely male or merely female, but must be the supreme unity of both. To realize this
unity or to create the true man, as a free unity of the male and
female principles, preserving their formal individualization but
having surmounted their material separateness and diver-
gence, this is the *problem* proper and the nearest task of love.
Having disentangled the conditions, which are demanded for

the effective solution of it, we are convinced that it is only the nonfulfillment of these conditions which brings love to perpetual shipwreck and constrains us to acknowledge it as an illusion. . . .

IV

The concern of genuine love is above all based on *faith*. The radical meaning of love, as has already been shown, consists in the acknowledgment for another creature of unconditional significance. But this creature in its empirical being as the subject of actual sensuous reception, is not possessed of unconditional significance: it is imperfect in its simplicity and transient as to its existence. Consequently, we can assert unconditional significance for it only by faith, which is the assurance of things hoped for, the conviction of things now seen. But to what does faith refer in the present instance? What does it strictly mean to believe in the unconditional—and, what is the same thing, everlasting—significance of this particular person? To assert, that he himself, as such, in his particularity and separateness, possesses absolute significance, would be as absurd as it is blasphemous. Of course the word "worship" is very generally used in the sphere of amorous relations, but then the word "madness" likewise possesses its legitimate application in this domain. So then, observing the logical law, which does not allow us to identify contradictory definitions, and likewise obeying the command of true religion, which forbids the worship of idols, we must, by faith in the object of our love, understand the affirmation of this object as it exists in God, and as in this sense possessing everlasting significance. It must be understood that this transcendent relation to the "other," this mental transference of it into the sphere of the Divine, presupposes the same relation in oneself, the same transference and affirmation of oneself in the sphere of the

absolute. I can only acknowledge the unconditional significance of a given person, or believe in him (without which
a true love is impossible), by affirming him in God, and therefore by belief in God Himself, and in myself, as possessing in
God the center and root of my own existence. This triune faith
is already a certain inward act, and by this act is laid the first
beginning of a true union of the man with his "other" and the
restoration in it, or in them, of the image of the triune God.
The act of faith, under the actual conditions of time and place,
is prayer (in the fundamental, not in the technical sense of the
word). The indissoluble union of oneself and another in this
relation is the first step towards an authentic union. In itself
this step is small, but without it nothing more advanced or
greater is possible.

Seeing that for God, the eternal and indivisible, all is together and at once, all is in one, then to affirm any individual
creature whatsoever in God signifies to affirm him not in his
separateness but in the All, or more accurately, in the unity of
the All. But seeing that this individual creature, in his given
actuality, does not enter into the unity of the All, but exists in
isolation as an individualized material phenomenon, the object
of our faith and love is necessarily to be distinguished from
the empirical object of our instinctive love, though it is also
inseparably bound up with it. It is one and the same person in
two dissimilar aspects, or in two different spheres of being—
the ideal and the real. The first is as yet only an idea. But by
the steadfast faith and insight of love we know that this idea is
not an arbitrary fiction of our own, but that it expresses the
truth of the object, only a truth as yet not realized in the
sphere of actual, external phenomena.

This true idea of the beloved object, though in the instant of
amorous feeling it shines through the actual phenomenon, is
yet manifested in a clearer aspect at first only as the object of
imagination. The concrete form of this imagination, the ideal

shape in which I clothe the beloved person at the given moment, is of course created by me, but it is not created out of nothing. And the subjectivity of this image as such, i.e., as it manifests itself here and now before the eyes of my soul, by no means exhibits what is itself subjective, i.e., a characteristic of an imaginary object which exists for me alone. If for me, who am myself on this side of the transcendent world, a certain ideal object appears to be only the product of my own imagination, this does not interfere with its full actuality in another and higher sphere of being. And though our actual existence is outside this higher sphere, yet our mind is not wholly alien to it, and we can possess a certain abstract comprehension of the laws of its being. And here is the first and fundamental law: If in our world separate and isolated existence is a fact and actuality, while unity is only a concept and an idea, there, on the contrary, actuality appertains to the unity, or more accurately, to the all-oneness, but separateness and individualization exists only potentially and subjectively.

And from this it follows, that the being of *this* person in the transcendent sphere is not individual, in the sense of real being in this world. There, i.e., in the truth, the individual person is only a living, and actual yet indivisible ray, of the one ideal light—the all-one reality. This ideal person, or embodiment of the idea, is only an individualization of the all-oneness, which is indivisibly present in each of its individualizations. So, when we imagine the ideal form of the beloved object, then under this form is communicated to us this same all-one reality.

19. SARTRE: The Self-Alienation of the Lover's Freedom

Jean Paul Sartre (1905–   ) was born in Paris and studied in Paris, Berlin and Freiburg. He entered the French army with the outbreak of the war in 1939, was captured by the Germans a year later and was released and returned to Paris during the German occupation of France. During the occupation he taught philosophy and was active in the resistance. His major philosophical work, **Being and Nothingness** (1943), was completed during these years. Since this period he has published a number of novels and plays and written on the relationship between Marxism and existentialism.

Why does the lover want to be *loved?* If Love were in fact a pure desire for physical possession, it could in many cases be

SOURCE: Jean Paul Sartre, "First Attitude toward Others: Love, Language, Masochism," in *Being and Nothingness,* trans, H. E. Barnes (New York: Philosophical Library, Inc., 1956), pp. 478–491. Copyright

easily satisfied. Proust's hero, for example, who installs his mistress in his home, who can see her and possess her at any hour of the day, who has been able to make her completely dependent on him economically, ought to be free from worry. Yet we know that he is, on the contrary, continually gnawed by anxiety. Through her consciousness Albertine escapes Marcel even when he is at her side, and that is why he knows relief only when he gazes on her while she sleeps. It is certain then that the lover wishes to capture a "consciousness." But why does he wish it? And how?

The notion of "ownership," by which love is so often explained, is not actually primary. Why should I want to appropriate the Other if it were not precisely that the Other makes me be? But this implies precisely a certain mode of appropriation; it is the Other's freedom as such that we want to get hold of. Not because of a desire for power. The tyrant scorns love, he is content with fear. If he seeks to win the love of his subjects, it is for political reasons; and if he finds a more economical way to enslave them, he adopts it immediately. On the other hand, the man who wants to be loved does not desire the enslavement of the beloved. He is not bent on becoming the object of passion which flows forth mechanically. He does not want to possess an automaton, and if we want to humiliate him, we need only try to persuade him that the beloved's passion is the result of a psychological determinism. The lover will then feel that both his love and his being are cheapened. If Tristan and Isolde fall madly in love because of a love potion, they are less interesting. The total enslavement of the beloved kills the love of the lover. The end is surpassed; if the beloved is transformed into an automaton, the lover finds himself alone. Thus the lover does not desire to possess the beloved as one possesses a thing; he demands a special type of appropriation. He wants to possess a freedom as freedom.

On the other hand, the lover can not be satisfied with that superior form of freedom which is a free and voluntary engagement. Who would be content with a love given as pure loyalty to a sworn oath? Who would be satisfied with the words, "I love you because I have freely engaged myself to love you and because I do not wish to go back on my word." Thus the lover demands a pledge, yet is irritated by a pledge. He wants to be loved by a freedom but demands that this freedom as freedom should no longer be free. He wishes that the Other's freedom should determine itself to become love— and this not only at the beginning of the affair but at each instant—and at the same time he wants this freedom to be captured *by itself,* to turn back upon itself, as in madness, as in a dream, so as to will its own captivity. This captivity must be a resignation that is both free and yet chained in our hands. In love it is not a determinism of the passions which we desire in the Other nor a freedom beyond reach; it is a freedom which *plays the role of* a determinism of the passions and which is caught in its own role. For himself the lover does not demand that he be the *cause* of this radical modification of freedom but that he be the unique and privileged occasion of it. In fact he could not want to be the cause of it without immediately submerging the beloved in the midst of the world as a tool which can be transcended. That is not the essence of love. On the contrary, in Love the Lover wants to be "the whole World" for the beloved. This means that he puts himself on the side of the world; he is the one who assumes and symbolizes the world; he is a *this* which includes all other *thises.* He is and consents to be an *object.* But on the other hand, he wants to be the object in which the Other's freedom consents to lose itself, the object in which the Other consents to find his being and his *raison d'être* as his second facticity—

the object-limit of transcendence, that toward which the Other's transcendence transcends all other objects but which it can in no way transcend. And everywhere he desires the circle of the Other's freedom; that is, at each instant as the Other's freedom accepts this limit to his transcendence, this acceptance is *already* present as the motivation of the acceptance considered. It is in the capacity of an end already chosen that the lover wishes to be chosen as an end. This allows us to grasp what basically the lover demands of the beloved; he does not want to *act* on the Other's freedom but to exist *a priori* as the objective limit of this freedom; that is, to be given at one stroke along with it and in its very upsurge as the limit which the freedom must accept in order to be free. By this very fact, what he demands is a limiting, a gluing down of the Other's freedom by itself; this limit of structure is in fact a *given*, and the very appearance of the given as the limit of freedom means that the freedom *makes itself exist* within the given by being its own prohibition against surpassing it. This prohibition is envisaged by the lover *simultaneously* as something lived—that is, something suffered (in a word, as a facticity) and as something freely consented to. It must be freely consented to since it must be effected only with the upsurge of a freedom which chooses itself as freedom. But it must be only what is lived since it must be an impossibility always present, a facticity which surges back to the heart of the Other's freedom. This is expressed psychologically by the demand that the free decision to love me, which the beloved formerly has taken, must slip in as a magically determining motivation *within* his present free engagement.

Now we can grasp the meaning of this demand: the facticity which is to be a factual limit for the Other in my demand to be loved and which is to result in being *his own* facticity—this is *my* facticity. It is in so far as I am the object which the Other makes come into being that I must be the inherent limit to his very transcendence. Thus the Other by his upsurge into being makes me be as unsurpassable and absolute, not as a nihilating For-itself but as a being-for-others-in-the-midst-of-the-world. Thus to want to be loved is to infest the Other with one's own facticity; it is to wish to compel him to re-create you perpetually as the condition of a freedom which submits itself and which is engaged; it is to wish both that freedom found fact and that fact have preeminence over freedom. If this end could be attained, it would result in the first place in my being *secure* within the Other's consciousness. First because the motive of my uneasiness and my shame is the fact that I apprehend and experience myself in my being-for-others as that which can always be surpassed toward something else, that which is the pure object of a value judgment, a pure means, a pure tool. My uneasiness stems from the fact that I assume necessarily and freely that being which another makes me be in an absolute freedom. "God knows what I am for him! God knows what he thinks of me!" This means "God knows what he makes me be." I am haunted by this being which I fear to encounter someday at the turn of a path, this being which is so strange to me and which is yet *my being* and which I know that I shall never encounter in spite of all my efforts to do so. But if the Other loves me then I become the *unsurpassable*, which means that I must be the absolute end. In this sense I am saved from *instrumentality*. My existence in the midst of the world becomes the exact correlate of my transcendence-for-myself since my independence is absolutely safeguarded. The object which the Other must make me be is an object-transcendence, an absolute center of reference around which all the instrumental-things of the world are ordered as pure *means*. At the same time, as the absolute limit of freedom—i.e., of the absolute source of all values—I am protected against any eventual devalorization. I am the absolute value. To the extent that I assume my being-for-others, I assume myself as value. Thus to

want to be loved is to want to be placed beyond the whole
system of values posited by the Other and to be the condition
of all valorization and the objective foundation of all values.
This demand is the usual theme of lovers' conversations,
whether as in *La Porte Etroite,* the woman who wants to be
loved identifies herself with an ascetic morality of self-surpass-
ing and wishes to embody the ideal limit of this surpassing—
or as more usually happens, the woman in love demands that
the beloved in his acts should sacrifice traditional morality for
her and is anxious to know whether the beloved would betray
his friends for her, "would steal for her," "would kill for her,"
etc.

From this point of view, my being must escape the *look* of
the beloved, or rather it must be the object of a look with
another structure. I must no longer be seen on the ground of
the world as a "this" among other "thises," but the world must
be revealed in terms of me. In fact to the extent that the
upsurge of freedom makes a world exist, I must be, as the
limiting-condition of this upsurge, the very condition of the
upsurge of a world. I must be the one whose function is to
make trees and water exist, to make cities and fields and other
men exist, in order to give them later to the Other who ar-
ranges them into a world, just as the mother in matrilineal
communities receives titles and the family name not to keep
them herself but to transfer them immediately to her children.
In one sense if I am to be loved, I am the object through
whose procuration the world will exist for the Other; in another sense I am the world. Instead of being a "this" detaching
itself on the ground of the world, I am the ground-as-object on
which the world detaches itself. Thus I am reassured; the
Other's look no longer paralyzes me with finitude. It no longer
fixes my being in *what I am.* I can no longer be *looked at* as
ugly, as small, as cowardly, since these characteristics necessarily represent a factual limitation of my being and an

apprehension of my finitude as finitude. To be sure, my possibles remain transcended possibilities, dead-possibilities; but I possess all possibles. I am all the dead-possibilities in the world; hence I cease to be the being who is understood from the standpoint of other beings or of its acts. In the loving intuition which I demand, I am to be given as an absolute totality in terms of which all its peculiar acts and all beings are to be understood. One could say, slightly modifying a famous pronouncement of the Stoics, that "the beloved can fail in three ways."[1] The ideal of the sage and the ideal of the man who wants to be loved actually coincide in this that both want to be an object-as-totality accessible to a global intuition which will apprehend the beloved's or the sage's actions in the world as partial structures which are interpreted in terms of the totality. Just as wisdom is proposed as a state to be attained by an absolute metamorphosis, so the Other's freedom must be absolutely metamorphosed in order to allow me to attain the state of being loved.

Up to this point our description would fall into line with Hegel's famous description of the Master and Slave relation. What the Hegelian Master is for the Slave, the lover wants to be for the beloved. But the analogy stops here, for with Hegel the Master demands the Slave's freedom only laterally and, so to speak, implicitly, while the lover wants the beloved's freedom *first and foremost*. In this sense if I am to be loved by the Other, this means that I am to be freely chosen as beloved. As we know, in the current terminology of love, the beloved is often called *the chosen one*. But this choice must not be relative and contingent. The lover is irritated and feels himself cheapened when he thinks that the beloved has chosen him *from among others*. "Then if I had not come into a certain city, if I had not visited the home of so and so, you would never

1. Translated literally, "can tumble three times."

have known me, you wouldn't have loved me?" This thought grieves the lover; his love becomes one love among others and is limited by the beloved's facticity and by his own facticity as well as by the contingency of encounters. It becomes *love in the world,* an object which presupposes the world and which in turn can exist for others. What he is demanding he expresses by the awkward and vitiated phrases of "fatalism." He says, "We were made for each other," or again he uses the expression "soul mate." But we must translate all this. The lover knows very well that "being made for each other" refers to an original choice. This choice can be God's, since he is the being who is absolute choice, but God here represents only the farthest possible limit of the demand for an absolute. Actually what the lover demands is that the beloved should make of him an absolute choice. This means that the beloved's being-in-the-world must be a being-as-loving. The upsurge of the beloved must be the beloved's free choice of the lover. And since the Other is the foundation of my being-as-object, I demand of him that the free upsurge of his being should have his choice of *me* as his unique and absolute end; that is, that he should choose to be for the sake of founding my object-state and my facticity.

Thus my facticity is *saved.* It is no longer this unthinkable and insurmountable given which I am fleeing; it is that for which the Other freely makes himself exist; it is as an end which he has given to himself. I have infected him with my facticity, but as it is in the form of freedom that he has been infected with it, he refers it back to me as a facticity taken up and consented to. He is the foundation of it in order that it may be his end. By means of this love I then have a different apprehension of my alienation and of my own facticity. My facticity—as for-others—is no longer a fact but a right. My existence *is* because it is *given a name.* I am because I give myself away. These beloved veins on my hands exist—beneficently. How good I am to have eyes, hair, eyebrows and to lavish them away tirelessly in an overflow of generosity to this tireless desire which the Other freely makes himself be. Whereas before being loved we were uneasy about that unjustified, unjustifiable protuberance which was our existence, whereas we felt ourselves "*de trop*," we now feel that our existence is taken up and willed even in its tiniest details by an absolute freedom which at the same time our existence conditions and which we ourselves will with our freedom. This is the basis for the joy of love when there is joy; we feel that our existence is justified.

By the same token if the beloved can love us, he is wholly ready to be assimilated by our freedom; for this being-loved which we desire is already the ontological proof applied to our being-for-others. Our objective essence implies the existence of the Other, and conversely it is the Other's freedom which founds our essence. If we could manage to interiorize the whole system, we should be our own foundation.

Such then is the real goal of the lover in so far as his love is an enterprise—i.e., a project of himself. This project is going to provoke a conflict. The beloved in fact apprehends the lover as one Other-as-object among others; that is, he perceives the lover on the ground of the world, transcends him, and utilizes him. The beloved is a *look*. He can not therefore employ his transcendence to fix an ultimate limit to his surpassings, nor can he employ his freedom to captivate itself. The beloved can not will to love. Therefore the lover must seduce the beloved, and his love can in no way be distinguished from the enterprise of seduction. In seduction I do not try to reveal my subjectivity to the Other. Moreover I could do so only by *looking at* the other; but by this look I should cause the Other's subjectivity to disappear, and it is exactly this which I want to assimilate. To seduce is to risk assuming my object-state completely for the Other; it is to put myself beneath his look and to make him look at me; it is to risk the danger of *being-seen* in order to effect a new departure and to appropriate the Other in and by means of my object-ness. I refuse to leave the level on which I make proof of my object-ness; it is on this level that I wish to engage in battle by making myself a *fascinating object*. In Part Two we defined fascination as a *state*. It is, we said, the non-ethic consciousness of being *nothing* in the presence of being. Seduction aims at producing in the Other the consciousness of his state of nothingness as he confronts the seductive object. By seduction I aim at constituting myself as a fullness of being and at making myself *recognized as such*. To accomplish this I constitute myself as a meaningful object. My acts must *point* in two directions: On the one hand, toward that which is wrongly called subjectivity and which is rather a depth of objective and hidden being; the act is not performed for itself only, but it points to an infinite, undifferentiated series of other real and possible acts which I give as constituting my objective, unperceived being. Thus I try to guide the transcendence which transcends me and to refer it to the infinity of my dead-possibilities precisely in order to be the unsurpassable and to the exact extent to which the only unsurpassable is the infinite. On the other hand, each of my acts tries to point to the great density of possible-world and must present me as bound to the vastest regions of the world. At the same time I *present* the world to the beloved, and I try to constitute myself as the necessary intermediary between her and the world; I manifest by my acts infinitely varied examples of my power over the world (money, position, "connections," *etc.*). In the first case I try to constitute myself as an infinity of depth, in the second case to identify myself with the world. Through these different procedures I propose myself as unsurpassable. This proposal could not be sufficient in itself; it is only a besieging of the Other. It can not take on value as fact without the consent of the Others' free-

dom, which I must capture by making it recognize itself as
nothingness in the face of my plenitude of absolute being.

Someone may observe that these various attempts at expression *presuppose* language. We shall not disagree with this.
But we shall say rather that they *are* language or, if you
prefer, a fundamental mode of language. For while psychological and historical problems exist with regard to the existence, the learning and the use of *a particular* language, there
is no special problem concerning what is called the discovery
or invention of language. Language is not a phenomenon
added on to being-for-others. It *is* originally being-for-others;
that is, it is the fact that a subjectivity experiences itself as an
object for the Other. In a universe of pure objects language
could under no circumstances have been "invented" since it
presupposes an original relation to another subject. In the
intersubjectivity of the for-others, it is not necessary to invent
language because it is already given in the recognition of the
Other. I *am* language. By the sole fact that whatever I may do,
my acts freely conceived and executed, my projects launched
toward possibilities have outside of them a meaning which
escapes me and which I experience. It is in this sense—and in
this sense only—that Heidegger is right in declaring that *I am
what I say.*[2] Language is not an instinct of the constituted
human creature, nor is it an invention of our subjectivity. But
neither does it need to be referred to the pure "being-outside-
of-self" of the *Dasein*. It forms part of the *human condition;* it

2. This formulation of Heidegger's position is that of A. de Waehlens.
La philosophie de Martin Heidegger. Louvain, 1942, p. 99. *Cf.* also
Heidegger's text, which he quotes: "Diese Bezeugung meint nicht hier
einen nachträglichen und beiher laufenden Ausdruck des Menschseins,
sondern sie macht das Dasein Menschen mit usw. (*Hölderlin und das
Wesen der Dichtung,* p. 6).

("This affirmation does not mean here an additional and supplementary
expression of human existence, but it does in the process make plain the
existence of man." Douglas Scott's translation. *Existence and Being,*
Chicago: Henry Regnery, 1949, p. 297.)

is originally the proof which a for-itself can make of its being-for-others, and finally it is the surpassing of this proof and the utilization of it toward possibilities which are my possibilities; that is, toward my possibilities of being this or that for the Other. Language is therefore not distinct from the recognition of the Other's existence. The Other's upsurge confronting me as a look makes language arise as the condition of my being. This primitive language is not necessarily seduction; we shall see other forms of it. Moreover we have noted that there is another primitive attitude confronting the Other and that the two succeed each other in a circle, each implying the other. But conversely seduction does not presuppose any earlier form of language; it is the complete realization of language. This means that language can be revealed entirely and at one stroke by seduction as a primitive mode of being of expression. Of course by language we mean all the phenomena of expression and not the articulated word, which is a derived and secondary mode whose appearance can be made the object of an historical study. Especially in seduction language does not *aim at giving to be known* but at causing to experience.

But in this first attempt to find a fascinating language I proceed blindly since I am guided only by the abstract and empty form of my object-state for·the Other. I can not even conceive what effect my gestures and attitudes will have since they will always be taken up and founded by a freedom which will surpass them and since they can have a meaning only if this freedom confers one on them. Thus the "meaning" of my expressions always escapes me. I never know exactly if I signify what I wish to signify nor even if I *am* signifying anything. It would be necessary that at the precise instant I should read in the Other what on principle is inconceivable. For lack of knowing what I actually express for the Other, I constitute my language as an incomplete phenomenon of flight outside myself. As soon as I express myself, I can only guess at the meaning of what I express—i.e., the meaning of what I am—since in this perspective to express and to be are one. The Other is always there, present and experienced as the one who gives to language its meaning. Each expression, each gesture, each word is on my side a concrete proof of the alienating reality of the Other. It is only the psychopath who can say, "someone has stolen my thought"—as in cases of psychoses of influence, for example.[3] The very fact of expression is a stealing of thought since thought needs the cooperation of an alienating freedom in order to be constituted as an object. That is why this first aspect of language—in so far as it is I who employ it for the Other—is *sacred*. The sacred object is an object which is in the world and which points to a transcendence beyond the world. Language reveals to me the freedom (the transcendence) of the one who listens to me in silence.

But at the same moment I remain for the Other a meaningful object—that which I have always been. There is no path which departing from my object-state can lead the Other to my transcendence. Attitudes, expressions, and words can only indicate to him other attitudes, other expressions, and other words. Thus language remains for him a simple property of a magical object—and this magical object itself. It is an action at a distance whose effect the Other exactly knows. Thus the word is *sacred* when I employ it and *magic* when the Other hears it. Thus I do not know my language any more than I know my body for the Other. I can not hear myself speak nor see myself smile. The problem of language is exactly parallel to the problem of bodies, and the description which is valid in one case is valid in the other.

Fascination, however, even if it were to produce a state of

3. Furthermore the psychosis of influence, like the majority of psychoses, is a special experience translated by myths, of a great metaphysical fact—here the fact of alienation. Even a madman in his own way realizes the human condition.

being-fascinated in the Other could not by itself succeed in producing love. We can be fascinated by an orator, by an actor, by a tightrope-walker, but this does not mean that we love him. To be sure we can not take our eyes off him, but he is still raised on the ground of the world, and fascination does not posit the fascinating object as the ultimate term of the transcendence. Quite the contrary, fascination *is* transcendence. When then will the beloved become in turn the lover?

The answer is easy: when the beloved projects being loved. By himself the Other-as-object never has enough strength to produce love. If love has for its ideal the appropriation of the Other qua Other (i.e., as a subjectivity which is looking at an object) this ideal can be projected only in terms of my encounter with the Other-as-subject, not with the Other-as-object. If the Other tries to seduce me by means of his object-state, then seduction can bestow upon the Other only the character of a *precious* object "to be possessed." Seduction will perhaps determine me to risk much to conquer the Other-as-object, but this desire to appropriate an object in the midst of the world should not be confused with love. Love therefore can be born in the beloved only from the proof which he makes of his alienation and his flight toward the Other. Still the beloved, if such is the case, will be transformed into a love only if he projects being loved; that is, if what he wishes to overcome is not a body but the Other's subjectivity as such. In fact the only way that he could conceive to realize this appropriation to make himself be loved. Thus it seems that to love is in essence the project of making oneself be loved. Hence this new contradiction and this new conflict: each of the lovers is entirely the captive of the Other inasmuch as each wishes to make himself loved by the Other to the exclusion of anyone else; but at the same time each one demands from the other a love which is not reducible to the "project of being-loved." What he demands in fact is that the Other without originally seeking to make himself be loved should have at once a contemplative and affective intuition of his beloved as the objective limit of his freedom, as the ineluctable and chosen foundation of his transcendence, as the totality of being and the supreme value. Love thus exacted from the other could not *ask for* anything; it is a pure engagement without reciprocity. Yet this love can not exist except in the form of a demand on the part of the lover.

The lover is held captive in a wholly different way. He is the captive of his very demand since love is the demand to be loved; he is a freedom which wills itself a body and which demands an outside, hence a freedom which imitates the flight toward the Other, a freedom which qua freedom lays claim to its alienation. The lover's freedom, in his very effort to make himself be loved as an object by the Other, is alienated by slipping into the body-for-others; that is, it is brought into existence with a dimension of flight toward the Other. It is the perpetual refusal to posit itself as pure selfness, for this affirmation of self as itself would involve the collapse of the Other as a look and the upsurge of the Other-as-object—hence a state of affairs in which the very possibility of being loved disappears since the Other is reduced to the dimension of objectivity. This refusal therefore constitutes freedom as dependent on the Other; and the Other as subjectivity becomes indeed an unsurpassable limit of the freedom of the for-itself, the goal and supreme end of the for-itself since the Other holds the key to its being. Here in fact we encounter the true ideal of love's enterprise: alienated freedom. But it is the one who wants to be loved who by the mere fact of wanting someone to love him alienates his freedom.

My freedom is alienated in the presence of the Other's pure subjectivity which founds my objectivity. It can never be alienated before the Other-as-object. In this form in fact the beloved's alienation, of which the lover dreams, would be contradictory since the beloved can found the being of the lover only by transcending it on principle toward other objects of the world; therefore this transcendence can constitute the object which it surpasses both as a transcended object and as an object limit of all transcendence. Thus each one of the lovers wants to be the object for which the Other's freedom is alienated in an original intuition; but this intuition which would be love in the true sense is only a contradictory ideal of the for-itself. Each one is alienated only to the exact extent to which he demands the alienation of the other. Each one wants the other to love him but does not take into account the fact that to love is to want to be loved and that thus by wanting the other to love him, he only wants the other to want to be loved in turn. Thus love relations are a system of indefinite reference—analogous to the pure "reflection-reflected" of consciousness—under the ideal standard of the value "love"; that is, in a fusion of consciousnesses in which each of them would preserve his otherness in order to found the other. This state of affairs is due to the fact that consciousnesses are separated by an insurmountable nothingness, a nothingness which is both the internal negation of the one by the other and a factual nothingness between the two internal negations. Love is a contradictory effort to surmount the factual negation while preserving the internal negation. I demand that the Other love me and I do everything possible to realize my project; but if the Other loves me, he radically deceives me by his very love. I demanded of him that he should found my being as a privileged object by maintaining himself as pure subjectivity confronting me; and as soon as he loves me he experiences me as subject and is swallowed up in his objectivity confronting my subjectivity.

The problem of my being-for-others remains therefore without solution. The lovers remain each one for himself in a total subjectivity; nothing comes to relieve them of their duty to make themselves exist each one for himself; nothing comes to relieve their contingency nor to save them from facticity. At least each one has succeeded in escaping danger from the Other's freedom—but altogether differently than he expected. He escapes not because the Other makes him be as the object-limit of his transcendence but because the Other experiences him as subjectivity and wishes to experience him only as such. Again the gain is perpetually compromised. At the start, each of the consciousnesses can at any moment free itself from its chains and suddenly contemplate the other as an *object*. Then the spell is broken; the Other becomes one mean among means. He is indeed an object for others as the lover desires but an object-as-tool, a perpetually transcended object. The illusion, the game of mirrors which makes the concrete reality of love, suddenly ceases. Later in the experience of love each consciousness seeks to shelter its being-for-others in the Other's freedom. This supposes that the other is beyond the world as pure subjectivity, as the absolute by which the world comes into being. But it suffices that the lovers should be looked *at* together by a third person in order for each one to experience not only his own objectivation but that of the other as well. Immediately the Other is no longer for me the absolute transcendence which founds me in my being; he is a transcendence-transcended, not by me but by another. My original relation to him—i.e., my relation of being the beloved for my lover, is fixed as a dead-possibility. It is no longer the experienced relation between a limiting object of all transcendence and the freedom which founds it; it is a love-as-object which is wholly alienated toward the third. Such is the true reason why lovers seek solitude. It is because the appearance of a third person, whoever he may be, is the destruction of their love. But factual solitude (e.g., we are alone in my room) is by no means a theoretical solitude. Even if nobody sees us, we exist for *all* consciousnesses and we are conscious of existing for all. The result is that love as a fundamental mode of being-for-others holds in its being-for-others the seed of its own destruction.

We have just defined the triple destructibility of love: in the first place it is, in essence, a deception and a reference to infinity since to love is to wish to be loved, hence to wish that the Other wish that I love him. A pre-ontological comprehension of this deception is given in the very impulse of love—hence the lover's perpetual dissatisfaction. It does not come, as is so often said, from the unworthiness of being loved but from an implicit comprehension of the fact that the amorous intuition is, as a fundamental-intuition, an ideal out of reach. The more I am loved, the more I lose my *being*, the more I am thrown back on my own responsibilities, on my own power to be. In the second place the Other's awakening is always possible; at any moment he can make me appear as an object—hence the lover's perpetual insecurity. In the third place love is an absolute which is perpetually *made relative* by others. One would have to be alone in the world with the beloved in order for love to preserve its character as an absolute axis of reference—hence the lover's perpetual shame (or pride—which here amounts to the same thing).

20. FROMM: Love and Economic Competition

Erich Fromm (1900–   ) was born in Frankfurt, Germany and received his doctorate from the University of Munich. From 1934 to 1939 he was associated with the International Institute for Social Research in New York. Since then he has been a faculty member and lecturer at several American colleges and universities including the National University of Mexico.

I

If love is a capacity of the mature, productive character, it follows that the capacity to love in an individual living in any given culture depends on the influence this culture has on the

SOURCE: Erich Fromm, "Love and Its Disintegration in Contemporary Western Society" and "The Practice of Love," in *The Art of Loving* (New York: Harper & Row, 1956), pp. 83–94, 128–133. Copyright © 1956 by Erich Fromm. Reprinted by permission of Harper & Row, Publishers, Inc. and George Allen & Unwin Ltd.

character of the average person. If we speak about love in contemporary Western culture, we mean to ask whether the social structure of Western civilization and the spirit resulting from it are conducive to the development of love. To raise the question is to answer it in the negative. No objective observer of our Western life can doubt, that love—brotherly love, motherly love, and erotic love—is a relatively rare phenomenon, and that its place is taken by a number of forms of pseudo-love which are in reality so many forms of the disintegration of love.

Capitalistic society is based on the principle of political freedom on the one hand, and of the market as the regulator of all economic, hence social relations, on the other. The commodity market determines the conditions under which commodities are exchanged, the labor market regulates the acquisition and sale of labor. Both useful things and useful human energy and skill are transformed into commodities which are exchanged without the use of force and without fraud under the conditions of the market. Shoes, useful and needed as they may be, have no economic value (exchange value) if there is no demand for them on the market; human energy and skill are without exchange value if there is no demand for them under existing market conditions. The owner of capital can buy labor and command it to work for the profitable investment of his capital. The owner of labor must sell it to capitalists under the existing market conditions, unless he is to starve. This economic structure is reflected in a hierarchy of values. Capital commands labor; amassed things, that which is dead, are of superior value to labor, to human powers, to that which is alive.

This has been the basic structure of capitalism since its beginning. But while it is still characteristic of modern capitalism, a number of factors have changed which give contemporary capitalism its specific qualities and which have a profound influence on the character structure of modern man. As the result of the development of capitalism we witness an ever-increasing process of centralization and concentration of capital. The large enterprises grow in size continuously, the smaller ones are squeezed out. The ownership of capital invested in these enterprises is more and more separated from the function of managing them. Hundreds of thousands of stockholders "own" the enterprise; a managerial bureaucracy which is well paid, but which does not own the enterprise, manages it. This bureaucracy is less interested in making maximum profits than in the expansion of the enterprise, and in their own power. The increasing concentration of capital and the emergence of a powerful managerial bureaucracy are paralleled by the development of the labor movement. Through the unionization of labor, the individual worker does not have to bargain on the labor market by and for himself; he is united in big labor unions, also led by a powerful bureaucracy which represents him vis-à-vis the industrial colossi. The initiative has been shifted, for better or worse, in the fields of capital as well as in those of labor, from the individual to the bureaucracy. An increasing number of people cease to be independent and become dependent on the managers of the great economic empires.

Another decisive feature resulting from this concentration of capital, and characteristic of modern capitalism, lies in the specific way of the organization of work. Vastly centralized enterprises with a radical division of labor lead to an organization of work where the individual loses his individuality, where he becomes an expendable cog in the machine. The human problem of modern capitalism can be formulated in this way:

Modern capitalism needs men who co-operate smoothly and in large numbers; who want to consume more and more; and whose tastes are standardized and can be easily influenced and anticipated. It needs men who feel free and independent, not subject to any authority or principle or conscience—yet willing to be commanded, to do what is expected of them, to fit into the social machine without friction; who can be guided without force, led without leaders, prompted without aim— except the one to make good, to be on the move, to function, to go ahead.

What is the outcome? Modern man is alienated from himself, from his fellow men, and from nature. He has been transformed into a commodity, experiences his life forces as an investment which must bring him the maximum profit obtainable under existing market conditions. Human relations are essentially those of alienated automatons, each basing his security on staying close to the herd, and not being different in thought, feeling or action. While everybody tries to be as close as possible to the rest, everybody remains utterly alone, pervaded by the deep sense of insecurity, anxiety and guilt which always results when human separateness cannot be overcome. Our civilization offers many palliatives which help people to be consciously unaware of this aloneness: first of all the strict routine of bureaucratized, mechanical work, which helps people to remain unaware of their most fundamental human desires, of the longing for transcendence and unity. Inasmuch as the routine alone does not succeed in this, man overcomes his unconscious despair by the routine of amusement, the passive consumption of sounds and sights offered by the amusement industry; furthermore by the satisfaction of buying ever new things, and soon exchanging them for others. Modern man is actually close to the picture Huxley describes in his *Brave New World:* well fed, well clad, satisfied sexually, yet without self, without any except the most superficial contact with his fellow men, guided by the slogans which Huxley formulated so succinctly, such as: "When the individual feels, the community reels"; or "Never put off till tomorrow the fun you can have today," or, as the crowning statement: "Everybody is happy nowadays." Man's happiness today consists in "having fun." Having fun lies in the satisfaction of consuming and "taking in" commodities, sights, food, drinks, cigarettes, people, lectures, books, movies—all are consumed, swallowed. The world is one great object for our appetite, a big apple, a big bottle, a big breast; we are the sucklers, the eternally expectant ones, the hopeful ones—and the eternally disappointed ones. Our character is geared to exchange and to receive, to barter and to consume; everything, spiritual as well as material objects, becomes an object of exchange and of consumption.

The situation as far as love is concerned corresponds, as it has to by necessity, to this social character of modern man. Automatons cannot love; they can exchange their "personality packages" and hope for a fair bargain. One of the most significant expressions of love, and especially of marriage with this alienated structure, is the idea of the "team." In any number of articles on happy marriage, the ideal described is that of the smoothly functioning team. This description is not too different from the idea of a smoothly functioning employee; he should be "reasonably independent," co-operative, tolerant, and at the same time ambitious and aggressive. Thus, the marriage counselor tells us, the husband should "understand" his wife and be helpful. He should comment favorably on her new dress, and on a tasty dish. She, in turn, should understand when he comes home tired and disgruntled, she should listen attentively when he talks about his business troubles, should not be angry but understanding when he forgets her birthday. All this kind of relationship amounts to is the well-oiled relationship between two persons who remain strangers all their lives, who never arrive at a "central relationship," but who treat each other with courtesy and who attempt to make each other feel better.

In this concept of love and marriage the main emphasis is on finding a refuge from an otherwise unbearable sense of aloneness. In "love" one has found, at last, a haven from aloneness. One forms an alliance of two against the world, and this egoism *à deux* is mistaken for love and intimacy.

The emphasis on team spirit, mutual tolerance and so forth is a relatively recent development. It was preceded, in the years after the First World War, by a concept of love in which mutual sexual satisfaction was supposed to be the basis for satisfactory love relations, and especially for a happy marriage. It was believed that the reasons for the frequent unhappiness in marriage were to be found in that the marriage partners had not made a correct "sexual adjustment"; the reason for this fault was seen in the ignorance regarding "correct" sexual behavior, hence in the faulty sexual technique of one or both partners. In order to "cure" this fault, and to help the unfortunate couples who could not love each other, many books gave instructions and counsel concerning the correct sexual behavior, and promised implicitly or explicitly that happiness and love would follow. The underlying idea was that love is the child of sexual pleasure, and that if two people learn how to satisfy each other sexually, they will love each other. It fitted the general illusion of the time to assume that using the right techniques is the solution not only to technical problems of industrial production, but of all human problems as well. One ignored the fact that the contrary of the underlying assumption is true.

Love is not the result of adequate sexual satisfaction, but sexual happiness—even the knowledge of the so-called sexual technique—is the result of love. If aside from everyday observation this thesis needed to be proved, such proof can be found in ample material of psychoanalytic data. The study of the most frequent sexual problems—frigidity in women, and the more or less severe forms of psychic impotence in men—

shows that the cause does not lie in a lack of knowledge of the right technique, but in the inhibitions which make it impossible to love. Fear of or hatred for the other sex are at the bottom of those difficulties which prevent a person from giving himself completely, from acting spontaneously, from trusting the sexual partner in the immediacy and directness of physical closeness. If a sexually inhibited person can emerge from fear or hate, and hence become capable of loving, his or her sexual problems are solved. If not, no amount of knowledge about sexual techniques will help.

But while the data of psychoanalytic therapy point to the fallacy of the idea that knowledge of the correct sexual technique leads to sexual happiness and love, the underlying assumption that love is the concomitant of mutual sexual satisfaction was largely influenced by the theories of Freud. For Freud, love was basically a sexual phenomenon. "Man having found by experience that sexual (genital) love afforded him his greatest gratification, so that it became in fact a prototype of all happiness to him, must have been thereby impelled to seek his happiness further along the path of sexual relations, to make genital eroticism the central point of his life." The experience of brotherly love is, for Freud, an outcome of sexual desire, but with the sexual instinct being transformed into an impulse with "inhibited aim." "Love with an inhibited aim was indeed originally full of sensual love, and in man's unconscious mind is so still." As far as the feeling of fusion, of oneness ("oceanic feeling"), which is the essence of mystical experience and the root of the most intense sense of union with one other person or with one's fellow men, is concerned, it was interpreted by Freud as a pathological phenomenon, as a regression to a state of an early "limitless narcissism."

It is only one step further that for Freud love is in itself an irrational phenomenon. The difference between irrational love, and love as an expression of the mature personality does not exist for him. He pointed out in a paper on transference love, that transference love is essentially not different from the "normal" phenomenon of love. Falling in love always verges on the abnormal, is always accompanied by blindness to reality, compulsiveness, and is a transference from love objects of childhood. Love as a rational phenomenon, as the crowning achievement of maturity, was, to Freud, no subject matter for investigation, since it had no real existence.

However, it would be a mistake to overestimate the influence of Freud's ideas on the concept that love is the result of sexual attraction, or rather that it is the *same* as sexual satisfaction, reflected in conscious feeling. Essentially the causal nexus proceeds the other way around. Freud's ideas were partly influenced by the spirit of the nineteenth century; partly they became popular through the prevailing spirit of the years after the First World War. Some of the factors which influenced both the popular and the Freudian concepts were, first, the reaction against the strict mores of the Victorian age. The second factor determining Freud's theories lies in the prevailing concept of man, which is based on the structure of capitalism. In order to prove that capitalism corresponded to the natural needs of man, one had to show that man was by nature competitive and full of mutual hostility. While economists "proved" this in terms of the insatiable desire for economic gain, and the Darwinists in terms of the biological law of the survival of the fittest, Freud came to the same result by the assumption that man is driven by a limitless desire for the sexual conquest of all women, and that only the pressure of society prevented man from acting on his desires. As a result men are necessarily jealous of each other, and this mutual jealousy and competition would continue even if all social and economic reasons for it would disappear.

Eventually, Freud was largely influenced in his thinking by the type of materialism prevalent in the nineteenth century.

One believed that the substratum of all mental phenomena was to be found in physiological phenomena; hence love, hate, ambition, jealousy were explained by Freud as so many outcomes of various forms of the sexual instinct. He did not see that the basic reality lies in the totality of human existence, first of all in the human situation common to all men, and secondly in the practice of life determined by the specific structure of society. (The decisive step beyond this type of materialism was taken by Marx in his "historical materialism," in which not the body, nor an instinct like the need for food or possession, serves as the key to the understanding of man, but the total life process of man, his "practice of life.") According to Freud, the full and uninhibited satisfaction of all instinctual desires would create mental health and happiness. But the obvious clinical facts demonstrate that men—and women— who devote their lives to unrestricted sexual satisfaction do not attain happiness, and very often suffer from severe neurotic conflicts or symptoms. The complete satisfaction of all instinctual needs is not only not a basis for happiness, it does not even guarantee sanity. Yet Freud's idea could only have become so popular in the period after the First World War because of the changes which had occurred in the spirit of capitalism, from the emphasis on saving to that on spending, from self-frustration as a means for economic success to consumption as the basis for an ever-widening market, and as the main satisfaction for the anxious, automatized individual. Not to postpone the satisfaction of any desire became the main tendency in the sphere of sex as well as in that of all material consumption.

It is interesting to compare the concepts of Freud, which correspond to the spirit of capitalism as it existed, yet unbroken, around the beginning of this century, with the theoretical concepts of one of the most brilliant contemporary psychoanalysts, the late H. S. Sullivan. In Sullivan's psychoanalytic system we find, in contrast to Freud's, a strict division between sexuality and love.

What is the meaning of love and intimacy in Sullivan's concept? "Intimacy is that type of situation involving two people which permits validation of all components of personal worth. Validation of personal worth requires a type of relationship which I call collaboration, by which I mean clearly formulated adjustments of one's behavior to the expressed needs of the other person in pursuit of increasingly identical— that is, more and more nearly mutual satisfactions, and in the maintenance of increasingly similar security operations." If we free Sullivan's statement from its somewhat involved language, the essence of love is seen in a situation of collaboration, in which two people feel: "We play according to the rules of the game to preserve our prestige and feeling of superiority and merit."

Just as Freud's concept of love is a description of the experience of the patriarchal male in terms of nineteenth-century capitalism, Sullivan's description refers to the experience of the alienated, marketing personality of the twentieth century. It is a description of an "egotism à *deux*," of two people pooling their common interests, and standing together against a hostile and alienated world. Actually his definition of intimacy is in principle valid for the feeling of any co-operating team, in which everybody "adjusts his behavior to the expressed needs of the other person in the pursuit of common aims" (it is remarkable that Sullivan speaks here of *expressed* needs, when the least one could say about love is that it implies a reaction to *unexpressed* needs between two people).

Love as mutual sexual satisfaction, and love as "teamwork" and as a haven from aloneness, are the two "normal" forms of the disintegration of love in modern Western society, the socially patterned pathology of love. There are many individualized forms of the pathology of love, which result in conscious suffering and which are considered neurotic by psychiatrists and an increasing number of laymen alike. . . .

II

One attitude, indispensable for the practice of the art of loving, which thus far has been mentioned only implicitly should be discussed explicitly since it is basic for the practice of love: *activity*. I have said before that by activity is not meant "doing something," but an inner activity, the productive use of one's powers. Love is an activity; if I love, I am in a constant state of active concern with the loved person, but not only with him or her. For I shall become incapable of relating myself actively to the loved person if I am lazy, if I am not in a constant state of awareness, alertness, activity. Sleep is the only proper situation for inactivity; the state of awakeness is one in which laziness should have no place. The paradoxical situation with a vast number of people today is that they are half asleep when awake, and half awake when asleep, or when they want to sleep. To be fully awake is the condition for not being bored, or being boring—and indeed, not to be bored or boring is one of the main conditions for loving. To be active in thought, feeling, with one's eyes and ears, throughout the day, to avoid inner laziness, be it in the form of being receptive, hoarding, or plain wasting one's time, is an indispensable condition for the practice of the art of loving. It is an illusion to believe that one can separate life in such a way that one is productive in the sphere of love and unproductive in all other spheres. Productiveness does not permit of such a division of labor. The capacity to love demands a state of intensity, awakeness, enhanced vitality, which can only be the result of a productive and active orientation in many other spheres of life. If one is not productive in other spheres, one is not productive in love either.

The discussion of the art of loving cannot be restricted to

the personal realm of acquiring and developing those characteristics and attitudes which have been described in this chapter. It is inseparably connected with the social realm. If to love means to have a loving attitude toward everybody, if love is a character trait, it must necessarily exist in one's relationship not only with one's family and friends, but toward those with whom one is in contact through one's work, business, profession. There is no "division of labor" between love for one's own and love for strangers. On the contrary, the condition for the existence of the former is the existence of the latter. To take this insight seriously means indeed a rather drastic change in one's social relations from the customary ones. While a great deal of lip service is paid to the religious ideal of love of one's neighbor, our relations are actually determined, at their very best, by the principle of *fairness*. Fairness meaning not to use fraud and trickery in the exchange of commodities and services, and in the exchange of feelings. "I give you as much as you give me," in material goods as well as in love, is the prevalent ethical maxim in capitalist society. It may even be said that the development of fairness ethics is the particular ethical contribution of capitalist society.

The reasons for this fact lie in the very nature of capitalist society. In precapitalist societies, the exchange of goods was determined either by direct force, by tradition, or by personal bonds of love or friendship. In capitalism, the all-determining factor is the exchange on the market. Whether we deal with the commodity market, the labor market, or the market of services, each person exchanges whatever he has to sell for that which he wants to acquire under the conditions of the market, without the use of force or fraud.

Fairness ethics lend themselves to confusion with the ethics of the Golden Rule. The maxim "to do unto others as you would like them to do unto you" can be interpreted as meaning "be fair in your exchange with others." But actually, it was formulated originally as a more popular version of the Biblical "Love thy neighbor as thyself." Indeed, the Jewish-Christian norm of brotherly love is entirely different from fairness ethics. It means to love your neighbor, that is, to feel responsible for and one with him, while fairness ethics means *not* to feel responsible, and one, but distant and separate; it means to respect the rights of your neighbor, but not to love him. It is no accident that the Golden Rule has become the most popular religious maxim today; because it can be interpreted in terms of fairness ethics it is the one religious maxim which everybody understands and is willing to practice. But the practice of love must begin with recognizing the difference between fairness and love.

Here, however, an important question arises. If our whole social and economic organization is based on each one seeking his own advantage, if it is governed by the principle of egotism tempered only by the ethical principle of fairness, how can one do business, how can one act within the framework of existing society and at the same time practice love? Does the latter not imply giving up all one's secular concerns and sharing the life of the poorest? This question has been raised and answered in a radical way by the Christian monks, and by persons like Tolstoi, Albert Schweitzer, and Simone Weil. There are others[1] who share the opinion of the basic incompatibility between love and normal secular life within our society. They arrive at the result that to speak of love today means only to participate in the general fraud; they claim that only a martyr or a mad person can love in the world of today, hence that all discussion of love is nothing but preaching. This very respectable viewpoint lends itself readily to a rationalization of cynicism. Actually it is shared implicitly by the average person who feels "I would like to be a good Christian—but I

1. Cf. Herbert Marcuse "The Social Implications of Psychoanalytic Revisionism," *Dissent* (summer, 1955).

would have to starve if I meant it seriously." This "radicalism" results in moral nihilism. Both the "radical thinkers" and the average person are unloving automatons and the only difference between them is that the latter is not aware of it, while the former knows it and recognizes the "historical necessity" of this fact.

I am of the conviction that the answer of the absolute incompatibility of love and "normal" life is correct only in an abstract sense. The *principle* underlying capitalistic society and the *principle* of love are incompatible. But modern society seen concretely is a complex phenomenon. A salesman of a useless commodity, for instance, cannot function economically without lying; a skilled worker, a chemist, or a physician can. Similarly, a farmer, a worker, a teacher, and many a type of businessman can try to practice love without ceasing to function economically. Even if one recognizes the principle of capitalism as being incompatible with the principle of love, one must admit that "capitalism" is in itself a complex and constantly changing structure which still permits of a good deal of nonconformity and of personal latitude.

In saying this, however, I do not wish to imply that we can expect the present social system to continue indefinitely, and at the same time to hope for the realization of the ideal of love for one's brother. People capable of love, under the present system, are necessarily the exceptions; love is by necessity a marginal phenomenon in present-day Western society. Not so much because many occupations would not permit of a loving attitude, but because the spirit of a production-centered, commodity-greedy society is such that only the nonconformist can defend himself successfully against it. Those who are seriously concerned with love as the only rational answer to the problem of human existence must, then, arrive at the conclusion that important and radical changes in our social structure are necessary, if love is to become a social and not a highly individualistic, marginal phenomenon. The direction of such changes can, within the scope of this book, only be hinted at.[2] Our society is run by a managerial bureaucracy, by professional politicians; people are motivated by mass suggestion, their aim is producing more and consuming more, as purposes in themselves. All activities are subordinated to economic goals, means have become ends; man is an automaton—well fed, well clad, but without any ultimate concern for that which is his peculiarly human quality and function. If man is to be able to love, he must be put in his supreme place. The economic machine must serve him, rather than he serve it. He must be enabled to share experience, to share work, rather than, at best, share in profits. Society must be organized in such a way that man's social, loving nature is not separated from his social existence, but becomes one with it. If it is true, as I have tried to show, that love is the only sane and satisfactory answer to the problem of human existence, then any society which excludes, relatively, the development of love, must in the long run perish of its own contradiction with the basic necessities of human nature. Indeed, to speak of love is not "preaching," for the simple reason that it means to speak of the ultimate and real need in every human being. That this need has been obscured does not mean that it does not exist. To analyze the nature of love is to discover its general absence today and to criticize the social conditions which are responsible for this absence. To have faith in the possibility of love as a social and not only exceptional-individual phenomenon, is a rational faith based on the insight into the very nature of man.

2. In *The Sane Society* (New York: Rinehart & Company, 1955), I have tried to deal with this problem in detail.

V

Sex, Morality and Society

In Western society questions concerning sex are closely related to views of morality. Any human action or activity can involve the issue of its morality if it occurs in some particular form or is part of some set of circumstances, the nature of which causes us to regard it in moral terms. Activities involved in such areas as work, business, the education of children, leisure, etc. can be discussed in morally neutral terms. We can refer to these activities and discuss their meaning in language that does not have direct moral connotations and that does not involve us in moral dispute. Ultimately all such activities, since they make up the human world, involve questions of value and are the subjects of great moral concern, but we can initially discuss them without specific moral direction to our speech. This is not true of sex.

When I speak of sex and the types of human sexual relationships, the language which I use takes me in one moral direction or another. If I speak of sexual activity in terms of marriage, monogamy, fidelity, etc., I am speaking the language of morality and convention. But if I wish to speak more broadly and include sexual relationships that lie outside these terms, I am suddenly involved in the language of depravity and deviation. The terms that lie outside the complex of marriage, monogamy and fidelity are terms such as adultery, fornication, sodomy, etc., each of which designates a particular type of sexual act or union and at the same time designates it as immoral or unnatural, and under some legal structures, it may also designate it as criminal. Behind this division in language is a model of the sex act and the relationship between the sexes that has its roots in the Judeo-Christian tradition (see Section II above).

At the center of this Judeo-Christian model is the view that the primary function for the sex act and the reason for its existence is its role in human procreation. Procreation is to take place only in terms of a lifetime bond of marriage between a man and a woman. The coupling of the marriage structure with the procreative model of the sex act provides the basis for a social framework through which the man and the woman assume particular economic roles. In this framework the roles of man-as-provider and woman-as-breeder are established as economic enactments of the spiritual doctrine of sex-as-procreation. The marriage structure is maintained by regarding all sexual acts outside the marital union or prior to it as sins and any sexual acts which are antithetical to procreation such as masturbation, homosexuality or sodomy as against nature and as criminal.

This entire model of sexual behavior and the marriage relationship, including the various modifications and liberalizations it has undergone since its exposition in Medieval Christian thought, has been called into question in modern thought and has broken down as a moral guide in large sectors of contemporary life. There are two questions which are central to the challenge of this traditional model of sexual ethics. One involves the right of society to legally regulate the sexual behavior of its members. The other involves the question of women's rights.

A central question in contemporary social and legal thought has involved the right of the society to have laws against abortion, homosexual and sodomous acts, adultery, fornication and other acts in which persons willfully engage as a result of their personal morality. Laws against such acts have behind them the Judeo-Christian model of the sex act as procreative and the fulfillment of its function through marriage. The circle which this model draws around man's sexual nature and which defines the forms in which he can morally exercise his sexual powers and those in which he morally cannot depends for its authority on a metaphysical and scriptural view of the nature of things and man's place in it. Laws which make acts such as adultery, sodomy, etc. crimes have for their moral justification the Judeo-Christian model of the sex act. The Judeo-Christian view of sexual morality has as its justification its theology of the ultimate nature of God and the world. This moral doctrine is overlaid with a spiritual doctrine and underlaid with legal codifications.

Counter to the Judeo-Christian model of sexual morality in contemporary Western society is the view that regards sex and sexual pleasure as natural to man and does not regard man's sexual activity as having intrinsically moral and immoral forms. This view does not derive its authority from a theological interpretation of the nature of things. It establishes its concept of moral and immoral actions through the evaluation of the effects any action has on others. This view is founded on the notion that persons in a society should be allowed to maximize the satisfaction of their desires and act as they see fit as long as their actions are not detrimental to the society as a whole or to the well-being of other individuals.

On this view sexual morality becomes largely the concern of the individual. The society does not have the need nor the right to make laws which regulate personal morality of any kind. However, on this view, society does not give up the right to make and enforce laws governing sexual actions that involve the well-being of others. Thus it can make laws in regard to rape and child molestation; it has the right to do so for the same reasons it can make laws against murder, theft and disturbance of the peace. This view generally grows out of the realization that laws which prohibit acts such as adultery, fornication and sodomy create "crimes without victims." That is, they are crimes in which either the "criminal" is himself the victim or his "victim" is himself a willing partner in the "crime." Sexual acts of this sort are not crimes according to any ordinary, socially practical criteria. They are only crimes if the Judeo-Christian model of sexual morality is accepted. They are thus seen as crimes because they are first seen as sinful or unnatural.

The question of women's rights is closely related to the question of the right of society to regulate personal morality as it grows out of another aspect of the Judeo-Christian model. The Judeo-Christian conception of the sex act in terms of procreation fosters the marriage relationship of man-as-provider and woman-as-breeder. On this conception of the sex act the man is seen as the active agent and the woman as the passive receiver. The woman is seen as a necessary adjunct part of the act of procreation initiated by the man, but she is not an equal partner in it. Society reflects this conception of roles in the sex act in the laws and customs that define the rights and social status of men and women. Men being the active agents in the sex act are the active agents economically, and as providers they enjoy particular status in society; e.g., although it is improper and often illegal to commit adultery, it is regarded as more serious for a woman to commit adultery than a man. Women, being conceived as the passive figure in the sex act, are assigned a passive role in society in which the realities of the social world are to be experienced by her through her husband-provider and family. Men define the cultural and economic realities of society, and women find themselves incorporated in it and assigned to particular roles and occupations.

The question of women's rights and the economic position of women in society has appeared with varying degrees of intensity as a social issue since the nineteenth century. The achievement of women's rights would seem to be tied to the overcoming of the Judeo-Christian model of the sex act which supports the roles of man-as-provider and female-as-breeder. The question of women's rights is closely tied to the question of society's legislation of sexual morality since the legislation of sex roles is involved in the legislation of sexual morality. The fundamental right that lies behind the question of women's rights is perhaps most obviously the *right* to have questions of right in a society resolved apart from its concepts of sex. However, behind the legal response to the question of women's rights is the redefinition of the actual role of women in society and in the sex act which would entail the building of a new set of identities for both man and woman in Western society.

The selections presented in this section are from the Marquis de Sade, Bertrand Russell, Simone de Beauvoir and Rollo May and show various perspectives on the questions of the relationship of sexual morality and society and the role of the sexes in it. De Sade is considerably separated in time from the other figures. Although de Sade's work dates from the late eighteenth century, it expresses with clarity a position regarding radical sexual freedom, parts of which are advocated today, but usually not with as much wit and literary ability as are present in de Sade's work.

The selection from de Sade is from *Philosophy in the Bedroom*. The work as a whole consists of a series of dialogues between a number of sexually liberated persons who alternate between engaging in sex acts of all kinds and discussing their pleasures and the nature of sex generally. The selection is part of a long discourse which occurs in the fifth dialogue in which de Sade proposes the principles upon which a truly republican state could be founded in which rationality and sensual pleasure would prevail. At the core of de Sade's theory is the concept of libertinage. Libertinage is based on the concept that man is essentially a pleasure-seeking being and is especially a seeker of sexual pleasure. De Sade argues that sodomy, fornication and homosexuality cannot be considered as acts which go against nature as it is nature which permits them and puts the inclination to engage in such acts in us in the beginning. De Sade asks the question: how can a "crime against nature" be committed when nature itself is the ultimate instigator of such "crimes"?

Because the enjoyment of sexual pleasure is natural to man, de Sade maintains, a true republic should be organized around the "right of enjoyment." All men should have a right to enjoy all women, and all women should have the right to indulge themselves in indefinite amounts of sensual pleasures. In fact, de Sade argues, in such a republic the woman who indulges the most in such pleasures will be regarded as the most virtuous. De Sade is quite modern in proposing the same, or at least similar, sexual rights for women as for men in his theory of libertinage. He is, however, even more radical than most current views on the equality of the sexes in that he would do away with concern for the paternity of children. In this he is quite close to Plato's view in the *Republic* in which one of the things "friends shall have in common" is their children (see

Section I above). De Sade is quite contemporary in his view that the state should not regulate the sexual morality of individuals. His view, however, is more extreme than contemporary views in that on his conception of the state licentiousness becomes a duty or at least a virtue.

The selection from Russell is the concluding chapter of *Marriage and Morals* which was first published in 1929. Some of his comments seem dated, but some are ahead of their time. His comment that contraceptives will become sufficiently perfected so that women can have sexual intercourse without virtually any risk of pregnancy is today a reality. But his view that the state will take over the care of children and the family will dissolve has not completely occurred, although something of this has developed in the form of child care programs in northern Europe, the United States and the U.S.S.R. More important than Russell's specific comments, which must be read against the less permissive conditions of the society of his day, is the tone and direction of his approach. Russell's approach insists that whatever sexual ethic a society is to have, it should not be simply one which is unreflectively taken over from past custom. It should be something which the society deliberately holds and which fits with the general relationships which it would like to see hold between all persons. Russell's position indicates that sexual ethics cannot be separated from ethics generally and must be considered as simply a particular part of it.

The selection from de Beauvoir is from *The Second Sex* which although published in 1949 is the most thorough and theoretically deep study done to date on the position of women in modern society. At the center of de Beauvoir's study is the argument that the secondary place women occupy in relation to men throughout the history of society is not due to their having natural "feminine" characteristics which suit them of necessity to occupy this position. Rather it is due to the social, educational and cultural structures of Western society, all of which interact to reinforce the patriarchal ideal. In the face of these structures, de Beauvoir maintains, women have failed to take places of human dignity as free beings alongside men, although there are signs in contemporary society that some women are coming to be able to do this. This is in large part because some women are able to achieve economic independence in contemporary society. De Beauvoir maintains that all civil liberties for women "remain theoretical as long as they are unaccompanied by economic freedom." She sees the economically independent woman as the vanguard in the liberation of women and the redefinition of the sexual roles of men and women in society.

The selection from May is taken from *Love and Will*. In this work May is concerned to raise questions about the possibilities for good and evil in contemporary technological life. May is ultimately concerned to explore ways in which the humane qualities of man's existence can be enhanced. The selection presents part of May's analysis of the problems of contemporary life, in particular the paradoxes or ambiguities of the contemporary experience of sex which revolve around the increase of internal anxieties about sex, emphasis on sexual technique and what May calls the "new puritanism." This selection from May leaves the question of sex, the relations between the sexes and the place of love in human affairs on a problematic note. It is, however, in such problematic form that these questions affect contemporary life. No solutions currently hold themselves out to us as simply for the taking. All roads toward their solution or analysis of them must begin with a feeling for their deeply problematic character and the way in which they have been problems in Western morality. As ethical questions they are open to any man's scrutiny, and their solutions, in the end, must be particular solutions developed by particular persons.

21. DE SADE: The Libertine—
Absolute Sexual Freedom

Marquis de Sade (1740–1814), whose full name was Donatien-Alphonse-Francois de Sade, is one of the most controversial figures in the history of the literature on sex. He was imprisoned for beating a girl named Rose Keller on Easter Sunday 1768, and as a result of other incidents of orgiastic violence, he spent various subsequent periods of his life in prison. His works are the result of considerable literary brilliance and are notorious for their unqualified advocation of debauchery and licentiousness. The term "sadism" takes its origin from his name.

First of all, what right have you to assert that women ought to be exempted from the blind submission to men's caprices Nature dictates? and, secondly, by what other right do you defend

SOURCE: Marquis de Sade, *Marquis de Sade: The Complete Justine, Philosophy in the Bedroom, and Other Writings,* comp. and trans. Richard Seaver and Austryn Wainhouse (New York: Grove Press, 1965), pp. 318–326. Copyright © 1965 by Richard Seaver and Austryn Wainhouse. Reprinted by permission of Grove Press, Inc.

their subjugation to a continence impossible to their physical structure and of perfect uselessness to their honor?

I will treat each of these questions separately.

It is certain, in a state of Nature, that women are born *vulguivaguous,* that is to say, are born enjoying the advantages of other female animals and belonging, like them and without exception, to all males; such were, without any doubt, both the primary laws of Nature and the only institutions of those earliest societies into which men gathered. *Self-interest, egoism,* and *love* degraded these primitive attitudes, at once so simple and so natural; one thought oneself enriched by taking a woman to wife, and with her the goods of her family: there we find satisfied the first two feelings I have just indicated; still more often, this woman was taken by force, and thereby one became attached to her—there we find the other of the motives in action, and in every case, injustice.

Never may an act of possession be exercised upon a free being; the exclusive possession of a woman is no less unjust than the possession of slaves; all men are born free, all have equal rights: never should we lose sight of those principles; according to which never may there be granted to one sex the legitimate right to lay monopolizing hands upon the other, and never may one of these sexes, or classes, arbitrarily possess the other. Similarly, a woman existing in the purity of Nature's laws cannot allege, as justification for refusing herself to someone who desires her, the love she bears another, because such a response is based upon exclusion, and no man may be excluded from the having of a woman as of the moment it is clear she definitely belongs to all men. The act of possession can only be exercised upon a chattel or an animal, never upon an individual who resembles us, and all the ties which can bind a woman to a man are quite as unjust as illusory.

If then it becomes incontestable that we have received from Nature the right indiscriminately to express our wishes to all women, it likewise becomes incontestable that we have the right to compel their submission, not exclusively, for I should then be contradicting myself, but temporarily.[1] It cannot be denied that we have the right to decree laws that compel woman to yield to the flames of him who would have her; violence itself being one of that right's effects, we can employ it lawfully. Indeed! has Nature not proven that we have that right, by bestowing upon us the strength needed to bend women to our will?

It is in vain women seek to bring to their defense either modesty or their attachment to other men; these illusory grounds are worthless; earlier, we saw how contemptible and factitious is the sentiment of modesty. Love, which may be termed the *soul's madness*, is no more a title by which their constancy may be justified: love, satisfying two persons only, the beloved and the loving, cannot serve the happiness of others, and it is for the sake of the happiness of everyone, and not for an egotistical and privileged happiness, that women have been given to us. All men therefore have an equal right of enjoyment of all women; therefore, there is no man who, in keeping with natural law, may lay claim to a unique and personal right over a woman. The law which will oblige them to prostitute themselves, as often and in any manner we wish, in the houses of debauchery we referred to a moment ago, and which will coerce them if they balk, punish them if they shirk or dawdle, is thus one of the most equitable of laws, against which there can be no sane or rightful complaint.

1. Let it not be said that I contradict myself here, and that after having established, at some point further above, that we have no right to bind a woman to ourselves, I destroy those principles when I declare now we have the right to constrain her; I repeat, it is a question of enjoyment only, not of property: I have no right of possession upon that fountain I find by the road, but I have certain rights to its use; I have the right to avail myself of the limpid water it offers my thirst; similarly, I have no real right of possession over such-and-such a woman, but I have incontestable rights to the enjoyment of her; I have the right to force from her this enjoyment, if she refuses me it for whatever the cause may be.

A man who would like to enjoy whatever woman or girl will henceforth be able, if the laws you promulgate are just, to have her summoned at once to duty at one of the houses; and there, under the supervision of the matrons of that temple of Venus, she will be surrendered to him, to satisfy, humbly and with submission, all the fancies in which he will be pleased to indulge with her, however strange or irregular they may be, since there is no extravagance which is not in Nature, none which she does not acknowledge as her own. There remains but to fix the woman's age; now, I maintain it cannot be fixed without restricting the freedom of a man who desires a girl of any given age.

He who has the right to eat the fruit of a tree may assuredly pluck it ripe or green, according to the inspiration of his taste. But, it will be objected, there is an age when the man's proceedings would be decidedly harmful to the girl's well-being. This consideration is utterly without value; once you concede me the proprietary right of enjoyment, that right is independent of the effects enjoyment produces; from this moment on, it becomes one, whether this enjoyment be beneficial or damaging to the object which must submit itself to me. Have I not already proven that it is legitimate to force the woman's will in this connection? and that immediately she excites the desire to enjoy she has got to expose herself to this enjoyment, putting all egotistical sentiments quite aside? The issue of her well-being, I repeat, is irrelevant. As soon as concern for this consideration threatens to detract from or enfeeble the enjoyment of him who desires her, and who has the right to appropriate her, this consideration for age ceases to exist; for what the object may experience, condemned by Nature and by the law to slake momentarily the other's thirst, is nothing to the point; in this study, we are only interested in what agrees with him who desires. But we will redress the balance.

Yes, we will redress it; doubtless we ought to. These women

we have just so cruelly enslaved—there is no denying we must recompense them, and I come now to the second question I proposed to answer.

If we admit, as we have just done, that all women ought to be subjugated to our desires, we may certainly allow then ample satisfaction of theirs. Our laws must be favorable to their fiery temperament. It is absurd to locate both their honor and their virtue in the antinatural strength they employ to resist the penchants with which they have been far more profusely endowed than we; this injustice of manners is rendered more flagrant still since we contrive at once to weaken them by seduction, and then to punish them for yielding to all the efforts we have made to provoke their fall. All the absurdity of our manners, it seems to me, is graven in this shocking paradox, and this brief outline alone ought to awaken us to the urgency of exchanging them for manners more pure.

I say then that women, having been endowed with considerably more violent penchants for carnal pleasure than we, will be able to give themselves over to it wholeheartedly, absolutely free of all encumbering hymeneal ties, of all false notions of modesty, absolutely restored to a state of Nature; I want laws permitting them to give themselves to as many men as they see fit; I would have them accorded the enjoyment of all sexes and, as in the case of men, the enjoyment of all parts of the body; and under the special clause prescribing their surrender to all who desire them, there must be subjoined another guaranteeing them a similar freedom to enjoy all they deem worthy to satisfy them.

What, I demand to know, what dangers are there in this license? Children who will lack fathers? Ha! what can that matter in a republic where every individual must have no other dam than the nation, where everyone born is the motherland's child. And how much more they will cherish her, they who, never having known any but her, will comprehend from birth that it is from her alone all must be expected. Do not suppose you are fashioning good republicans so long as children, who ought to belong solely to the republic, remain immured in their families. By extending to the family, to a restricted number of persons, the portion of affection they ought to distribute amongst their brothers, they inevitably adopt those persons' sometimes very harmful prejudices; such children's opinions, their thoughts are particularized, malformed, and the virtues of a Man of the State become completely inaccessible to them. Finally abandoning their heart altogether to those by whom they have been given breath, they have no devotion left for what will cause them to mature, to understand, and to shine, as if these latter blessings were not more important than the former! If there is the greatest disadvantage in thus letting children imbibe interests from their family often in sharp disagreement with those of their country, there is then the most excellent argument for separating them from their family; and are they not naturally weaned away by the means I suggest, since in absolutely destroying all marital bonds, there are no longer born, as fruits of the woman's pleasure, anything but children to whom knowledge of their father is absolutely forbidden, and with that the possibility of belonging to only one family, instead of being, as they must be, purely *les enfants de la patrie*.

There will then be houses intended for women's libertinage and, like the men's, under the government's protection; in these establishments there will be furnished all the individuals of either sex women could desire, and the more constantly they frequent these places the higher they will be esteemed. There is nothing so barbarous or so ludicrous as to have identified their honor and their virtue with the resistance women show the desires Nature implants in them, and which continually inflame those who are hypocrite enough to pass

censure on them. From the most tender age,[2] a girl released
from her paternal fetters, no longer having anything to preserve for marriage (completely abolished by the wise laws I
advocate), and superior to the prejudices which in former
times imprisoned her sex, will therefore, in the houses created
for the purpose, be able to indulge in everything to which her
constitution prompts her; she will be received respectfully,
copiously satisfied, and, returned once again into society, she
will be able to tell of the pleasures she tasted quite as publicly
as today she speaks of a ball or promenade. O charming sex,
you will be free: as do men, you will enjoy all the pleasures of
which Nature makes a duty, from not one will you be withheld. Must the diviner half of humankind be laden with irons
by the other? Ah, break those irons; Nature wills it. For a
bridle have nothing but your inclinations, for laws only your
desires, for morality Nature's alone; languish no longer under
brutal prejudices which wither your charms and hold captive
the divine impulses of your hearts;[3] like us, you are free, the
field of action whereon one contends for Venus' favors is as
open to you as it is to us; have no fear of absurd reproaches;
pedantry and superstition are things of the past; no longer will
you be seen to blush at your charming delinquencies; crowned
with myrtle and roses, the esteem we conceive for you will be
henceforth in direct proportion to the scale you give your
extravagances.

2. The Babylonians scarcely awaited their seventh year to carry their
first fruits to the temple of Venus. The first impulse to concupiscence a
young girl feels is the moment when Nature bids her prostitute herself,
and without any other kind of consideration she must yield instantly
Nature speaks; if she resists, she outrages Nature's law.

3. Women are unaware to what point their lasciviousness embellishes
them. Let one compare two women of roughly comparable age and
beauty, one of whom lives in celibacy, and the other in libertinage: it
will be seen by how much the latter exceeds in éclat and freshness; all
violence done Nature is far more wearing than the abuse of pleasures;
everyone knows beds improve a woman's looks.

What has just been said ought doubtless to dispense us from examining adultery; nevertheless, let's cast a glance upon it, however nonexistent it be in the eyes of the laws I am establishing. To what point was it not ridiculous in our former institutions to consider adultery criminal! Were there anything absurd in the world, very surely it is the timelessness ascribed to conjugal relations; it appears to me it is but necessary to scrutinize, or sense the weight of, those bonds in order to cease to view as wicked the act which lightens them; Nature, as we remarked recently, having supplied women with a temper more ardent, with a sensibility more profound, than she awarded persons of the other sex, it is unquestionably for women that the marital contract proves more onerous.

Tender women, you ablaze with love's fire, compensate yourselves now, and do so boldly and unafraid; persuade yourselves that there can exist no evil in obedience to Nature's promptings, that it is not for one man she created you, but to please them all, without discrimination. Let no anxiety inhibit you. Imitate the Greek republicans; never did the philosophers whence they had their laws contrive to make adultery a crime for them, and nearly all authorized disorderliness among women. Thomas More proves in his *Utopia* that it becomes women to surrender themselves to debauchery, and that great man's ideas were not always pure dreams.[4]

Amongst the Tartars, the more profligate a woman, the more she was honored; about her neck she publicly wore a certain jewelry attesting to her impudicity, and those who were not at all decorated were not at all admired. In Peru, families cede their wives and daughters to the visiting traveler; they are rented at so much the day, like horses, or carriages! Volumes, finally, would not suffice to demonstrate that lewd behavior

4. The same thinker wished affianced couples to see each other naked before marriage. How many alliances would fail, were this law enforced! It might be declared that the contrary is indeed what is termed purchase of merchandise sight unseen.

has never been held criminal amongst the illuminated peoples of the earth. Every philosopher knows full well it is solely to the Christian impostors we are indebted for having puffed it up into crime. The priests had excellent cause to forbid us lechery: this injunction, by reserving to them acquaintance with and absolution for these private sins, gave them an incredible ascendancy over women, and opened up to them a career of lubricity whose scope knew no limits. We know only too well how they took advantage of it and how they would again abuse their powers, were they not hopelessly discredited.

Is incest more dangerous? Hardly. It loosens family ties and the citizen has that much more love to lavish on his country; the primary laws of Nature dictate it to us, our feelings vouch for the fact; and nothing is so enjoyable as an object we have coveted over the years. The most primitive institutions smiled upon incest; it is found in society's origins: it was consecrated in every religion, every law encouraged it. If we traverse the world we will find incest everywhere established. The blacks of the Ivory Coast and Gabon prostitute their wives to their own children; in Judah, the eldest son must marry his father's wife; the people of Chile lie indifferently with their sisters, their daughters, and marry mother and daughter at the same time. I would venture, in a word, that incest ought to be every government's law—every government whose basis is fraternity. How is it that reasonable men were able to carry absurdity to the point of believing that the enjoyment of one's mother, sister, or daughter could ever be criminal? Is it not, I ask, an abominable view wherein it is made to appear a crime for a man to place higher value upon the enjoyment of an object to which natural feeling draws him close? One might just as well say that we are forbidden to love too much the individuals Nature enjoins us to love best, and that the more she gives us a hunger for some object, the more she orders us

away from it. These are absurd paradoxes; only people bestial-
ized by superstition can believe or uphold them. The community of women I am establishing necessarily leading to incest,
there remains little more to say about a supposed misde-
meanor whose inexistence is too plainly evident to warrant
further pursuit of the matter, and we shall turn our attention
to rape, which at first glance seems to be, of all libertinage's
excesses, the one which is most dearly established as being
wrong, by reason of the outrage it appears to cause. It is certain, however, that rape, an act so very rare and so very
difficult to prove, wrongs one's neighbor less than theft, since
the latter is destructive to property, the former merely damaging to it. Beyond that, what objections have you to the
ravisher? What will you say, when he replies to you that, as a
matter of fact, the injury he has committed is trifling indeed,
since he has done no more than place a little sooner the object
he has abused in the very state in which she would soon have
been put by marriage and love.

But sodomy, that alleged crime which will draw the fire of
heaven upon cities addicted to it, is sodomy not a monstrous
deviation whose punishment could not be severe enough? Ah,
sorrowful it is to have to reproach our ancestors for the judi-
ciary murders in which, upon this head, they dared indulge
themselves. We wonder that savagery could ever reach the
point where you condemn to death an unhappy person all of
whose crime amounts to not sharing your tastes. One shudders
to think that scarce forty years ago the legislators' absurd thinking had not evolved beyond this point. Console yourselves,
citizens; such absurdities are to cease: the intelligence of your
lawmakers will answer for it. Thoroughly enlightened upon
this weakness occurring in a few men, people deeply sense
today that such error cannot be criminal, and that Nature, who
places such slight importance upon the essence that flows in

our loins, can scarcely be vexed by our choice when we are pleased to vent it into this or that avenue.

What single crime can exist here? For no one will wish to maintain that all the parts of the body do not resemble each other, that there are some which are pure, and others defiled; but, as it is unthinkable such nonsense be advanced seriously, the only possible crime would consist in the waste of semen. Well, is it likely that this semen is so precious to Nature that its loss is necessarily criminal? Were that so, would she every day institute those losses? and is it not to authorize them to permit them in dreams, to permit them in the act of taking one's pleasure with a pregnant woman? Is it possible to imagine Nature having allowed us the possibility of committing a crime that would outrage her? Is it possible that she consent to the destruction by man of her own pleasures, and to his thereby becoming stronger than she? It is unheard of—into what an abyss of folly one is hurled when, in reasoning, one abandons the aid of reason's torch! Let us abide in our unshakable assurance that it is as easy to enjoy a woman in one manner as in another, that it makes absolutely no difference whether one enjoys a girl or a boy, and as soon as it is clearly understood that no inclinations or tastes can exist in us save the ones we have from Nature, that she is too wise and too consistent to have given us any which could ever offend her.

22. RUSSELL: Reason in Sexual Ethics

Bertrand Russell (1872–1970) was born of a distinguished family and educated at Cambridge. His work with A. N. Whitehead on **Principia Mathematica,** which appeared in 1910–1913, places him among the most important figures in the development of modern mathematics and logic. His frequent stands on social issues and world peace made him one of the most publicly concerned thinkers of our time. His works, which are considerable in number, can be divided into those dealing with technical philosophical issues and those which treat social and political questions.

In the course of our discussion we have been led to certain conclusions, some historical, some ethical. Historically, we found that sexual morality, as it exists in civilized societies, has

SOURCE: Bertrand Russell, *Marriage and Morals* (New York: Liveright Publishers, 1956), pp. 303–320. Copyright © 1956 by Bertrand Russell. Reprinted by permission of Liveright Publishers, New York, and George Allen & Unwin Ltd., London.

been derived from two quite different sources, on the one hand desire for certainty as to fatherhood, on the other an ascetic belief that sex is wicked, except in so far as it is necessary for propagation. Morality in pre-Christian times, and in the Far East down to the present day, had only the former source, except in India and Persia, which are the centers from which asceticism appears to have spread. The desire to make sure of paternity does not, of course, exist in those backward races which are ignorant of the fact that the male has any part in generation. Among them, although masculine jealousy places certain limitations upon female license, women are on the whole much freer than in early patriarchal societies. It is clear that in the transition there must have been considerable friction, and the restraints upon women's freedom were doubtless considered necessary by men who took an interest in being the fathers of their own children. At this stage, sexual morality existed only for women. A man might not commit adultery with a married woman, but otherwise he was free.

With Christianity, the new motive of avoidance of sin enters in, and the moral standard becomes in theory the same for men as for women, though in practice the difficulty of enforcing it upon men has always led to a greater toleration of their failings than of those of women. Early sexual morality had a plain biological purpose, namely to ensure that the young should have the protection of two parents during their early years and not only of one. The purpose was lost sight of in Christian theory, though not in Christian practice.

In quite modern times there have been signs that both the Christian and the pre-Christian parts of sexual morality are undergoing modification. The Christian part has not the hold that it formerly had, because of the decay of religious orthodoxy and the diminishing intensity of belief even among those who still believe. Men and women born during the present century, although their unconsciousness is apt to retain the old attitudes, do not, for the most part, consciously believe that fornication as such is sin. As for the pre-Christian elements in sexual ethics, these have been modified by one factor, and are in process of being modified by yet another. The first of these factors is the use of contraceptives, which are making it increasingly possible to prevent sexual intercourse from leading to pregnancy, and are therefore enabling women, if unmarried, to avoid children altogether, and if married, to have children only by their husbands, without in either case finding it necessary to be chaste. This process is not yet complete, because contraceptives are not yet wholly reliable, but one may, I think, assume that before very long they will become so. In that case, assurance of paternity will become possible without the insistence that women shall have no sexual intercourse outside marriage. It may be said that women could deceive their husbands on the point, but after all it has been possible from the earliest times for women to deceive their husbands, and the motive for deception is much less strong when the question is merely who shall be the father than when it is whether there shall be intercourse with a person who may be passionately loved. One may, therefore, assume that deceit as to paternity, though it may occasionally occur, will be less frequent than deceit as to adultery has been in the past. It is also by no means impossible that the jealousy of husbands should, by a new convention, adapt itself to the new situation, and arise only when wives propose to choose some other man as the father of their children. In the East, men have always tolerated liberties on the part of eunuchs which most European husbands would resent. They have tolerated them because they introduce no doubt as to paternity. The same kind of toleration might easily be extended to liberties accompanied by the use of contraceptives.

The bi-parental family may, therefore, survive in the future without making such great demands upon the continence of

women as it had to make in the past. A second factor, however, in the change which is coming over sexual morals, is
liable to have more far-reaching effects. This is the increasing
participation of the State in the maintenance and education of
children. This factor, so far, operates in Europe more than in
America, and affects mainly the wage-earning classes, but
they, after all, are a majority of the population, and it is quite
likely that the substitution of the State for the father, which is
gradually taking place where they are concerned, will ultimately extend to the whole population. The part of the father,
in animal families as with the human family, has been to
provide protection and maintenance, but in civilized communities protection is provided by the police, and maintenance
may come to be provided wholly by the State, so far, at any
rate, as the poorer sections of the population are concerned. If
that were so, the father would cease to serve any obvious
purpose. With regard to the mother, there are two possibilities. She may continue her ordinary work and have her
children cared for in institutions, or she may, if the law so
decides, be paid by the State to care for her children while
they are young. If the latter course is adopted, it may be used
for a while to bolster up traditional morality, since a woman
who is not virtuous may be deprived of payment. But if she is
deprived of payment she will be unable to support her children unless she goes to work, and it will, therefore, be
necessary to put her children in some institution. It would
seem probable, therefore, that the operation of economic
forces may lead to the elimination of the father, and even to a
great extent of the mother, in the care of children whose
parents are not rich. If so, all the traditional reasons for traditional morality will have disappeared, and new reasons will
have to be found for a new morality.

The break-up of the family, if it comes about, will not be, to
my mind, a matter for rejoicing. The affection of parents is

important to children, and institutions, if they exist on a large scale, are sure to become very official and rather harsh. There will be a terrible degree of uniformity when the differentiating influence of different home environments is removed. And unless an international government is previously established, the children of different countries will be taught a virulent form of patriotism which will make it nearly certain that they will exterminate each other when grown up. The necessity for an international government arises also in regard to population, since in its absence nationalists have a motive for encouraging a greater increase of numbers than is desirable, and, with the progress of medicine and hygiene, the only remaining method of disposing of excessive numbers will be war.

While the sociological questions are often difficult and complicated, the personal questions are, to my mind, quite simple. The doctrine that there is something sinful about sex is one which has done untold harm to individual character—a harm beginning in early childhood and continuing throughout life. By keeping sex love in a prison, conventional morality has done much to imprison all other forms of friendly feeling, and to make men less generous, less kindly, more self-assertive and more cruel. Whatever sexual ethic may come to be ultimately accepted must be free from superstition and must have recognizable and demonstrable grounds in its favor. Sex cannot dispense with an ethic, any more than business or sport or scientific research or any other branch of human activity. But it can dispense with an ethic based solely upon ancient prohibitions propounded by uneducated people in a society wholly unlike our own. In sex, as in economics and in politics, our ethic is still dominated by fears which modern discoveries have made irrational, and the benefit to be derived from those discoveries is largely lost through failure of psychological adaptation to them.

It is true that the transition from the old system to the new has its own difficulties, as all transitions have. These who advocate any ethical innovation are invariably accused, like Socrates, of being corrupters of youth; nor is this accusation always wholly unfounded, even when in fact the new ethic which they preach would, if accepted in its entirety, lead to a better life than the old ethic which they seek to amend. Every one who knows the Mahometan East asserts that those who have ceased to think it necessary to pray five times a day have also ceased to respect other moral rules which we consider more important. The man who proposes any change in sexual morality is especially liable to be misinterpreted in this way, and I am conscious myself of having said things which some readers may have misinterpreted.

The general principle upon which the newer morality differs from the traditional morality of puritanism is this: we believe that instinct should be trained rather than thwarted. Put in these general terms, the view is one which would win very wide acceptance among modern men and women, but it is one which is fully valid only when accepted with its full implications and applied from the earliest years. If in childhood instinct is thwarted rather than trained, the result may be that it has to be to some extent thwarted throughout later life, because it will have taken on highly undesirable forms as a result of thwarting in early years. The morality which I should advocate does not consist simply of saying to grown-up people or to adolescents: "Follow your impulses and do as you like." There has to be consistency in life; there has to be continuous effort directed to ends that are not immediately beneficial and not at every moment attractive; there has to be consideration for others; and there should be certain standards of rectitude. I should not, however, regard self-control as an end in itself, and I should wish our institutions and our moral conventions to be such as to make the need for self-control a minimum rather than a maximum. The use of self-control is like the use of brakes on a train. It is useful when you find yourself going in the wrong direction, but merely harmful when the direction is right. No one would maintain that a train ought always to be run with the brakes on, yet the habit of difficult self-control has a very similar injurious effect upon the energies available for useful activity. Self-control causes these energies to be largely wasted on internal friction instead of external activity; and on this account it is always regrettable, though sometimes necessary.

The degree to which self-control is necessary in life depends upon the early treatment of instinct. Instincts, as they exist in children, may lead to useful activities or harmful ones, just as the steam in a locomotive may take it toward its destination or into a siding where it is smashed by an accident. The function of education is to guide instinct into the directions in which it will develop useful rather than harmful activities. If this task has been adequately performed in early years, a man or woman will, as a rule, be able to live a useful life without the need of severe self-control, except, perhaps, at a few rare crises. If on the other hand early education has consisted in a mere thwarting of instinct, the acts to which instinct prompts in later life will be partly harmful, and will therefore have to be continually restrained by self-control.

These general considerations apply with peculiar force to sexual impulses, both because of their great strength and because of the fact that traditional morality has made them its peculiar concern. Most traditional moralists appear to think that, if our sexual impulses were not severely checked, they would become trivial, anarchic and gross. I believe this view to be derived from observation of those who have acquired the usual inhibitions from their early years and have subsequently attempted to ignore them. But in such men the early prohibitions are still operative even when they do not succeed in prohibiting. What is called conscience, that is to say the unreasoning and more or less unconscious acceptance of precepts learnt in early youth, causes men still to feel that whatever the conventions prohibit is wrong, and this feeling may persist in spite of intellectual convictions to the contrary. It thus produces a personality divided against itself, one in which instinct and reason no longer go hand in hand, but instinct has become trivial and reason has become anemic. One finds in the modern world various different degrees of revolt against conventional teaching. The commonest of all is the revolt of the man who intellectually acknowledges the ethical truth of the morality he was taught in youth, but confesses, with a more or less unreal regret, that he is not sufficiently heroic to live up to it. For such a man there is little to be said. It would be better that he should alter either his practice or his beliefs in such a way as to bring harmony between them. Next comes the man whose conscious reason has rejected much that he learnt in the nursery, but whose unconscious still accepts it in its entirety. Such a man will suddenly change his line of conduct under the stress of any strong emotion, especially fear. A serious illness or an earthquake may cause him to repent and to abandon his intellectual convictions as the result of an uprush of infantile beliefs. Even at ordinary times his behavior will be inhibited, and the inhibitions may take an undesirable form. They will not prevent him from acting in ways that are condemned by traditional morals, but they will prevent him from doing so in a whole-hearted way, and will thus eliminate from his actions some of the elements that would have given them value. The substitution of a new moral code for the old one can never be completely satisfactory unless the new one is accepted with the whole personality, not only with that top layer which constitutes our conscious thought. To most people this is very difficult if throughout their early years they have been exposed to the old morality. It is therefore impossible to judge a new morality fairly until it has been applied in early education.

Sex morality has to be derived from certain general principles, as to which there is perhaps a fairly wide measure of agreement, in spite of the wide disagreement as to the consequences to be drawn from them. The first thing to be secured is that there should be as much as possible of that deep, serious love between man and woman which embraces the whole personality of both and leads to a fusion by which each is enriched and enhanced. The second thing of importance is that there should be adequate care of children, physical and psychological. Neither of these principles in itself can be considered in any way shocking, yet it is as a consequence of these two principles that I should advocate certain modifications of the conventional code. Most men and women, as things stand, are incapable of being as wholehearted and as generous in the love that they bring to marriage as they would be if their early years had been less hedged about with taboos. They either lack the necessary experience, or they have gained it in furtive and undesirable ways. Moreover, since jealousy has the sanction of moralists, they feel justified in keeping each other in a mutual prison. It is, of course, a very good thing when a husband and wife love each other so completely that neither is ever tempted to unfaithfulness; it is not, however, a good thing that unfaithfulness, if it does occur, should be treated as something terrible, nor is it desirable to go so far as to make all friendship with persons of the other sex impossible. A good life cannot be founded upon fear, prohibition, and mutual interference with freedom. Where faithfulness is achieved without these, it is good, but where all this is necessary it may well be that too high a price has been paid, and that a little mutual toleration of occasional lapses would be better. There can be no doubt that mutual jealousy, even where there is physical faithfulness, often causes more unhappiness in a marriage than would be caused if there were more confidence in the ultimate strength of a deep and permanent affection.

The obligations of parents toward children are treated far more lightly than seems to me right by many persons who consider themselves virtuous. Given the present system of the biparental family, as soon as there are children it is the duty of both parties to a marriage to do everything that they can to preserve harmonious relations, even if this requires considerable self-control. But the control required is not merely, as conventional moralists pretend, that involved in restraining every impulse to unfaithfulness; it is just as important to control impulses to jealousy, ill-temper, masterfulness, and so on. There can be no doubt that serious quarrels between parents are a very frequent cause of nervous disorders in children; therefore whatever can be done to prevent such quarrels should be done. At the same time, where one or both parties have not sufficient self-control to prevent disagreements from coming to the knowledge of the children, it may well be better that the marriage should be dissolved. It is by no means the case that the dissolution of a marriage is invariably the worst thing possible from the point of view of the children; indeed it is not nearly so bad as the spectacle of raised voices, furious accusations, perhaps even violence, to which many children are exposed in bad homes.

It must not be supposed that the sort of thing which a sane advocate of greater freedom desires is to be achieved at once by leaving adults, or even adolescents, who have been brought up under the old severe restrictive maxims, to the unaided promptings of the damaged impulses which are all the moralists have left to them. This is a necessary stage, since otherwise they will bring up their children as badly as they were brought up; but it is no more than a stage. Sane freedom must be learnt from the earliest years, since otherwise the only freedom possible will be a frivolous, superficial freedom, not freedom of the whole personality. Trivial impulses will lead to physical excesses, while the spirit remains in fetters. Instinct rightly trained from the first can produce something much better than what results from an education inspired by a Calvinistic belief in original sin, but when such an education has been allowed to do its evil work, it is exceedingly difficult to undo the effect in later years. One of the most important benefits which psychoanalysis has conferred upon the world is its discovery of the bad effects of prohibitions and threats in early childhood; to undo this effect may require all the time and technique of a psychoanalytic treatment. This is true not only of those obvious neurotics who have suffered damage visible to every one; it is true also of most apparently normal people. I believe that nine out of ten of those who have had a conventional upbringing in their early years have become in some degree incapable of a decent and sane attitude toward marriage and sex generally. The kind of attitude and behavior that I should regard as the best has been rendered impossible for such people; the best that can be done is to make them aware of the damage that they have sustained and to persuade them to abstain from maiming their children in the same way in which they have been maimed.

The doctrine that I wish to preach is not one of license; it involves exactly as much self-control as is involved in the conventional doctrine. But self-control will be applied more to abstaining from interference with the freedom of others than to restraining one's own freedom. It may, I think, be hoped that with the right education from the start this respect for the personality and freedom of others may become comparatively easy; but for those of us who have been brought up to believe that we have a right to place a veto upon the actions of others in the name of virtue, it is undoubtedly difficult to forgo the exercise of this agreeable form of persecution. It may even be impossible. But it is not to be inferred that it would be impossible to those who had been taught from the first a less restrictive morality. The essence of a good marriage is respect for each other's personality combined with that deep intimacy, physical, mental, and spiritual, which makes a serious love between man and woman the most fructifying of all human experiences. Such love, like everything that is great and precious, demands its own morality, and frequently entails a sacrifice of the less to the greater; but such sacrifice must be voluntary, for, where it is not, it will destroy the very basis of the love for the sake of which it is made.

23. DE BEAUVOIR:
Women's Liberation

Simone de Beauvoir (1908–   ) was born in Paris and studied
at the Sorbonne, taking her degree in philosophy in 1929. Since
her student days she has been a friend and associate of Sartre.
She, with Sartre, has been one of the leading proponents of the
existentialist movement and has edited the existentialist magazine
Les Temps Modernes. Her writings include both works of fiction
and philosophical essays.

According to French law, obedience is no longer included
among the duties of a wife, and each woman citizen has the
right to vote; but these civil liberties remain theoretical as long
as they are unaccompanied by economic freedom. A woman

SOURCE: From *The Second Sex*, by Simone de Beauvoir, trans. H. M.
Parshley. Copyright 1952 by Alfred A. Knopf, Inc. Reprinted by permission of the publisher, and Jonathan Cape Ltd.

supported by a man—wife or courtesan—is not emancipated from the male because she has a ballot in her hand; if custom imposes less constraint upon her than formerly, the negative freedom implied has not profoundly modified her situation; she remains bound in her condition of vassalage. It is through gainful employment that woman has traversed most of the distance that separated her from the male; and nothing else can guarantee her liberty in practice. Once she ceases to be a parasite, the system based on her dependence crumbles; between her and the universe there is no longer any need for a masculine mediator.

The curse that is upon woman as vassal consists, as we have seen, in the fact that she is not permitted to do anything; so she persists in the vain pursuit of her true being through narcissism, love, or religion. When she is productive, active, she regains her transcendence; in her projects she concretely affirms her status as subject; in connection with the aims she pursues, with the money and the rights she takes possession of, she makes trial of and senses her responsibility. Many women are aware of these advantages, even among those in very modest positions. I heard a charwoman declare, while scrubbing the stone floor of a hotel lobby: "I never asked anybody for anything; I succeeded all by myself." She was as proud of her self-sufficiency as a Rockefeller. It is not to be supposed, however, that the mere combination of the right to vote and a job constitutes a complete emancipation: working, today, is not liberty. Only in a socialist world would woman by the one attain the other. The majority of workers are exploited today. On the other hand, the social structure has not been much modified by the changes in woman's condition; this world, always belonging to men, still retains the form they have given it.

We must not lose sight of those facts which make the question of woman's labor a complex one. An important and thoughtful woman recently made a study of the women in the Renault factories; she states that they would prefer to stay in the home rather than work in the factory. There is no doubt that they get economic independence only as members of a class which is economically oppressed; and, on the other hand, their jobs at the factory do not relieve them of housekeeping burdens. If they had been asked to choose between forty hours of work a week in the factory and forty hours of work a week in the home, they would doubtless have furnished quite different answers. And perhaps they would cheerfully accept both jobs, if as factory workers they were to be integrated in a world that would be theirs, in the development of which they would joyfully and proudly share. At the present time, peasants apart, the majority of women do not escape from the traditional feminine world; they get from neither society nor their husbands the assistance they would need to become in concrete fact the equals of the men. Only those women who have a political faith, who take militant action in the unions, who have confidence in their future, can give ethical meaning to thankless daily labor. But lacking leisure, inheriting a traditional submissiveness, women are naturally just beginning to develop a political and social sense. And not getting in exchange for their work the moral and social benefits they might rightfully count on, they naturally submit to its constraints without enthusiasm.

It is quite understandable, also, that the milliner's apprentice, the shopgirl, the secretary, will not care to renounce the advantages of masculine support. I have already pointed out that the existence of a privileged caste, which she can join by merely surrendering her body, is an almost irresistible temptation to the young woman; she is fated for gallantry by the fact that her wages are minimal while the standard of living expected of her by society is very high. If she is content to get along on her wages, she is only a pariah: ill lodged, ill dressed, she will be denied all amusement and even love. Virtuous people preach asceticism to her, and, indeed, her dietary regime is often as austere as that of a Carmelite. Unfortunately, not everyone can take God as a lover: she has to please men if she is to succeed in her life as a woman. She will therefore accept assistance, and this is what her employer cynically counts on in giving her starvation wages. This aid will sometimes allow her to improve her situation and achieve a real independence; in other cases, however, she will give up her work and become a kept woman. She often retains both sources of income and each serves more or less as an escape from the other; but she is really in double servitude: to job and to protector. For the married woman her wages represent only pin money as a rule; for the girl who "makes something on the side" it is the masculine contribution that seems extra; but neither of them gains complete independence through her own efforts.

There are, however, a fairly large number of privileged women who find in their professions a means of economic and social autonomy. These come to mind when one considers woman's possibilities and her future. This is the reason why it is especially interesting to make a close study of their situation, even though they constitute as yet only a minority; they continue to be a subject of debate between feminists and antifeminists. The latter assert that the emancipated women of today succeed in doing nothing of importance in the world and that furthermore they have difficulty in achieving their own inner equilibrium. The former exaggerate the results obtained by professional women and are blind to their inner confusion. There is no good reason, as a matter of fact, to say they are on the wrong road; and still it is certain that they are not tranquilly installed in their new realm: as yet they are only halfway there. The woman who is economically emancipated from man is not for all that in a moral, social, and psychological situation identical with that of man. The way she carries on her profession and her devotion to it depend on the context supplied by the total pattern of her life. For when she begins her adult life she does not have behind her the same past as does a boy; she is not viewed by society in the same way; the universe presents itself to her in a different perspective. The fact of being a woman today poses peculiar problems for an independent human individual.

The advantage man enjoys, which makes itself felt from his childhood, is that his vocation as a human being in no way runs counter to his destiny as a male. Through the identification of phallus and transcendence, it turns out that his social and spiritual successes endow him with a virile prestige. He is not divided. Whereas it is required of woman that in order to realize her femininity she must make herself object and prey, which is to say that she must renounce her claims as sovereign subject. It is this conflict that especially marks the situation of the emancipated woman. She refuses to confine herself to her role as female, because she will not accept mutilation; but it would also be a mutilation to repudiate her sex. Man is a human being with sexuality; woman is a complete individual, equal to the male, only if she too is a human being with sexuality. To renounce her femininity is to renounce a part of her humanity. Misogynists have often reproached intellectual women for "neglecting themselves"; but they have also preached this doctrine to them: if you wish to be our equals, stop using make-up and nail-polish.

This piece of advice is nonsensical. Precisely because the concept of femininity is artificially shaped by custom and fashion, it is imposed upon each woman from without; she can be transformed gradually so that her canons of propriety approach those adopted by the males: at the seashore—and often elsewhere—trousers have become feminine. That changes nothing fundamental in the matter: the individual is still not free to do as she pleases in shaping the concept of femininity. The woman who does not conform devaluates herself sexually and hence socially, since sexual values are an integral feature of society. One does not acquire virile attributes by rejecting feminine attributes; even the transvestite fails to make a man of herself—she is a travesty. As we have seen, homosexuality constitutes a specific attitude: neutrality is impossible. There is no negative attitude that does not imply a positive counterpart. The adolescent girl often thinks that she can simply scorn convention; but even there she is engaged in public agitation; she is creating a new situation entailing consequences she must assume. When one fails to adhere to an accepted code, one becomes an insurgent. A woman who dresses in an outlandish manner lies when she affirms with an air of simplicity that she dresses to suit herself, nothing more. She knows perfectly well that to suit herself is to be outlandish.

Inversely, a woman who does not wish to appear eccentric will conform to the usual rules. It is injudicious to take a defiant attitude unless it is connected with positively effective action: it consumes more time and energy than it saves. A woman who has no wish to shock or to devaluate herself socially should live out her feminine situation in a feminine manner; and very often, for that matter, her professional success demands it. But whereas conformity is quite natural for a man—custom being based on his needs as an independent and active individual—it will be necessary for the woman who also is subject, activity, to insinuate herself into a world that has doomed her to passivity. This is made more burdensome because women confined to the feminine sphere have grossly magnified its importance: they have made dressing and housekeeping difficult arts. Man hardly has to take thought of his clothes, for they are convenient, suitable to his active life, not necessarily elegant; they are scarcely a part of his personality. More, nobody expects him to take care of them himself: some kindly disposed or hired female relieves him of this bother.,

Woman, on the contrary, knows that when she is looked at she is not considered apart from her appearance: she is judged, respected, desired, by and through her toilette. Her clothes were originally intended to consign her to impotence, and they have remained unserviceable, easily ruined: stockings get runs, shoes get down at the heel, light-colored blouses and frocks get soiled, pleats get unpleated. But she will have to make most of the repairs herself; other women will not come benevolently to her assistance and she will hesitate to add to her budget for work she could do herself: permanents, setting hair, make-up materials, new dresses, cost enough already. When they come in after the day's work, students and secretaries always have a stocking with a run to be fixed, a blouse to wash, a skirt to press. A woman who makes a good income will spare herself this drudgery, but she will have to maintain a more complicated elegance; she will lose time in shopping, in having fittings, and the rest. Tradition also requires even the single woman to give some attention to her lodgings. An official assigned to a new city will easily find accommodations at a hotel; but a woman in the same position will want to settle down in a place of her own. She will have to keep it scrupulously neat, for people would not excuse a negligence on her part which they would find quite natural in a man.

It is not regard for the opinion of others alone that leads her to give time and care to her appearance and her housekeeping. She wants to retain her womanliness for her own satisfaction. She can regard herself with approval throughout her present and past only in combining the life she has made for herself with the destiny that her mother, her childhood games, and her adolescent fantasies prepared for her. She has entertained narcissistic dreams; to the male's phallic pride she still opposes her cult of self; she wants to be seen, to be attractive. Her mother and her older sisters have inculated the liking for a nest: a home, an "interior," of her own! That has always been basic in her dreams of independence; she has no intention of discarding them when she has found liberty by other roads. And to the degree in which she still feels insecure in the masculine universe, she tends to retain the need for a retreat, symbolical of that interior refuge she has been accustomed to seeking within herself. Obedient to the feminine tradition, she will wax her floors, and she will do her own cooking instead of going to eat at a restaurant as a man would in her place. She wants to live at once like a man and like a woman, and in that way she multiplies her tasks and adds to her fatigue.

If she intends to remain fully feminine, it is implied that she also intends to meet the other sex with the odds as favorable as possible. Her most difficult problems are going to be posed in the field of sex. In order to be a complete individual, on an equality with man, woman must have access to the masculine world as does the male to the feminine world, she must have access to the *other;* but the demands of the *other* are not symmetrical in the two symmetrical cases. Once attained, fame and fortune, appearing like immanent qualities, may increase woman's sexual attractiveness; but the fact that she is a being of independent activity wars against her femininity, and this she is aware of. The independent woman—and above all the intellectual, who thinks about her situation—will suffer, as a female, from an inferiority complex; she lacks leisure for such minute beauty care as that of the coquette whose sole aim in life is to be seductive; follow the specialists' advice as she may, she will never be more than an amateur in the domain of elegance. Feminine charm demands that transcendence, degraded into immanence, appear no longer as anything more than a subtle quivering of the flesh; it is necessary to be spontaneously offered prey.

But the intellectual knows that she is offering herself, she knows that she is a conscious being, a subject; one can hardly dull one's glance and change one's eyes into sky-blue pools at will; one does not infallibly stop the surge of a body that is straining toward the world and change it into a statue animated by vague tremors. The intellectual woman will try all the more zealously because she fears failure; but her conscious zeal is still an activity and it misses its goal. She makes mistakes like those induced by the menopause: she tries to deny her brain just as the woman who is growing older tries to deny her age; she dresses like a girl, she overloads herself with flowers, furbelows, fancy materials; she affects childish tricks of surprised amazement. She romps, she babbles, she pretends flippancy, heedlessness, sprightliness.

But in all this she resembles those actors who fail to feel the emotion that would relax certain muscles and so by an effort of will contract the opposing ones, forcing down their eyes or the corners of their mouths instead of letting them fall. Thus in imitating abandon the intellectual woman becomes tense. She realizes this, and it irritates her; over her blankly naïve face, there suddenly passes a flash of all too sharp intelligence; lips soft with promise suddenly tighten. If she has trouble in pleasing, it is because she is not, like her slavish little sisters, pure will to please; the desire to seduce, lively as it may be, has not penetrated to the marrow of her bones. As soon as she feels awkward, she becomes vexed at her abjectness; she wants to take her revenge by playing the game with masculine weapons: she talks instead of listening, she displays subtle thoughts, strange emotions; she contradicts the man instead of agreeing with him, she tries to get the best of him. Mme de Staël won some resounding victories: she was almost irresistible. But the challenging attitude, very common among American women, for example, irritates men more often than it conquers them; and there are some men besides, who bring it upon themselves by their own defiant air. If they would be willing to love an equal instead of a slave—as, it must be added, do those among them who are at once free from arrogance and without an inferiority complex—women would not be as haunted as they are by concern for their femininity; they would gain in naturalness, in simplicity, and they would find themselves women again without taking so much pains, since, after all, that is what they are.

The fact is that men are beginning to resign themselves to the new status of woman; and she, not feeling condemned in advance, has begun to feel more at ease. Today the woman who works is less neglectful of her femininity than formerly, and she does not lose her sexual attractiveness. This success, though already indicating progress toward equilibrium, is not yet complete; it continues to be more difficult for a woman than for a man to establish the relations with the other sex that she desires. Her erotic and affectional life encounters numerous difficulties. In this matter the unemancipated woman is in no way privileged: sexually and affectionally most wives and courtesans are deeply frustrated. If the difficulties are more evident in the case of the independent woman, it is because she has chosen battle rather than resignation. All the problems of life find a silent solution in death; a woman who is busy with living is therefore more at variance with herself than is she who buries her will and her desires; but the former will not take the latter as a standard. She considers herself at a disadvantage only in comparison with man.

24. MAY: The Sexual Paradoxes of Contemporary Life

Rollo May (1909–   ), American clinical psychologist, received his Ph.D. at Columbia in 1949. He has been a member of the faculty of various colleges and universities and is the author of a number of widely read books, among which are **Man's Search for Himself** and **Love and Will.**

There are four kinds of love in Western tradition. One is *sex*, or what we call lust, libido. The second is *eros*, the drive of love to procreate or create—the urge, as the Greeks put it, toward higher forms of being and relationship. A third is *philia*, or friendship, brotherly love. The fourth is *agape* or

SOURCE: Rollo May, "Paradoxes of Sex and Love," in *Love and Will* (New York: W. W. Norton & Co., Inc., 1969), pp. 37–48. Copyright © 1969 by W. W. Norton & Company, Inc. Reprinted by permission of W. W. Norton & Company, Inc., and Souvenir Press of London.

caritas as the Latins called it, the love which is devoted to the welfare of the other, the prototype of which is the love of God for man. Every human experience of authentic love is a blending, in varying proportions, of these four.

We begin with sex not only because that is where our society begins but also because that is where every man's biological existence begins as well. Each of us owes his being to the fact that at some moment in history a man and a woman leapt the gap, in T. S. Eliot's words, "between the desire and the spasm." Regardless of how much sex may be banalized in our society, it still remains the power of procreation, the drive which perpetuates the race, the source at once of the human being's most intense pleasure and his most pervasive anxiety. It can, in its daimonic form, hurl the individual into sloughs of despond, and, when allied with eros, it can lift him out of his despondency into orbits of ecstasy.

The ancients took sex, or lust, for granted just as they took death for granted. It is only in the contemporary age that we have succeeded, on a fairly broad scale, in singling out sex for our chief concern and have required it to carry the weight of all four forms of love. Regardless of Freud's overextension of sexual phenomena as such—in which he is but the voice of the struggle of thesis and antithesis of modern history—it remains true that sexuality is basic to the ongoing power of the race and surely has the *importance* Freud gave it, if not the *extension*. Trivialize sex in our novels and dramas as we will, or defend ourselves from its power by cynicism and playing it cool as we wish, sexual passion remains ready at any moment to catch us off guard and prove that it is still the *mysterium tremendum*.

But as soon as we look at the relation of sex and love in our time, we find ourselves immediately caught up in a whirlpool of contradictions. Let us, therefore, get our bearings by beginning with a brief phenomenological sketch of the strange paradoxes which surround sex in our society.

Sexual Wilderness

In Victorian times, when the denial of sexual impulses, feelings, and drives was the mode and one would not talk about sex in polite company, an aura of sanctifying repulsiveness surrounded the whole topic. Males and females dealt with each other as though neither possessed sexual organs. William James, that redoubtable crusader who was far ahead of his time on every other topic, treated sex with the polite aversion characteristic of the turn of the century. In the whole two volumes of his epoch-making *Principles of Psychology*, only one page is devoted to sex, at the end of which he adds, "These details are a little unpleasant to discuss. . . ."[1] But William Blake's warning a century before Victorianism, that "He who desires but acts not, breeds pestilence," was amply demonstrated by the later psychotherapists. Freud, a Victorian who did look at sex, was right in his description of the morass of neurotic symptoms which resulted from cutting off so vital a part of the human body and the self.

Then, in the 1920s, a radical change occurred almost overnight. The belief became a militant dogma in liberal circles that the opposite of repression—namely, sex education, freedom of talking, feeling, and expression—would have healthy effects, and obviously constituted the only stand for the enlightened person. In an amazingly short period following World War I, we shifted from acting as though sex did not exist at all to being obsessed with it. We now placed more emphasis on sex than any society since that of ancient Rome, and some scholars believe we are more preoccupied with sex than any other people in all of history. Today, far from not

1. William James, *Principles of Psychology* (New York: Dover Publications, 1950; originally published by Henry Holt, 1890), 2:439.

talking about sex, we might well seem, to a visitor from Mars dropping into Times Square, to have no other topic of communication.

And this is not solely an American obsession. Across the ocean in England, for example, "from bishops to biologist, everyone is in on the act." A perceptive front-page article in *The Times Literary Supplement*, London, goes on to point to the "whole turgid flood of post-Kinsey utilitarianism and post-Chatterley moral uplift. Open any newspaper, any day (Sunday in particular), and the odds are you will find some pundit treating the public to his views on contraception, abortion, adultery, obscene publications, homosexuality between consenting adults or (if all else fails) contemporary moral patterns among our adolescents."[2]

Partly as a result of this radical shift, many therapists today rarely see patients who exhibit repression of sex in the manner of Freud's pre-World War I hysterical patients. In fact, we find in the people who come for help just the opposite: a great deal of talk about sex, a great deal of sexual activity, practically no one complaining of cultural prohibitions over going to bed as often or with as many partners as one wishes. But what our patients do complain of is lack of feeling and passion. "The curious thing about this ferment of discussion is how little anyone seems to be *enjoying* emancipation."[3] So much sex and so little meaning or even fun in it!

Where the Victorian didn't want anyone to know that he or she had sexual feelings, we are ashamed if we do not. Before 1910, if you called a lady "sexy" she would be insulted; nowadays, she prizes the compliment and rewards you by turning her charms in your direction. Our patients often have the problems of frigidity and impotence, but the strange and

2. *Atlas* (November, 1965), p. 302. Reprinted from *The Times Literary Supplement*, London.
3. *Ibid.*

poignant thing we observe is how desperately they struggle not to let anyone find out they don't feel sexually. The Victorian nice man or woman was guilty if he or she did experience sex; now we are guilty if we *don't*.

One paradox, therefore, is that enlightenment has not solved the sexual probems in our culture. To be sure, there are important positive results of the new enlightenment, chiefly in increased freedom for the individual. Most external problems are eased: sexual knowledge can be bought in any bookstore, contraception is available everywhere except in Boston where it is still believed, as the English countess averred on her wedding night, that sex is "too good for the common people." Couples can, without guilt and generally without squeamishness, discuss their sexual relationship and undertake to make it more mutually gratifying and meaningful. Let these gains not be underestimated. External social anxiety and guilt have lessened; dull would be the man who did not rejoice in this.

But *internal* anxiety and guilt have increased. And in some ways these are more morbid, harder to handle, and impose a heavier burden upon the individual than external anxiety and guilt.

The challenge a woman used to face from men was simple and direct—would she or would she not go to bed?—a direct issue of how she stood vis-à-vis cultural mores. But the question men ask now is no longer, "Will she or won't she?" but "Can she or can't she?" The challenge is shifted to the woman's personal adequacy, namely, her own capacity to have the vaunted orgasm—which should resemble a *grand mal* seizure. Though we might agree that the second question places the problem of sexual decision more where it should be, we cannot overlook the fact that the first question is much easier for the person to handle. In my practice, one woman was afraid to go to bed for fear that the man "won't find me very good at making love." Another was afraid because "I don't even know how to do it," assuming that her lover would hold this against her. Another was scared to death of the second marriage for fear that she wouldn't be able to have the orgasm as she had not in her first. Often the woman's hesitation is formulated as, "He won't like me well enough to come back again."

In past decades you could blame society's strict mores and preserve your own self-esteem by telling yourself what you did or didn't do was society's fault and not yours. And this would give you some time in which to decide what you do want to do, or to let yourself grow into a decision. But when the question is simply how you can perform, your own sense of adequacy and self-esteem is called immediately into question, and the whole weight of the encounter is shifted inward to how you can meet the test.

College students, in their fights with college authorities about hours girls are to be permitted in the men's rooms, are curiously blind to the fact that rules are often a boon. Rules give the student time to find himself. He has the leeway to consider a way of behaving without being committed before he is ready, to try on for size, to venture into relationships tentatively—which is part of any growing up. Better to have the lack of commitment direct and open rather than to go into sexual relations under pressure—doing violence to his feelings by having physical commitment without psychological. He may flaunt the rules; but at least they give some structure to be flaunted. My point is true whether he obeys the rule or not. Many contemporary students, understandably anxious because of their new sexual freedom, repress this anxiety ("one should *like* freedom") and then compensate for the additional anxiety the repression gives them by attacking the parietal authorities for not giving them more freedom!

What we did not see in our short-sighted liberalism in sex was that throwing the individual into an unbounded and empty sea of free choice does not in itself give freedom, but is more apt to increase inner conflict. The sexual freedom to which we were devoted fell short of being fully human.

In the arts, we have also been discovering what an illusion it was to believe that mere freedom would solve our problem. Consider, for example, the drama. In an article entitled "Is Sex Kaput?," Howard Taubman, former drama critic of *The New York Times*, summarized what we have all observed in drama after drama: "Engaging in sex was like setting out to shop on a dull afternoon; desire had nothing to do with it and even curiosity was faint."[4] Consider also the novel. In the "revolt against the Victorians," writes Leon Edel, "the extremists have had their day. Thus far they have impoverished the novel rather than enriched it."[5] Edel perceptively brings out the crucial point that in sheer realistic "enlightenment" there has occured a *dehumanization* of sex in fiction. There are "sexual encounters in Zola," he insists, "which have more truth in them than any D. H. Lawrence described—and also more humanity."[6]

The battle against censorship and for freedom of expression surely was a great battle to win, but has it not become a new straitjacket? The writers, both novelists and dramatists, "would rather hock their typewriters than turn in a manuscript without the obligatory scenes of unsparing anatomical documentation of their characters' sexual behavior. . . ."[7] Our "dogmatic enlightenment" is self-defeating: it ends up destroying the very sexual passion it set out to protect. In the great tide of realistic chronicling, we forgot, on the stage and in the novel and even in psychotherapy, that imagination is the life-blood of eros, and that realism is neither sexual nor erotic.

4. Howard Taubman, "Is Sex Kaput?," *New York Times*, sect. 2, January 17, 1965.
5. Leon Edel, "Sex and the Novel," *New York Times*, sect. 7, pt. I, November 1, 1964.
6. *Ibid.*
7. See Taubman, "Is Sex Kaput?"

Indeed, there is nothing *less* sexy than sheer nakedness, as a random hour at any nudist camp will prove. It requires the infusion of the imagination (which I shall later call intentionality) to transmute physiology and anatomy into *interpersonal* experience—into art, into passion, into eros in a million forms which has the power to shake or charm us.

Could it not be that an "enlightenment" which reduces itself to sheer realistic detail is itself an escape from the anxiety involved in the relation of human imagination to erotic passion?

Salvation through Technique

A second paradox is that *the new emphasis on technique in sex and love-making backfires.* It often occurs to me that there is an inverse relationship between the number of how-to-do-it books perused by a person or rolling off the presses in a society and the amount of sexual passion or even pleasure experienced by the persons involved. Certainly nothing is wrong with technique as such, in playing golf or acting or making love. But the emphasis beyond a certain point on technique in sex makes for a mechanistic attitude toward love-making, and goes along with alienation, feelings of loneliness, and depersonalization.

One aspect of the alienation is that the lover, with his age-old art, tends to be superseded by the computer operator with his modern efficiency. Couples place great emphasis on book-keeping and timetables in their love-making—a practice confirmed and standardized by Kinsey. If they fall behind schedule they become anxious and feel impelled to go to bed whether they want to or not. My colleague, Dr. John Schimel, observes, "My patients have endured stoically, or without noticing, remarkably destructive treatment at the hands of their spouses, but they have experienced falling behind in the sexual time-table as a loss of love."[8] The man feels he is some-how losing his masculine status if he does not perform up to schedule, and the woman that she has lost her feminine attractiveness if too long a period goes by without the man at least making a pass at her. The phrase "between men," which women use about their affairs, similarly suggests a gap in time like the *entr'acte.* Elaborate accounting- and ledger-book lists —how often this week have we made love? did he (or she) pay the right amount of attention to me during the evening? was the foreplay long enough?—make one wonder how the spontaneity of this most spontaneous act can possibly survive. The computer hovers in the stage wings of the drama of love-making the way Freud said one's parents used to.

It is not surprising then, in this preoccupation with tech-niques, that the questions typically asked about an act of love-making are not, Was there passion of meaning or pleasure in the act? but, How well did I perform?[9] Take, for example, what Cyril Connolly calls "the tyranny of the orgasm," and the preoccupation with achieving a simultaneous orgasm, which is another aspect of the alienation. I confess that when people talk about the "apocalyptic orgasm," I find myself wondering, Why do they have to try so hard? What abyss of self-doubt, what inner void of loneliness, are they trying to cover up by this great concern with grandiose effects?

Even the sexologists, whose attitude is generally the more sex the merrier, are raising their eyebrows these days about

---

8. John L. Schimel, "Ideology and Sexual Practices," *Sexual Behavior and the Law,* ed. Ralph Slovenko (Springfield, Ill.: Charles C. Thomas, 1965), pp. 195, 197.

9. Sometimes a woman patient will report to me, in the course of de-scribing how a man tried to seduce her, that he cites as part of his seduc-tion line how efficient a lover he is, and he promises to perform the act eminently satisfactorily for her. (Imagine Mozart's Don Giovanni offering such an argument!) In fairness to elemental human nature, I must add that as far as I can remember, the women reported that this "advance billing" did not add to the seducers' chances of success.

the anxious overemphasis on achieving the orgasm and the great importance attached to "satisfying" the partner. A man makes a point of asking the woman if she "made it," or if she is "all right," or uses some other euphemism for an experience for which obviously no euphemism is possible. We men are reminded by Simone de Beauvoir and other women who try to interpret the love act that this is the last thing in the world a woman wants to be asked at that moment. Furthermore, the technical preoccupation robs the woman of exactly what she wants most of all, physically and emotionally, namely the man's spontaneous abandon at the moment of climax. This abandon gives her whatever thrill or ecstasy she and the experience are capable of. When we cut through all the rigmarole about roles and performance, what still remains is how amazingly important the sheer fact of intimacy of relationship is—the meeting, the growing closeness with the excitement of not knowing where it will lead, the assertion of the self, and the giving of the self—in making a sexual encounter memorable. Is it not this intimacy that makes us return to the event in memory again and again when we need to be warmed by whatever hearths life makes available?

It is a strange thing in our society that what goes into building a relationship—the sharing of tastes, fantasies, dreams, hopes for the future, and fears from the past—seems to make people more shy and vulnerable than going to bed with each other. They are more wary of the tenderness that goes with psychological and spiritual nakedness than they are of the physical nakedness in sexual intimacy.

The New Puritanism

The third paradox is that our highly-vaunted sexual freedom has turned out to be a new form of puritanism. I spell it with a small "p" because I do not wish to confuse this with the original Puritanism. That, as in the passion of Hester and Dimmesdale in Hawthorne's *The Scarlet Letter,* was a very different thing.[10] I refer to puritanism as it came down via our Victorian grandparents and became allied with industrialism and emotional and moral compartmentalization.

10. That the actual Puritans in the sixteenth and seventeenth centuries were a different breed from those who represented the deteriorated forms in our century can be seen in a number of sources. Roland H. Bainton in the chapter "Puritanism and the Modern Period," of his book *What Christianity Says about Sex, Love and Marriage* (New York: Reflection Books, Association Press, 1957), writes "The Puritan ideal for the relations of man and wife was summed up in the words, 'a tender respectiveness.'" He quotes Thomas Hooker: "The man whose heart is endeared to the woman he loves, he dreams of her in the night, hath her in his eye and apprehension when he awakes, museth on her as he sits at table, walks with her when he travels and parlies with her in each place he comes." Ronald Mushat Frye, in a thoughtful paper, "The Teachings of Classical Puritanism on Conjugal Love," *Studies from the Renaissance,* II (1955), submits conclusive evidence that Classical Puritanism inculcated a view of sexual life in marriage as the "Crown of all our bliss," "Founded in Reason, Loyal, Just, and Pure" (p. 149). He believes that "the fact remains that the education of England in a more liberal view of married love in the sixteenth and early seventeenth centuries was in large part the work of that party within English Protestantism which is called Puritan" (p. 149). The Puritans were against lust and acting on physical attraction outside of marriage, but they as strongly believed in the sexual side of marriage and believed it the duty of all people to keep this alive all their lives. It was a later confusion which associated them with the asceticism of continence in marriage. Frye states, "In the course of a wide reading of Puritan and other Protestant writers in the sixteenth and early seventeenth centuries, I have found nothing but opposition to this type of ascetic 'perfection'" (p. 152).

One has only to look carefully at the New England churches built by the Puritans and in the Puritan heritage to see the great refinement and dignity of form which surely implies a passionate attitude toward life. They had the dignity of controlled passion, which may have made possible an actual living with passion in contrast to our present pattern of expressing and dispersing all passion. The deterioration of Puritanism into our modern secular attitudes was caused by the confluence of three trends: industrialism, Victorian emotional compartmentalization, and the secularization of all religious attitudes. The first introduced the specific mechanical model; the second introduced the emotional dishonesty which Freud analyzed so well; and the third took away the depth dimensions of religion and made the concerns how one "behaved" in such matters as smoking, drinking, and sex in the superficial forms which we are attacking above. (For a view of the delightful love letters between husband and wife in this period, see the two volume biography of John Adams by Page Smith. See also the writings on the Puritans by Perry Miller.)

I define this puritanism as consisting of three elements. First, *a state of alienation from the body*. Second, *the separation of emotion from reason*. And third, *the use of the body as a machine*.

In our new puritanism, bad health is equated with sin.[11] Sin used to mean giving in to one's sexual desires; it now means not having full sexual expression. Our contemporary puritan holds that it is immoral *not* to express your libido. Apparently this is true on both sides of the ocean: "There are few more depressing sights," the London *Times Literary Supplement* writes, "than a progressive intellectual determined to end up in bed with someone from a sense of moral duty. . . . There is no more high-minded puritan in the world than your modern advocate of salvation through properly directed passion. . . ."[12] A woman used to be guilty if she went to bed with a man; now she feels vaguely guilty if after a certain number of dates she still refrains; her sin is "morbid repression," refusing to "give." And the partner, who is always completely enlightened (or at least pretends to be) refuses to allay her guilt by getting overtly angry at her (if she could fight him on the issue, the conflict would be a lot easier for her). But he stands broadmindedly by, ready at the end of every date to undertake a crusade to assist her out of her fallen state. And this, of course, makes her "no" all the more guilt-producing for her.

This all means, of course, that people not only have to learn to perform sexually but have to make sure, at the same time, that they can do so without letting themselves go in passion or unseemly commitment—the latter of which may be interpreted as exerting an unhealthy demand upon the partner. *The Victorian person sought to have love without falling into*

11. This formulation was originally suggested to me by Dr. Ludwig Lefebre.

12. *Atlas* (November, 1965), p. 302.

sex; the modern person seeks to have sex without falling into love.

I once diverted myself by drawing an impressionistic sketch of the attitude of the contemporary enlightened person toward sex and love. I would like to share this picture of what I call the new sophisticate:

> The new sophisticate is not castrated by society, but like Origen is self-castrated. Sex and the body are for him not something to be and live out, but tools to be cultivated like a T.V. announcer's voice. The new sophisticate expresses his passion by devoting himself passionately to the moral principle of dispersing all passion, loving everybody until love has no power left to scare anyone. He is deathly afraid of his passions unless they are kept under leash, and the theory of total expression is precisely his leash. His dogma of liberty is his repression; and his principle of full libidinal health, full sexual satisfaction, is his denial of eros. The old Puritans repressed sex and were passionate; our new puritan represses passion and is sexual. His purpose is to hold back the body, to try to make nature a slave. The new sophisticate's rigid principle of full freedom is not freedom but a new straitjacket. He does all this because he is afraid of his body and his compassionate roots in nature, afraid of the soil and his procreative power. He is our latter-day Baconian devoted to gaining power *over* nature, gaining knowledge in order to get more power. And you gain power over sexuality (like working the slave until all zest for revolt is squeezed out of him) precisely by the role of full expression. Sex becomes our tool like the caveman's bow and arrows, crowbar, or adz. Sex, the new machine, the *Machina Ultima.*

This new puritanism has crept into contemporary psychiatry and psychology. It is argued in some books on the counseling of married couples that the therapist ought to use only the term "fuck" when discussing sexual intercourse, and to insist the patients use it; for any other word plays into the patients' dissimulation. What is significant here is not the use of the term itself: surely the sheer lust, animal but self-conscious,

and bodily abandon which is rightly called fucking is not to be
left out of the spectrum of human experience. But the interesting thing is that the use of the once-forbidden word is now
made into an *ought*—a duty for the moral reason of honesty. To
be sure, it *is* dissimulation to deny the biological side of
copulation. But it is also dissimulation to use the term fuck for
the sexual experience when what we seek is a relationship of
personal intimacy which is more than a release of sexual ten-
sion, a personal intimacy which will be remembered tomorrow
and many weeks after tomorrow. The former is dissimulation
in the service of inhibition; the latter is dissimulation in the
service of alienation of the self, a defense of the self against
the anxiety of intimate relationship. As the former was the
particular problem of Freud's day, the latter is the particular
problem of ours.

The new puritanism brings with it a depersonalization of
our whole language. Instead of making love, we "have sex"; in
contrast to intercourse, we "screw"; instead of going to bed,
we "lay" someone or (heaven help the English language as
well as ourselves!) we "are laid." This alienation has become
so much the order of the day that in some psychotherapeutic
training schools, young psychiatrists and psychologists are
taught that it is "therapeutic" to use solely the four-letter
words in sessions; the patient is probably masking some repression if he talks about making love; so it becomes our
righteous duty—the new puritanism incarnate!—to let him
know he only fucks. Everyone seems so intent on sweeping
away the last vestiges of Victorian prudishness that we entirely forget that these different words refer to different kinds
of human experience. Probably most people have experienced
the different forms of sexual relationship described by the
different terms and don't have much difficulty distinguishing
among them. I am not making a value judgment among these
different experiences; they are all appropriate to their own

kinds of relationship. Every woman wants at some time to be "laid"—transported, carried away, "made" to have passion when at first she has none, as in the famous scene between Rhett Butler and Scarlett O'Hara in *Gone with the Wind*. But if being "laid" is all that ever happens in her sexual life, then her experience of personal alienation and rejection of sex are just around the corner. If the therapist does not appreciate these diverse kinds of experience, he will be presiding at the shrinking and truncating of the patient's consciousness, and will be confirming the narrowing of the patient's bodily awareness as well as his or her capacity for relationship. This is the chief criticism of the new puritanism: it grossly limits feelings, it blocks the infinite variety and richness of the act, and it makes for emotional impoverishment.

Index